Anatomy of
Cross-Examination

Anatomy of Cross-Examination

Second Edition

Leonard E. Davies

Copyright © 2003 by Leonard E. Davies.

ISBN: Softcover   1-4134-3199-2

All rights reserved. No part of this book may be reproduced or transmitted in any form or by any means, electronic or mechanical, including photocopying, recording, or by any information storage and retrieval system, without permission in writing from the copyright owner.

This book was printed in the United States of America.

To order additional copies of this book, contact:
Xlibris Corporation
1-888-795-4274
www.Xlibris.com
Orders@Xlibris.com

CRITICAL ACCLAIM FOR
ANATOMY OF CROSS-EXAMINATION

"Many years ago, my grandfather, in an effort to make me decide to go to law school, gave me a book, *The Art of Cross-Examination,* by Francis Wellman, a celebrated New York trial attorney. Although it had little to do with my eventual decision, its precepts became my Bible from the moment I started trying criminal cases. Now my old friend and colleague, Leonard E. Davies, has come up with a worthy successor, and one that should help to educate today's practitioners in the fine art of employing what many consider the greatest courtroom truth-seeker—cross-examination"

William Kunstler, Defense attorney for the Chicago Seven

"The unlimited permutations and combinations of events confronting the cross-examiner cannot be managed by a lengthy list of do's and don'ts. Leonard Davies instead provides an antenna, a series of sensitive feelers than can guide the litigator through the minefield of inevitable surprises that he or she is sure to meet.

"This book should not be in the lawyer's library, it should be on his nightstand."

Shelby Yastrow, Former General Counsel for the McDonald's Corporation.

"*Anatomy of Cross-Examination* by Leonard E. Davies is the finest work which I have ever read on this topic. Its unique organization provides not only the basic principles, but also thoughtful illustrative examples drawn from many sources, including some based on the actual trial experiences of this noted advocate. It is a veritable primer and an essential companion which ever lawyer should read and have by his or her side when they must cross-examine. Every trial lawyer, both the novice and the expert, will need this essential work."

E. Donald Shapiro, former Dean,
and Joseph Solomon Distinguished Professor of
Law at New York Law School.

"The trial of a lawsuit is the most difficult, emotionally painful, and intellectually demanding thing I have ever done. Finally there is a book written by one of the best trial lawyers in the country, which clearly guides the trial lawyer through this complex process and gives real assistance in the most difficult part of the trial, cross-examination.

Lonn E. Berney, Esq., Trial Lawyer, Writer, Lecturer

Cross-examination is the most exciting and anxiety-provoking time in every trial. Because it is a powerful tool in the search for truth, it is what every trial lawyer should live for. But many lawyers fear it. Leonard Davies' *Anatomy of Cross-Examination* provides an analytical view of cross-examination that should greatly alleviate many of these lawyer's fears.

It is not so much that Davies has something new to say but how he organizes the subject and illustrates points with historical examples that make his work a valuable addition to a trial advocacy library. The table of contents alone is an outstanding outline of the essentials of any case or cross-examination. And the examples used by Davies, some going back to biblical times, should be a source of comfort—they show that although trial practice has changed in many ways over the years, the fundamentals of cross-examination remain unchanged.

But Davies work covers much more than just cross-examination. He is from the school that views a trial as a series of integrated elements, all of which must be carefully coordinated to make a persuasive case. The book covers the entire trial process from the moment the parties enter the courtroom to the final rebuttal argument. It shows how cross-examination is integrated into the larger whole of the trial process.

As he points out, cross-examination is more than simply questioning a witness and, with luck, scoring some points. It should be used to persuade the jury and obtain evidence for final argument. Conducting a winning cross-examination that does not advance the client's chance of success serves no purpose. Attorneys should not even plan cross-examination without first determining its objectives.

On the subject of conducting the cross-examination itself, Davies covers issues of technique, style, and strategy. Fundamental to any cross-examination is the need to understand the witness, and the author offers many insightful ideas on witness evaluation.

Davies presents many strategies to deal with witnesses, including the most reluctant or evasive ones. As Davies points out, at times it is necessary to allow a witness to make the questioner look foolish in order to lay the trap that will eventually expose the lie. At other times, either a single question may suffice or the examiner may have to ignore the "rules". The examples used are instructive. For example, Davies recounts how Daniel exposed the wicked elders in Chapter 13 or the Book of Daniel and how Max Steuer revealed the fabrication of Kate Alterman in the Triangle Shirtwaist Company fire case by asking her to repeat her testimony, which revealed discrepancies in her stories.

. . . . [F]or the novice, Davies' work is a valuable teaching tool. For the experienced trial lawyer, it is an entertaining refresher course.

Larry S. Stewart is a Miami attorney and former president of the American Trial Lawyers Association

CONTENTS

Acknowledgments 33
Forward 35
Introduction 37

PART ONE: SIZING UP THE TERRAIN 45

PRINCIPLE ONE: THE OBJECT OF CROSS-EXAMINATION IS TO CAST DOUBT ON THE WITNESSES AND EVIDENCE PRESENTED BY THE OPPOSITION USING ALL THE RHETORICAL SKILLS AVAILABLE 47

> Cross-examination is more than asking questions. Cross-examination is the strategy of words and actions the advocate employs during the presentation of evidence by the opposition that serves to cast doubt. To be an effective cross-examiner the advocate must employ all the rhetorical skills. The advocate must establish his own character, he must put the jury in a receptive frame of mind, and he must cast doubt on witnesses and evidence of the opposition.

PRINCIPLE TWO: THE ADVOCATE MUST CREATE A FAVORABLE TRIAL ATMOSPHERE FOR EFFECTIVE CROSS-EXAMINATION 52

> If the advocate has failed to create a favorable atmosphere his cross-examination will fail. Establish a rapport with the court as quickly as possible. Include the jury in the proceedings a quickly as possible. Establish the boundaries

of your case. Present your theme and strategy to the jury at the earliest possible moment. Pay as much attention to your form as to your substance.

PRINCIPLE THREE: THE APPEAL TO THE JURORS BEGINS WHEN THEY ENTER THE COURTROOM FOR THE FIRST TIME AND ENDS WITH CLOSING ARGUMENT 59

Juries should be made allies at the first possible moment. The jury must be made aware of the importance of their role in the trial. The jury should be impressed with the skills of the advocate. Engage the jury in arriving at a joint conclusion. The advocate must never lose sight of the appeal to the jury. The tools for voir dire are growing and the opportunity to use them shrinking. The advocate must develop his skills and priorities to use the time available in the best way possible.

PRINCIPLE FOUR: ASSUME THE JURY IS WATCHING YOU 65

One or more of the jurors will monitor every act of the advocate, The advocate should not say or do anything in the courtroom that betrays a weakness in the case. Never let the jury lose sight of the positive aspects of the case. Always convey a sense of confidence in your client and the case.

PRINCIPLE FIVE: CROSS-EXAMINATION IS MEASURED BY QUALITY NOT QUANTITY 71

Brevity is a goal all cross-examinations should strive for. Every question asked provides the potential for a harmful answer. The lawyer must have the confidence and grasp of his case to such a degree that he can feel confident in not asking every question imaginable. Daniel needed only one question to save Susanna from the death penalty.

PRINCIPLE SIX: A JUDGES SLIGHTEST WORD OR GESTURE MAY CARRY MORE WEIGHT WITH THE JURY THAN ALL THE ELOQUENCE YOU CAN MUSTER 78

A judge devoid of prejudice is the exception rather than the rule. Jurors take their clues from the judge. Judges can manipulate the case without appearing to do so on the record. The advocate must learn ways to resist the judicial manipulation of the jury.

PRINCIPLE SEVEN: THE CLOSING ARGUMENT SHOULD BE FORMULATED AT THE OUTSET OF THE CASE 85

Cross-examination must be undertaken with the closing argument in mind. It is never too soon to begin to formulate the closing argument. The closing argument is subject to constant revision. The advocate must have a clear idea of the question before he can elicit an answer. Never try and alter the evidence to fit the argument.

PRINCIPLE EIGHT: AVOID UNNECESSAY NOTE TAKING 90

Time spent writing notes is time away from watching the case. The advocate should develop techniques that will minimize note taking. A smooth, continuous flow in the case is desired and constant reference to notes destroys the flow. A good memory can be developed and is indispensable to the advocate.

PART TWO: PLOTTING THE STRATEGY 97

PRINCIPLE ONE: SHOULD YOU CROSS-EXAMINE AT ALL? 99

Cross-examination should be the last resort. Did the witness hurt your case? Can you deal with the testimony better through another witness or in closing argument? Is the potential for harm greater any benefits to be achieved. Can the goals be achieved in ways other than impeaching the witness? Does the jury expect cross-examination? If you dismiss the witness without cross-examination do so in a manner that is beneficial.

PRINCIPLE TWO: STIPULATE TO TESTIMONY AND EVIDENCE WHEREVER POSSIBLE 105

Keeping the judge and jury focused on the important issues will help your case. If information is irrelevant to the central issue of the case much can be gained by stipulating to its admission. Don't appear to the jury as being an obstructionist. The impact of harmful testimony may be blunted through stipulation.

PRINCIPLE THREE: KNOW WHAT YOU SEEK TO ACCOMPLISH IN YOUR CROSS-EXAMINATION 109

Cross-examination requires improvisation which must be built on a firm understanding of the case. Inadequate preparation may lead to erroneous improvisation. If the cross-examiner doesn't know exactly where he is going it will be impossible to know when to stop.

PRINCIPLE FOUR: ALWAYS OBSERVE THE WITNESS DURING DIRECT EXAMINATION 112

> From the entrance into the courtroom until the final word of direct examination the witness will speak with more than just words. Analysis of the witness requires more than listening to the testimony. Everything the witness does will give some clue as to what cross-examination strategy will work. The tone of voice, the body language, and moments of hesitation may indicate a point of vulnerability. The reaction to the witness by judges, jurors, the opposition, and the spectators will help in formulating the attack on the witness.

PRINCIPLE FIVE: EACH OBJECTION SHOULD BE A STATEMENT TO THE JURY 115

> An objection should be used as a rhetorical device. Objections should be used to make points with the jury. Objections should never simply state the rule. Objections should always give the jury the commonsense reason for the objection. Objections should be made to the jury through the judge. Objections should be used as tactical devices to upset the pace and rhythm of the opposition. Too many objections is like crying wolf.

PRINCIPLE SIX: NEVER OBJECT TO YOUR OWN QUESTIONS 119

> There are no indiscreet questions-only indiscreet answers. The job of the advocate is to ask questions, the answers to which will help his client; it is the job of the opposition to object. If the other side fails to object the question is proper. The rules of evidence are too elastic to assume you know that the ruling on an objection will be against you. Sometimes the tactic is the question and not the answer.

PRINCIPLE SEVEN: DO NOT ALLOW THE WITNESS TO REPEAT ON CROSS-EXAMINATION EVERYTHING HE SAID ON DIRECT EXAMINATION 122

>A frequent mistake of trial lawyers is to allow the witness to repeat his direct examination on cross-examination. The advocate must have goals for his cross and a well articulated plan for achieving them. Allowing the witness to repeat his direct most often happens with the witness that can do the most damage. Falling into this trap most often happens to lawyers who do not understand their case. There are techniques for avoiding the problem.

PRINCIPLE EIGHT: VICTORIES ACHIEVED ON CROSS-EXAMINATION MAY BE LOST ON THE JURY 126

>The jury may not be aware that a point has been made. Never be satisfied that since you see the point everyone else does. You should have tactics to use before and after the trap is sprung. The quarry should be made to squirm—but not too much. Every opportunity should be seized to reiterate points to the jury.

PRINCIPLE NINE: IF YOU AREN'T PREPARED FOR THE ANSWER DON'T ASK THE QUESTION 130

>Forget the rule of don't ask a question if you don't know the answer. This is an impossible rule to follow. New matters always come up in trial that must be explored even if you don't know precisely where they may lead. Ask a series of foundation questions that will tell you the answer to the critical question before the jury is aware of it, this will let you retreat if you don't like what you see. Don't ask the crucial question until you have the witness in the position of answering your way or looking foolish. Ask a series of tangential

questions that will force the witness to answer the critical question your way.

PART THREE: SELECTING THE TACTICS 135

PRINCIPLE ONE: TACTICS IN CROSS-EXAMINATION MUST BE BASED ON THE ENTIRE CASE 137

Tactics may be available to you that are not appropriate to the situation. The tactics selected must have some relationship to the objectives of the cross-examination. Conduct the cross-examination with confidence and without hesitancy. Avoid lengthy cross-examination. Even the witness whose testimony is not vulnerable may have something that will help you. Don't cross on collateral matters unless you are sure it will lead to something beneficial. Pay close attention to the direct regardless of how insignificant you the think the witness is.

PRINCIPLE TWO: KNOWING THE REACTION OF THE JURY IS VITAL TO CROSS-EXAMINATION 144

Always monitor the jurors for their reaction. You may think you are doing well and the find the jury disapproves. Put yourself in the shoes of the jurors. Wherever possible consider yourself an advocate for the jury. Courts won't tell the jury it can nullify a law; the clever lawyer can. Peter Zenger and Alexander Hamilton.

PRINCIPLE THREE: THERE SHOULD BE ON HESITATION IN CROSS-EXAMINATION 147

Advocates should have a pace, rhythm, and flow to their cross-examination. Among the choices available to the advocate are: begin with a minor subject and advance to the crucial ones; attack the opposition's case immediately when they may be vulnerable; or use silence to unnerve the witness. Regardless of the choice the advocate must accomplish it in a commanding way.

PRINCIPLE FOUR: LENGTHY CROSS-EXAMINATION EXAGGERATES THE VALUE OF THE DIRECT EXAMINATION 151

> Be as brief as possible. Effective cross-examination will not be unduly long. Lengthy cross-examination can be avoided by knowing the options. Even when long cross-examination is unavoidable it should remain focused and to the point.

PRINCIPLE FIVE: RESPOND TO A HARMFUL ANSWER BY IMMEDIATELY POSING ANOTHER QUESTION 154

> In every case there is a witness that will deliver a harmful response. The advocate must develop the rhetorical skills to deal with the damaging response. An effective reply is available for most harmful responses.

PRINCIPLE SIX: NO CROSS-EXAMANITION DOESN'T ALWAYS MEAN NO QUESTIONS 159

> Even where the decision is not to cross-examine there may be good reason to question the witness. Don't squander opportunities to make telling points to the jury. Most opposition witnesses can be used to help your case. Use the opportunity to repeat favorable testimony from other witnesses. Make a statement to the jury in the form of a question.

PRINCIPLE SEVEN: AVOID EXAGGERATING TRIFLING DISCREPANCIES 164

> The sympathy of the jury is usually with the witness. It won't help your cause to show up the witness in some minor way. Minor inconsistencies should be probed in case they lead to larger ones.

PRINCIPLE EIGHT: CROSS-EXAMINATION SHOULD NOT BE CONDUCTED FROM WRITTEN QUESTIONS 167

> Repeated reference to notes will lose the attention of the jury. The questioning should have as few pauses as possible. The advocate should ask the question; the witness should answer "yes" or "no". Ways to avoid excessive use of notes.

PRINCIPLE NINE: EXPOSING THE LIE DOES NOT COMPLETE THE CROSS-EXAMINATION 172

> The lie must be firmly placed in the minds of the jurors. Just because you are aware of lie doesn't mean the jury is. Once you expose the lie, be sure you leave no loose ends. The witness should be left with no plausible answer when the other side seeks to rehabilitate him. Choose carefully the right moment to expose the lie. Abraham Lincoln and the murder in the moonlight.

PART FOUR: ACHIEVING THE OBJECTIVE 179

PRINCIPLE ONE: THE OBJECT OF THE EXAMINATION MUST BE CLEARLY DEFINED BEFORE CONFRONTING THE WITNESS 181

End the cross-examination when the objectives have been reached. Because the cross-examination doesn't always go as planned, flexibility is important. Changing the focus of the cross in mid-stream requires ingenuity and discipline. New areas that may lead to damage should be abandoned without the jury being aware of the damage. Questions should require 'yes' or 'no' answers. Don't lose control of the witness.

PRINCIPLE TWO: THE OBJECTIVES OF CROSS-EXAMINATION OFTEN EXCEED IMPEACHING THE WITNESS 185

Did the witness cause any damage? Can it be dealt with in a way other than cross-examination? Are there other goals besides impeachment? How to pursue new matters that arise. Discover whether the new area is beneficial or harmful before the jury does . . . .

PRINCIPLE THREE: TIMING IS EVERYTHING 188

The how and when of the question is as important as the subject of the question. A damaging concession from a witness may be lost on the jury because of timing. The advocate should strive for a sense of the dramatic in his presentation. The wide latitude allowed in cross-examination is important to a dramatic presentation. Judges will be quick to limit the cross-examination if it is tedious and unfocused. The cross-examination of Reader by Francis Wellman.

PRINCIPLE FOUR: DECIDE WHETHER THE OBJECT OF YOUR CROSS-EXAMINATION IS TO DISCREDIT THE WITNESS OR DISCREDIT THE TESTIMONY 208

Juries are usually sympathetic to the witness. Attacking the testimony is safer than attacking the witness. If the prejudice of the witness is clear an attack on him can be justified. If the decision is to attack the witness decide whether is for the purpose of discrediting him or destroying him. Discredit means an attack on the motives the witness has for testifying; destroying the witness means to attack him at every level of his life. Louis Nizer cross-examines Judge Austin in the Paul Crump commutation hearing.

PRINCIPLE FIVE: CROSS-EXAMINATION SHOULD NOT OPEN A SUBJECT OTHERWISE CLOSED TO THE OTHER SIDE.. 219

Some prejudicial matters may not be raised by one side unless the other side raises them. The cross-examination must be censored to avoid falling into this trap. A close rein on the witness will help. The advocate should do the testifying and the witness should be required to agree or disagree.

PRINCIPLE SIX: THE JURY MUST BE MADE AWARE OF ANY MISTAKES.. 222

The opposition or a witness will make a mistake in such a way that the jury will not be aware of its significance. The mistake must be reiterated in a variety of ways until its impact is felt by the jury. Some judges will try and prevent you from doing so. Some techniques for bringing the mistakes home to the jury.

PRINCIPLE SEVEN: NEVER ASK A QUESTION THAT CONTAINS THE WORD "WHY" EITHER EXPRESS OR IMPLIED 224

If there is one inviolable rule of cross-examination it is to never ask a question that contains the word 'why'. All the common interrogatives (who, what, where, when, how) should be avoided. The advocate should testify and force the witness to agree or disagree.

PRINCIPLE EIGHT: QUESTIONS SHOULD BE SIMPLE AND UNAMBIGUOUS 229

Complicated questions confuse the jury and the witness. A complicated question inevitably gives the witness the opportunity to elaborate. Ten syllables is the ideal length for a question. Divide long questions into several short ones. Simple questions maintain the interest and focus of the jury. The question is a rhetorical device.

PART FIVE: DEVELOPING A STYLE 233

PRINCIPLE ONE: THE ADVOCAT MUST CONTROL THE SUBJECT MATTER AND PACE OF CROSS-EXAMINATION 235

Giving the jury a coherent and well structured case requires controlling the case. Questions must have clear goals in mind. Learn to upset the pace and rhythm of the opposition. Learn to deal with the opposition attempts to disrupt you. Throw the opposition off stride with objections and diversions. Turn the opposition's efforts to throw you off stride to your advantage. Earl Rogers and the cigar. Irving Andrews leaves the courtroom.

PRINCIPLE TWO: BEGIN THE CROSS-EXAMINATION COURTEOUSLY 239

Being a lady or gentleman in court will always be to your benefit. Use aggression or feigned anger sparingly and only when clearly justified. It is easy to go from courteous to aggressive but not vice versa. Righteous indignation is a useful tool.

PRINCIPLE THREE: DON'T CONFUSE CROSS-EXAMINATION WITH EXAMINING CROSSLY ... 242

Bullying and browbeating the witness are not styles used by good cross-examiners. The jury sees the contest as being heavily in favor of the lawyer. The harsh style causes valid points to be lost on the jury. Confusing and humiliating the witness is not effective cross-examination. Earl Rogers cross-examines a pathologist.

PRINCIPLE FOUR: NEVER OPEN WITH THE LAST SUBJECT COVERED RED IN DIRECT EXAMINATION 247

The rule does not apply to housekeeping witnesses. The opposition will try and end with their strongest point and the witness will be ready to defend it. Take time to impeach on other subjects before attacking on the strongest one. When the advocate has devastating impeaching material it may serve to go strait to the attack. Jerry Giesler defends Erroll Flynn.

PRINCIPLE FIVE: NEVER FALSELY REPRESENT WHAT A WITNESS HAS SAID 253

Exalting over minor victories gives the jury the impression of childishness. Showing pleasure when scoring easy points serves to diminish important victories. If the witness is honest and trustworthy the jury will recognize it. Attempts at impeaching this witness will affect the advocate's credibility with the jury. Resist any temptation to misrepresent what a witness has said. A classic example of a judge's reaction to this tactic.

PRINCIPLE SIX: NEVER USE VIOLENT OR ABUSIVE LANGUAGE TO THE WITNESS 258

Juries usually believe the direct examination. The advocate must take this into account even though he knows the witness is a liar. First, the advocate must convince the jury that its confidence in the witness is misplaced. Jurors may at first resist this and the subject must be approached with caution. Forcefulness and indignation may be used but never violent or abusive language. Lord Russell cross-examines Richard Pigott.

PRINCIPLE SEVEN: HIDE YOUR WOUNDS 266

Never react negatively to damaging statements. Jurors are keenly aware of the advocate's reaction to testimony. Often the damage occurs when the advocate is at his most vulnerable. Maintaining self control is a must. Some ways to deal with damage.

PRINCIPLE EIGHT: MAINTAIN A SERENE APPEARANCE 268

Retain your composure. Keep the jury tightly focused on the unfolding drama. Louis Nizer cross-examines Westbrook Pegler.

PART SIX: UNDERSTANDING WITNESSES 287

PRINCIPLE ONE: ANALYSIS OF THE WITNESS IS A PREREQUISITE TO FORMULATING STRATEGY 289

Understand what motivates the witness and where any weaknesses may lie. Once there is an understanding of the witness several strategies present themselves. Shift the burden of proof from the advocate to the witness. Put the witness on the defensive. Give the witness room to roam and gain details for impeachment at a later time. Use of timing and change of emotional direction to keep the witness off stride. Make use of assault on the witness as a tactic. Establish a bad memory as to some items and then attack the witness on other matters using this show of bad memory as a rationale. Use timing to put the witness on the defensive.

PRINCIPLE TWO: MONEY WILL BRIBE A FEW: HATE, BIAS, INTEREST, ANGER, OR FEAR WILL BRIBE MANY 304

Witnesses who would never consider selling their testimony for money often do so for other reasons. These witnesses rarely know themselves what they are doing. The witness may be harboring a grudge for a wrong done him or someone he knows, and is using this case to redress the previous wrong. Their testimony may be subconsciously colored sympathy. In the hands of a clever investigator or attorney a witness may be led to remember things that did not happen.

PRINCIPLE THREE: THE MEMORY OF THE WITNESS IS MADE UP WHAT HE SEES AND WHAT HE THINKS 314

The memory is a creative process and is subject to great inaccuracy. The advocate must understand the memory creation process and be able to point out the fallacies. Even the eye witness doesn't always see the things he says he sees. Edward Carson and the Archer-Shee case.

PRINCIPLE FOUR: WITNESSES OFTEN TAKE A POSITION AND THEN REMEMBER FACTS TO SUPPORT THE POSITION 319

Witnesses allow selective perception to guide their memory of events. Even trained professionals, investigating a crime, will reach a conclusion and then seek evidence to support the conclusion. This type of witness is relatively easy to cross-examine. Injecting the facts overlooked by the witness into the cross-examination makes it readily apparent the testimony is not trustworthy. Lloyd Paul Stryker and the divorcee.

PRINCIPLE FIVE: WITNESSES TEND TO MINIMIZE OR ENLARGE FACTS 322

Once the witness reaches a conclusion he tends to minimize facts that are unsupportive and enlarge on those that are supportive of his position. The advocate should encourage this tendency and encourage the witness to exaggerate until the witness conflicts with the common-sense of the jury. The use of incredulity, and posing questions in the negative, is a useful technique. Lord Russell and the Baccarat Case.

PRINCIPLE SIX: THE INDIRECT ATTACK IS BEST AGAINST THE STRONG OR VIGOROUS WITNESS 335

The testimony of this witness must be chipped away at. Irony is a good technique with this witness. The advocate must have a strong enough ego to take some blows from the witness before bringing the witness down. Patience is a key. Edward Carson shows how in his cross-examination of Oscar Wilde.

PRINCIPLE SEVEN: NEVER TRY AND IMPEACH AN APPARENTLY TRUTHFUL WITNESS 346

Most witnesses are honest and testify in a straight-forward manner. This is usually apparent to the jury. To use impeachment to try and cast such a witness in a different light serves to enhance the value of the testimony. The advocate should adopt this witness as his own in some way. Marshall-Hall and Dr. Wilcox in the Seddon case.

PRINCIPLE EIGHT: ALWAYS END THE CROSS-EXAMINATION ON A HIGH NOTE 350

> The last impression of the witness may be the most important. If the advocate has one or more telling points he should make them at the end of the cross-examination. If the advocate makes his most telling points early in the cross-examination he should return to them at the close; reconstruct them; and then end. Earl Rogers defends Clarence Darrow.

PART SEVEN: THINKING ON YOUR FEET 355

PRINCIPLE ONE: SIZING UP A WITNESS REQUIRES ON-THE-SPOT DECISION MAKING 357

> No amount of preparation removes the need of spontaneous decision making. Don't be a slave to pre-planned approaches. The ability to improvise is most crucial during the cross-examination itself. Successful improvisation depends on a complete understanding of the rules of evidence. Why witnesses may be wrong. Clues for reading the witness on the stand.

PRINCIPLE TWO: THE WHOLE IS NOT ALWAYS EQUAL TO THE SUM OF THE PARTS 362

> Testimony often includes undisclosed conclusions. Without the conclusions the story may be vulnerable. Seek to separate the conclusions from the facts. Attack the testimony by attacking each individual fact.

PRINCIPLE THREE: EMBROIDERY OF THE FACTS IS OFTEN THE DOWNFALL OF THE WITNESS 368

Some dissembling witnesses will not leave well enough alone. Their need to exaggerate often puts them in an untenable position. The advocate must be able to discern fact from fantasy. Probe the subject for signs of exaggeration before launching a full scale attack.

PRINCIPLE FOUR: ASK A CRUCIAL QUESTION WHEN THE WITNESS IS EBULLIENT 371

The witness's defenses are lowest when he feels good about himself and his performance. His vulnerability is high and he should be attacked at this point. Building the witness's self-esteem often requires permitting your own to suffer temporarily.

PRINCIPLE FIVE: THE LYING WITNESS CANNOT INVENT LIES AS QUICKLY AS THE LAWYER CAN INVENT QUESTIONS 373

A lie, no matter how small, will lead to a witness's downfall. Don't attack the lie when it is first disclosed. Ignore the lie and make the witness commit to several positions relying on the lie. When the lie is exposed after the witness is made to commit himself to details the lawyer has several avenues of attack if the witness tries to extricate himself.

PRINCIPLE SIX: THE WITNESS MAY BE HIDING A PERSONALITY DISORDER 378

Much more is now known about personality disorders and their symptoms than ever before. Knowing the symptoms and exploiting them can be valuable.

PRINCIPLE SEVEN: HOW THE QUESTION IS ASKED MAY EFFECT THE TRUTH OF THE ANSWER 384

The form of the question may effect the answer. The question to the witness may suggest the advocate does or does not have certain impeaching information. The witness may enlarge or minimize the facts to your advantage because of the manner of the question. Your tone of voice, emphasis on words, sequence of questions, and body language can be used to lead the witness on a false trail.

PRINCIPLE EIGHT: PRIOR INCONSISTENT ACTS OR STATEMENTS BY THE WITNESS MUST BE DEMONSTRATED TO THE JURY 387

If the witness has failed to do something, or done something inconsistent with the testimony it should be brought to the attention of the jury. Acts of omission are more difficult to demonstrate than acts of commission. Show the witness to have had an opportunity to ratify his testimony and recollection but failed to do so.

PRINCIPLE NINE: TEST THE WITNESS'S ABILITY TO SEE, THE EXACTITUDE OF HIS MEMORY, AND HIS ABILITY TO ARTICULATE WHAT HE KNOWS 391

Was the witness able to see the events he testified to? Can the witness remember the events in a reliable way? Is the memory of the event consistent with other events in the witness's life? Is the witness able to communicate what he saw and remembers in a credible way? Max Steuer and the Triangle Waist Company fire.

PRINCIPLE TEN: EVERY WITNESS SHOULD BE DAMAGED OR NEUTRALIZED ON CROSS-EXAMINATION 403

Witnesses that must be cross-examined must be damaged or neutralized. The advocate striking out on cross-examination is unacceptable. When the cross-examination is over the advocate must have gained something he can use in closing argument. Home runs are rare; the advocate must settle for the double, the single, the bunt, or the sacrifice. The advocate must be patient. Sometimes neutralizing the witness is all the advocate can do.

PART EIGHT: THE EXPERT WITNESS 409

PRINCIPLE ONE: THE EXPERT IS EASIER TO CROSS-EXAMINE THAN IS USUALLY SUPPOSED 409

Experts testify in nearly every trial. Experts have special leeway in their testimony. The expert can be impeached like any other witness. Some ways to impeach the expert. The law gives the advocate some special tools for cross-examining the expert. The learned treatise rule always provides a way to impeach the expert.

PRINCIPLE TWO: THE EXPERT SHOULD IMPEACHED WITH THE SAME TOOLS USED ON ANY OTHER WITNESS 411

Begin the cross-examination of the expert by exploring the ways to impeach any other witness. Ask the expert the questions the jury would ask. Always examine the expert in language the jury understands. Thomas Murphy cross-examines Dr. Binger in the Hiss-Chambers case.

PRINCIPLE THREE: THE SUPERSTRUCTURE SHOULD BE BROUGHT DOWN WITH AN ATTACK ON THE NUTS AND BOLTS 422

Attack the superstructure of the opinion by attacking the nuts and bolts. This is the same technique used with lay witnesses and is equally effective with experts. Exploit the arrogance and complacency of most experts. Don't confuse the expertise of a particular subject with the expertise of the cross-examiner. Louis Nizer shows 'Rum and Coca-Cola' is a fraud.

PRINCIPLE FOUR: CONTRAST THE EXPERT WITH THE WITNESS WHO HAS FIRST HAND KNOWLEDGE 433

Usually the expert is giving an opinion on facts that other witnesses testify to. The jury should be made aware that your eye-witnesses are more reliable the opponent's expert. Medalie cross-examines Dr. Jelliffe in the Harriman case.

PRINCIPLE FIVE: DO NOT ALLOW THE WITNESS TO EXPAND ON THE OPINION 446

The expert must be kept on a tighter leash than other witnesses. As someone trained in forensics the expert will seize every opportunity to elaborate on his opinion. Simulated ignorance is an effective tool. It helps to lull the expert into a false sense of security. Ask questions that require 'yes' or 'no' answers. Stryker cross-examines a doctor.

PRINCIPLE SIX: THERE ARE FEW EXPERT OPINIONS THAT HAVE NOT BEEN QUESTIONED BY ANOTHER EXPERT 452

> The learned treatise exception to the hearsay rule. Make a distinction in the expert's testimony between statements of fact and conclusions based on the facts. Most expert opinions can be challenged using authoritative writings. This is a powerful weapon since the opponent usually cannot cross-examine the authority. The expert should admit the authoritativeness of the treatise the advocate uses or appear foolish to the jury.

PRINCIPLE SEVEN: FORCE THE EXPERT TO COMMIT AS MUCH AS POSSIBLE BEFORE IMPEACHING THE OPINION 456

> A forensic expert is trained to testify in court. This expert will be more adept at explaining inconsistencies and avoiding traps than most witnesses. This expert must be made to commit as much a possible to the foundation of his opinion before he is confronted with inconsistencies. Vincent Hallinan cross-examines a doctor.

Epilogue: When To End May Be The Most Difficult Question Of All 461

Bibliography 465

This Work, As With All That I Do That Is Worthwhile, Is Dedicated To My Family

ACKNOWLEDGMENTS

Everything we do is inextricably entwined with every event of our experience. this book is no exception. It is impossible to give everyone and everything proper credit. There are those who deserve special mention. Judge John Kane, Jr. has been a good friend and great help, Joseph Saint Veltri has always been there in support, Walter Gerash gave encouragement when it was needed most. A special note of appreciation to my friends and mentors Gresham and Carla Sykes, and to my first editor, Dan Mangan, who taught me so much about writing. Many people read this book and have offered worthwhile suggestions and help. Special thanks to Governor Richard Lamm, Darrell Kuelpman at Evergreen International Aviation, and Shelby Yastrow. Finally, I want to acknowledge two late great lawyers and friends: William Kunstler the great champion of justice, and Irving Andrews the best trial lawyer I ever saw.

Forward

Some years ago I was a partner in a fairly large-sized law firm. My practice was confined to trial and appellate work, but the firm was divided into specialized departments. Newly hired associates would rotate through these departments until they felt comfortable with an area of specialty to which they would be permanently assigned.

At the end of his rotation period, a particularly brilliant young associate asked me for some guidance. He was most interested in trial work. He had been a law clerk to a judge on the Tenth Circuit Court of Appeals. He had graduated first in his class from law school and had received numerous awards for excellence in scholarship. "Nothing I have studied," he said, "informs me of what I need to become a trial lawyer. What should I read?"

I did not tell him what he would soon learn for himself; that for a trial lawyer, law school is a test of endurance, not of talent. Instead, I told him that he must learn the rules of evidence by rote—much as a violinist learns the scales—and he would have to observe as many trials as he possibly could to get a sense of heft and the feel of it all. As for reading, I suggested that he must begin and end with Aristotle's "Rhetoric" and "Poetics". Of course, every trial lawyer must read Francis Wellman's "The Art of Cross-Examination" and then I added a short list of my personal favorites, Brill's "Introductory Lectures on the Psychoanalytic Method", Viktor Frankel's "Man's Search for Meaning", Clausewitz's "War, Politics and Power", "The Heptameron" by Marguerite de Navarre, and Ruth Whitman's "Becoming a Poet".

In addition, there is a profusion of reports of famous trials available in almost any library. The Sacco-Vanzetti case, the trials of Oscar Wilde, Crippen's Case and the Lindbergh kidnapping

35

case come readily to mind. At the time I talked with this young lawyer, however, I could not include in my list "Anatomy of Cross-Examination" by Leonard E. Davies. Now That Mr. Davies has written this excellent work, I will begin my list with it.

It is hardly heresy to recognize the obvious: Advocacy is not law anymore than a piano is music. Trial lawyering is a craft the performance of which can occasionally rise to artistic experience. Being a trial lawyer is its own reward and its own punishment. It takes a combination of thorough painstaking preparation, intense concentration, talent and normal measure of fortuity. Reading Mr. Davies's book or any other works I have mentioned will not miraculously transform the reader into an accomplished trial lawyer, but it will certainly pave the way; it will chart the course.

Davies' title, "Anatomy of Cross-Examination", is indeed well chosen. There is a tendency to think of the several aspects of trial as if they were separate and unrelated much as traditional allopathic physicians are said to treat broken bones rather than the whole patient. Cross-examination is integral to every other aspect of trial. It cannot be done well or successfully in the absence of a comprehension of the entire case. It depends on the opening statement; it adheres to the direct examination and it foreshadows the closing argument. Altogether, advocacy depends on the creation of personal style which cannot be achieved by mimicry or slavish repetition of programmed formulas. Style is the product of total dedication. If you want to develop the style necessary for effective advocacy, your success will be determined in large measure by your effort. Davies' book should help you achieve maximum efficiency with your efforts.

John L. Kane, Jr.
United States Senior District Judge
Denver, Colorado

Introduction

When I began the practice of law in 1966 it was the beginning of an era of civil disobedience in America that would burn literally and figuratively for most of following decade. As a young lawyer whose sole purpose in gaining admission to the bar was to advance the cause of civil liberties it was a fortuitous circumstance.

As the immigrant son of a Welsh coal miner I had grown up on tales of the oppression of the worker and the stirring speeches of John L. Lewis the fiery orator who led the coal miner's union. I was inspired in many ways by accounts of the great lawyers in our history who had fought for and advanced the defense of civil liberties, Thomas Erskine, Clarence Darrow, Earl Rogers, Andrew Hamilton of Philadelphia, James Otis, Sam Liebowitz, and George Davis, to name but a few. I was somewhat shocked in my innocence and ignorance when I discovered that law school was not concerned with the exploits of people such as these and insisted instead that I spend time on contracts, real estate and trusts, subjects that I was surprised to discover were part of the law and which held little interest for me.

After the shock wore off, I tackled these subjects with the attitude that they were simply unpleasant obstacles I had to deal with to get to the real thing. I continued to read all I could get my hands on that dealt with the subject of a trial and of trial lawyers. The thought that one day I would have the chance to do what they had done to advance the cause of justice sustained me through some rather boring, tedious, and economically difficult times.

In the third year, I took advantage of an existing program in the state of Colorado that permitted senior law students to appear in the county courts to represent indigent defendants charged with misdemeanors. By the time I graduated and was admitted to the bar I was already the veteran of more than a dozen jury trials. I also gained a comprehensive knowledge of the law and tactics of jury trials from reading the exploits of Howe and Hummell, Moman Pruitt, Jerry Geisler, William Fallon, Jake Ehrlich, Vincent Hallinan, Rufus Choate, Max Steuer, Louis Nizer, Edward Bennett Williams, and Francis Wellman among others.

My sense of justice motivated me to use my talents as a lawyer to advance the cause of civil rights, leading me to a decade of constant work in the court room and the trial of some of the most interesting cases of that era.

These clients and causes included the Black Panther party in Denver and elsewhere; Rudolpho "Corky" Gonzales and his Crusade for Justice and later the La Raza Unida; the migrant laborer of Northern Colorado and corrupt municipal courts that perverted justice by using the plight of the migrants to fill the city coffers; Reies Tijerina and the New Mexico Land Grant Movement; the students of Denver University who took over the dean's office; the students of the University of Colorado who were insulted by S.I.Hayakawa until they reacted as he wanted them to and were then arrested; the San Francisco Mime Troupe and their right to exercise free speech in the theater; and protesters of the war in Vietnam.

The skills I developed as a trial lawyer on behalf of these and other clients were forged in the county and municipal courts, honed in the district courts, and polished in the federal courts.

From this experience I am convinced that the mechanics of advocacy can be taught in the law schools, but that an understanding of the true nature of the trial lawyer's task and the secrets of great cross-examination can only be found in the study of those who have gone before. For the trial lawyer's knowledge must extend beyond legal subjects. The trial lawyer must be knowledgeable in history, psychology, literature, and the arts and sciences, and have the ability to bring this knowledge to bear in such a way as to persuade a jury.

Just as the surgeon must understand human anatomy and the circulatory system before performing heart bypass surgery, so must the trial lawyer have a clear understanding of the dynamics of a trial before he can understand the role of cross-examination in the entire drama.

The trial lawyer must understand that our justice system is fragile, that it combines the imprecision of the law and the imperfection of man. Everyone involved in the system, judges, juries, police, lawyers, and witnesses, is capable of making mistakes and concealing prejudices, sometimes unknowingly.

Jurors who spend all theirs lives in a world where, for the most part, they are permitted to indulge a wide range of prejudices, are asked in court where they are deciding the fate of another person to set aside these prejudices and adopt a set of strict values defined over centuries. They may find some of these concepts difficult to accept or understand, and the trial lawyer must convince them to give up their everyday notions of concepts such as reasonable doubt or presumption of innocence and replace them with definitions of these concepts that are dictated by the law.

Juries are fallible and they make mistakes. Many advocates assume too much about the ability of jurors to set aside everyday assumptions and adopt the strictures of the law. Most jurors, for instance, believe that a defendant has done something wrong or he wouldn't be in the courtroom, and that if he doesn't take the stand in his own behalf he is guilty. Both of these concepts are contrary to the law but they are deeply ingrained in most peoples' everyday thought patterns. The trial lawyer must recognize this problem and develop strategies and tactics to overcome these common attitudes.

Our system of determining the truth about the past is subject to will and caprice. It is a form of art and not of science. Judges have great latitude in exercising discretion and have the opportunity to sway a jury to a conclusion they want. Prosecutors usually have professional witnesses to depend on and they too exercise a great latitude in influencing the jury. Consequently fundamental notions of justice must be impressed on the jury. While the law says that a defendant is presumed innocent the reality is the defendant is presumed guilty, meaning that at the outset of the case the cards are stacked against him. Cross-examination becomes the greatest aid in determining the truth. Without it the task of representing a client in a trial would be hopeless.

Cross-examination can only be successful if the jury has been prepared for it. They must be educated by the lawyer long before the stage of cross-examination in a trial is reached. Before the advocate can educate a jury he must educate himself and develop a keen understanding of what people are likely to think, what their prejudices may be, and how to overcome them, and what kinds of emotion or presentation may appeal to the individual jurors. Being able to do this requires a great empathy for all levels of human experience.

A deep understanding of the roots of our system of justice is required to give flesh and blood to constitutional ideals such as the presumption of innocence and proof beyond a reasonable doubt because fundamental principles are constantly in danger of being eroded in the name of some higher goal.

People don't give up their liberty but under some illusion. Whether it be the fight against terrorism, the desire for safe streets, or the war on drugs and crime, there are always those who think the quick fix is forgetting about constitutional protections. These people believe that the fist and bludgeon of law enforcement will only be used against someone who is guilty and that invasion of one's home for a search will only happen to those who are guilty of a crime. As frustrations mount, the view that constitutional safeguards are a luxury gains currency.

No one who is charged with enforcing laws and administering justice is immune from this temptation. These people, from judges down to the security guard at the airport, are constantly bombarded with the message that lawbreakers are walking the streets because society has given them legal rights they do not deserve.

Jurors are not immune to this kind of thinking and in fact have more right to feel this way. They do not work in an environment that requires them on a daily basis to consider the problem of balancing the quick fix against the long term considerations of constitutional protections and they have no mechanism in their everyday lives to balance this desire to rid themselves and society of crime against the long range effects of the quick fix.

It falls to the trial lawyer as much as anyone to insure that our system of justice does not succumb to these pressures. Of all the tools available to the advocate none is more important than cross-examination. It is a complex subject that resists being taught. Some commentators simply throw up their hands and exclaim that great cross-examiners are born not made. I suppose this is true to the same extent that some of us can study a foreign language forever and never become truly fluent while others gain fluency quite rapidly. On the other hand we can all learn the vocabulary and the idioms and be more proficient than had we never learned at all. The subject is complex but the more one understands what others have said and done about it the more likely there will be success.

Cross-examination is a complex and multifaceted subject. Some of the many themes this book will explore include the following:

- Cross-examination is the single most important weapon in determining the truth at trial. If the testimony of one side remains intact while that of the other is put into question, the failure of cross-examination usually results in a failure to win the case.
- Cross-examination is the trial skill acquired with the most difficulty; nevertheless there have been no great trial lawyers who have not been great cross-examiners. Although there is no single formula for becoming a great cross-examiner, studying the great ones in history and working with those having the skills and experience is indispensable.
- Only cross-examination involves face to face confrontation between witness and lawyer. For this reason juries await the moment with keen anticipation and the ensuing defeats and victories are magnified in their impression of who should win.
- Often the outcome of the case depends on this confrontation between one side's witnesses and the other's lawyer and the lawyer must enter this battle while keeping the entire case

in mind. While concentrating on the witness the lawyer must constantly be aware of the effect the testimony is having on other participants in the case and formulate questions and strategy quickly to assure his points are being driven home.

Cross-examination is a battle of wits producing tension, cleverness, suspense, and humor, and requires the spontaneous formulation of strategy. The cross-examiner must be perceptive while exercising ingenuity and logical thought and must intuitively read the mind of the witness while judging motives. Quickness of mind, control of one's self, control of the witness, and thinking on one's feet, is demanded in the face of the unexpected. The cross-examiner must be able to make an instant analysis and formulate a method of attack while asking questions.

- Jurors believe their individual interests are universally shared and the advocate undertaking cross-examination must weave into the fabric of his presentation some thread that will appeal to each.
- Effective cross-examination proceeds from a mastery of the subject matter of the trial and a keen understanding of human nature, thus the trial lawyer must have an inquisitive mind and thirst for learning in a wide range of subjects. The advocate should keep in mind that words are weapons and books the battlements from which they are hurled. All great advocates have been avid readers of works that plumb the experiences of mankind.

The idea for this book stemmed from a desire to reduce the subject of cross-examination to a series of principles that the cross-examiner could review before a trial. The principles are divided into eight parts.

Part one (Sizing Up the Terrain) gives an overview of the issues common to most trials that the cross-examiner must be aware of, and deal with, if he expects to be successful. Why the cross-examination really begins before the jury enters the courtroom.

The need to create a favorable courtroom atmosphere if your cross-examination is to succeed.

Part two (Plotting the Strategy) addresses the general considerations of cross-examination common to any case. Deciding when and if you should cross-examine, and how to set and maintain the focus of the case.

Part three (Selecting Tactics) focuses on specific tactics that should be employed in the cross-examination. Ways the advocate can deflect damage, maintain control, and put the jury on his side.

Part four (Achieving the Objective) discusses particular ways to define and achieve your objectives during cross-examination.

Part five (Developing a Style) raises issues with respect to ways the cross-examiner should conduct himself during cross-examination that will be most helpful in his search for victory.

Part six (Understanding Witnesses) Provides insights into the forces that operate on a witness that result in their testimony and some ways to attack the witness.

Part seven (Thinking on Your Feet) gives some hints and advice about the spontaneous innovation every advocate must be able to do in order to be a successful cross-examiner.

Part eight (Questioning the Expert Witness) explores some of the special considerations that exist with respect to dealing with the expert witness. It takes some of the mystery out of this area of cross-examination and shows why the expert is in many ways no more difficult to cross-examine than any other witness.

PART ONE
Sizing Up The Terrain

PRINCIPLE ONE

The Object Of Cross-Examination Is To Cast Doubt On The Witnesses And Evidence Presented By The Opposition Using All The Rhetorical Skills Available

Cross-examination is more than asking questions. A definition of cross-examination limited to the dramatic confrontation between witness and advocate fails to take into consideration additional elements I believe necessary to the training of the cross-examiner. While this confrontation is the main thrust of cross-examination and the most dramatic. The advocate must keep in mind that cross-examination entails a great deal more. Cross-examination is the strategy of words and actions the advocate employs during the presentation of evidence by the opposition that serves to cast doubt on the opponent's case. Consequently the cross-examiner must possess an understanding and a mastery of skills and techniques beyond the methods of actually questioning witnesses if he is to use cross-examination to its fullest.

It is my belief that the cross-examiner who does not realize there are factors in the skill of cross-examination that go beyond merely learning to question a witness will be at a disadvantage.

A great cross-examiner formulates a comprehensive strategy for use during the presentation of evidence by the other side, a strategy that includes a great many more things than planning questions to ask the witness when it is his turn. He pays close attention to his own behavior, that of his client and that of any supporter of the client who may be present. He knows that this expressions and body language during the testimony of opposing witness are themselves a form of cross-examination. He factors his treatment of others in the courtroom into his general attack on the opposition's case. He watches the jurors to determine their thoughts and reactions to the testimony. He maintains eye contact with the jurors when possible. He understands the judicious use of various emotions such as silence, indifference, indignation or incredulity.

THREE FORMS OF CLASSICAL RHETORIC

If the advocate is to use all the techniques of cross-examination effectively he must be well grounded in all facets of the trial and have a clear understanding of exactly what trials are meant to accomplish. It is not the object of this work to give a comprehensive discussion of the development of the trial to its present day status. It is important however to give some attention to basic notions of what we as advocates are seeking to do in a trial through the artful use of rhetoric and drama. A fundamental understanding of what a trial is and therefore what cross-examination seeks to accomplish can be gained from a reading of Aristotle's Rhetoric. Something I suggest every trial lawyer do.

Aristotle points out that rhetoric is the use of verbal arts to persuade others to believe certain things. There are three kinds of rhetoric: political rhetoric, ceremonial rhetoric, and forensic rhetoric.

Political rhetoric seeks to persuade a civic decision maker such as an electorate what the future of the state should be and what action must be taken to accomplish it. Ceremonial rhetoric, by contrast, is not used to persuade the listener but to state as eloquently as possible that which the listener already understands. A funeral oration is a good example of ceremonial rhetoric. The third form of rhetoric, and the one that the trial lawyer must be thoroughly familiar with, is forensic rhetoric.

Forensic rhetoric seeks to convince decision makers that events in the past occurred a particular way. This is all a trial is about.

Each side to a case is seeking to convince a jury that events in the past occurred in a certain way. Was the traffic light red or green when the accident occurred? Was it negligent to fail to diagnose cancer in a patient? Did the client pull the trigger in self defense or did he kill with premeditation? It is the advocate's job to persuade the fact finder that the answer to these questions are the answers he proposes and not those which the opposition proposes.

Aristotle goes on to tell us that "rhetoric may be defined as the faculty of observing in any given case the available means of persuasion". It does not depend on the mastery of the subject matter of the persuasion. If the case is about medicine, or involves geometry, or engineering the advocate need not be an expert in those subjects to be able to persuade the decision maker. But the advocate must be able to discern the means of persuasion on almost any subject presented.

There are three types of persuasion proved by the spoken word. There is persuasion which depends on the personal character of the speaker. The verbal presentation must be made in such a way as to make the audience believe that the speaker is credible. We believe good men more readily and fully than others, and this is particularly true in matters where exact certainty is impossible and opinion is divided. Second, there is persuasion that puts the listener in a certain frame of mind. It is easier to convince a jury of certain facts if they are friendly and receptive than if they are hostile and resistant. Third, there is persuasion by the proof, or apparent proof. In a trial this is the quality of the evidence and the credibility of the witnesses.

The advocate must keep in mind the fact that cross-examination is just one of several opportunities during to trial to employ his skills in forensic rhetoric. The success of any one will depend on the success of the others. In order to effectively employ those skills of cross-examination the advocate must be firmly grounded in an understanding of the other means of persuasion.

The skills of the advocate first come into play during jury selection. It is the phase of the trial in which the advocate not only tries to select a jury that is impartial, but also presents a chance to plant the seeds of his version of past events and to establish those elements of human interaction that will make the jury want to accept his version of past events rather than those of opposing counsel.

The second opportunity presents itself in the opening statement during which the advocate is permitted great latitude in outlining for the jury what he expects his case to prove. The third opportunity is the presentation of his proof through witnesses and exhibits.

The fourth and most crucial is opportunity to cast doubt on the direct evidence of the other side by words and actions throughout the trial that help cast doubt on the case of the other side. This is cross-examination.

Finally the advocate has the opportunity to convince the fact finder through his summation or closing argument.

The advocate must remember that all of Aristotle's modes of rhetorical persuasion are common to these various stages; character of the speaker, putting the audience in a receptive mood, and proof or apparent proof which is the evidence and the credibility of the witnesses. Often the advocate will concentrate on the third mode in cross-examination and neglect the first two. More often than not this oversight will lead to disaster. The advocate must constantly pay attention to the role of the character of the speaker and keeping the jury in a receptive mood if his attack on the credibility of the witnesses and the evidence is to succeed.

Context Of Cross-Examination

While cross-examination is a vital stage in the advocate's goal of persuading a jury, it cannot stand alone. The cross-examination has better chance of success if all the other stages of the trial are approached with the same attention to detail. Even the most brilliant of cross-examinations may fail to convince the jury if other aspects of the case have been neglected. The great advocate will not concentrate on only one aspect of the case at the expense of any other. Building a solid foundation through voir dire and the opening statement will put the jury in a frame of mind to absorb and understand the points the advocate hopes to make during cross-examination.

The advocate must view the trial as a blank canvas, which, by the time summation comes around, will appear to the jury as a completed picture, a picture that makes sense to the jury and is understandable in all its aspects. To do this effectively the advocate must begin the creation of this picture at the very outset of the case and have a clear idea that he can project to the jury at every stage.

The advocate must be able to separate the material from the extraneous. He must not confuse activity for action, movement for direction, or form for substance. To accomplish this, the advocate must begin the preparation of his closing argument from the moment he accepts a case destined for trial. By the time the jury panel files into the courtroom and the voir dire begins, the advocate must have a clear idea of the points he wishes to make with the jury and a way of doing it that the jury will readily understand.

To get and maintain the jury's focus, the advocate must create an atmosphere beneficial to him and to his client. This requires a fair understanding of the dramatic arts. The advocate is the producer, director, stage manager, and lead actor. How well he performs these roles will play a large part in determining the outcome of the case.

Principle Two

The Advocate Must Create A Favorable Trial Atmosphere For Effective Cross-Examination

The most brilliant and effective cross-examination in the world may fail to win the jury to your side if it is conducted in a hostile atmosphere. The advocate who does not pay attention to all the dynamics of the courtroom may lose in spite of how good the case is or how wonderful his cross-examination might be.

The "Personality" Of The Courtroom

At the outset of a trial the advocate should have an understanding of the personality of the courtroom where he is trying the case. If he has not appeared in the particular court before or is unfamiliar with judge and the court personnel he should familiarize himself as much as possible with the situation. He can do this by discussing the matter with other lawyers who have practiced in that particular court; attending proceedings in the court as an observer; obtaining a letter of introduction from a mutual friend of the judge (preferably another judge); and seeking to meet the court personnel and establishing a rapport with them.

All courts have a distinct "personality". This is a combination of the personalities of the judge, his secretary, the clerk, the court reporter, and the bailiff. They live together every working day. They share in each others' lives, the tragedies, the joys, the ups and downs. It is a formidable club for which, in most cases, the advocate is an intruder. The greater the intrusion, the more difficult for the advocate to gain acceptance. The advocate should do everything in his power to diffuse any resentment that may naturally occur and make himself a welcome addition to the court.

In criminal cases, the advocate usually must face the additional fact that the district attorney assigned to that courtroom has had the opportunity to gain entry into the group and (assuming he has made the most of it) will have that added advantage over you. You, on the other hand, must establish a similar position.

Gaining Admittance To The Official Circle

As an advocate, about to try a case, you are entering into a well defined mini-society as a stranger. Add to this the fact that you will soon be faced with a jury panel full of people who have been thrown together for the first time, assembled in a large room, and literally marched through the halls together to enter a courtroom which is daunting in design and setting. These strangers will be nervous and keenly attuned to the dynamics of the situation they are entering. Their perception that you too are an outsider will present you with another obstacle to overcome.

Before the trial begins the advocate should know as much as he can about the idiosyncrasies of the court. He can gain this knowledge through his own experience or through discussions with other lawyers. He should visit the court on one pretext or another and introduce himself to the personnel. If possible he should attend some proceedings in the court as an observer and establish some sense of the dynamics of that particular court.

Judge's Pet Procedures And Unwritten Rules

Every court has its pet procedures. The advocate should be familiar with them before the trial. Often these are in written form and can be obtained from the court clerk. One should also endeavor to discover whether the court has particular rules that are not written anywhere but which will incur the wrath of the judge or the bailiff when violated and will serve to embarrass you and put you off stride.

Some years ago there was a judge in this jurisdiction who presided in a courtroom in which the seal of the state was woven into the carpet just in front of the bench. The judge, who was cantankerous in general, would fly into a rage when any lawyer stepped on the seal. Presumably the judge felt such conduct signified disrespect. Unfortunately, the seal was so placed that in the normal conduct of a trial it would inevitably be in the path of the lawyers.

It was standing procedure among the bar that lawyers new to the court would not be told of this unwritten but vigorously enforced rule. Inevitably an uninitiated lawyer would step on the seal and the judge would immediately interrupt and admonish the offending culprit in the most derogatory language possible right in front of the jury. It usually had a devastating effect on the lawyer.

Other judges have similar rules written and unwritten that are usually brought to the attention of the offending lawyer at the moment he is in full stride. For example, many judges do not want attorneys practicing before them to leave the podium during their presentations and will admonish and interrupt you if it happens, thereby destroying your concentration during the examination of a witness.

Knowing these problems in advance will save the advocate considerable embarrassment in front of the jury. This is important because the favorable atmosphere you must create will be difficult to achieve if the jury feels you have not been welcomed into the court's circle.

Overcoming these various obstacles usually takes little more than the exercise of common courtesy and civility. Make a point of being able to address each of the court personnel by name. Pay attention to what is happening. If the reporter needs help with her chair or in carrying something, there is no rule against offering to help. Quite the contrary. Good manners require it. Personal greetings each day before the start of the trial should be mandatory. Discovering through conversation some common interest with the court personnel also helps establish rapport. If the personnel in the court like you, the jury will be aware of it, and it will help them like you as well.

INVOLVING THE JURORS FROM THE OUTSET

A trial is an unfolding drama of which cross-examination is only one part. In order for the advocate to be successful with the cross-examination, the jury must be prepared from the earliest stage for each step in the presentation of his case and be favorably disposed to its validity.

Successful cross-examination must be built on a foundation of juror interest, trust, and understanding for the lawyer and the case. Building this foundation must begin at the very outset of the case and is accomplished by creating a sympathetic atmosphere through word and gesture by the lawyer and the client.

The lawyer must be aware that having gained the attention of the jury through dress or eloquence of speech, he will be scrutinized by them throughout the case, some to reinforce an early opinion and others to find a flaw. The lawyer must assume the jury will see everything he does and says and he must conduct himself in a manner calculated to have an impact.

It should not be forgotten that for most jurors the trial will be a new experience. They will enter the courtroom well aware of the solemnity of the proceedings which they should not be permitted to forget. The advocate should maintain an attitude that is respectful but not condescending, one that shows confidence as well as humility conveys to the jury a sense of their importance to the case.

It is frustrating for jurors who are otherwise active participants outside the courtroom to be relegated to the role of mute observers. To the extent the advocate can include them in the events of the trial they will feel a warm sense of camaraderie with him and, by extension, with his client.

We are far from understanding the exact dynamics of jury behavior and decision making. Experience tells me that jurors try to focus on the facts of the case but are nevertheless swayed by small incidents. I remember an accident case in which the clients were husband and wife. Each day the husband opened the door for the wife, held her chair when she sat or rose, and was otherwise solicitous of her comfort. After the case one of the jurors explained the basis of the verdict for us in terms of the facts of the case but mentioned several times that he was impressed with the behavior of the husband towards the wife.

Some advocates behave towards the jurors in a very polite solicitous way when they address them or exchange looks with them only to destroy the resulting goodwill by badgering their clients or browbeating others in the court. If the advocate is aloof, cold, poorly dressed, or abrasive in word or gesture, the jury will be aware of it. Behaving poorly towards anyone in the court room will have a negative effect on the jury.

Having a clear idea of the strategy of the case at the outset is necessary to gain the confidence and interest of the jury. If counsel is unprepared, or unable to articulate the case in a short space, this limitation will be conveyed to the jury and there will be a lack of understanding and confidence.

Lincoln was asked how he achieved such clarity of ideas in his speech and responded this way:

> *I never went to school more than six months in my life, but I can say this, that among my earliest recollections I remember how, when a mere child, I used to get irritated when anybody talked to me in a way I could not understand. I do not think I ever got angry at anything else in my life, but that always disturbed my temper and has ever since. I can remember going to my little bedroom after hearing the neighbors talk of an evening with my father and spending no small part of the night walking up and down and trying to make out what was the exact meaning of*

> *some of their to me dark sayings. I could not sleep, although I tried to. When I got on such a hunt for an idea, and until I got it, or I thought I had got it I was not satisfied until I had repeated it over and over, until I had put it in language plain enough, as I thought, for any boy I knew to comprehend. This was a kind of passion with me. It has stuck by me, for I am never easy now when I am handling a case until I have bounded it north, and bounded it south, and bounded it east, and bounded it west.*

Before the jury panel ever enters the courtroom the advocate should have a clear and concise idea of strategy, tactics, objectives, and his closing argument. Once the jurors are present for selection the advocate should begin to impress upon them his theory of the case. If the defense is that the client performed some or all of the acts alleged but did not have the necessary criminal intent, then this simple theme should constantly be brought to the attention of the jury. This may take the form of a statement to the judge that alludes to intention and the difficulty of defining it. Or an opportunity may present itself where the opposing counsel says or does something that is incorrect or creates a problem however small. You can express the sentiment in the presence of the jury panel that you are sure he did not intend the result and that we all agree that it is difficult at best to impute a negative intent to anyone.

This same result may be achieved by accepting responsibility for some act or omission in the case, such as being a few minutes late. In doing so, stress can be placed on the fact that there was no disrespect intended. This observation points out that we can all be guilty of acts that may be negative but do not necessarily carry any criminal intent.

The lawyer should be aware that the drama of a trial has equal measures of form and substance and to present the substance while overlooking the form can be disastrous. This difficulty should not be confused with the problem of allowing form to be a substitute for substance. Rather it is a recognition that even an advocate whose case is strong on substantive merits will very likely fail if he ignores the form in which his presentation is delivered to the jury.

Being well dressed and groomed, and demonstrating good manners, will always have a positive effect on jurors, while the failure in these areas will always have a negative effect. Jurors expect the trial lawyer to be different from them, just as they would like their politicians to be different. They expect the lawyer to be more articulate, better dressed, and more knowledgeable. The key for the successful advocate it to be all these things without being condescending.

A favorable atmosphere is created through courtesy towards everyone; civility in your relations with opposing counsel, the judge, and witnesses, articulate speech, precision in argument, concision in presentment of evidence, and control of the situation.

Principle Three

The Appeal To The Jurors Begins When They Enter The Courtroom For The First Time And Ends With Closing Argument

Many advocates believe that the jury is not an active participant in the case and somehow should be approached as an inanimate observer with whom there is no personal interaction. This is a major mistake. Every attempt should be made to create a alliance with the jury as if the advocate and the jury were embarking together on a voyage of discovery and drama.

It should be the advocate's practice to begin the appeal at the moment the panel from which the ultimate jury will be selected enters the courtroom. The advocate should stop what he is doing at that moment and stand if he is seated. He should attempt to make eye contact with as many as possible and induce as many as possible to share a smile with him. It should be remembered that these men and women are strangers in a strange environment and need reassurance and friendliness. Every attempt should be made to charm the jury on a personal level by showing interest in them as individuals.

SIGNIFICANCE OF VOIR DIRE

The first opportunity to have interaction with them verbally, is the voir dire examination. I make it a practice to spend the time during the judges voir dire and the opponent's if I am defending the case, to memorize the name of each juror who is called to the box. I believe that when I rise to conduct voir dire and can call each prospective juror by name it accomplishes two things. First it gives each one the sense that I know him or her and puts them at ease. It also gives them the sense that if I can call each by name this quickly I must have a good memory, and thus at other times in the case when I recite my recollection of the testimony they will already have evidence of the quality of my memory.

It is important to keep in mind the fact that there are four functions in voir dire: one, to discover any factual information about the juror that requires their discharge for legal reasons; two, to discover facts about them that will give counsel basis for excluding them from the panel peremptorily; three, to establish your character as a speaker as one means of persuasion; and four, to put the jury in a certain frame of mind for the purposes of persuasion.

At the end of the voir dire examination the jury should be disposed towards your case and have made individual and collective promises that in exchange for your doing something (establishing reasonable doubt for instance they will do another (return a verdict of not guilty for instance).

The vast majority of jurors when first entering the courtroom are resentful of having to give up their other activities, especially earning a living, to sit for hours in a courtroom. The advocate that can make this experience an interesting and enjoyable one will have gone a long way in winning the jury to his side of the case.

The use of voir dire to establish your personal character and to put the jury in a frame of mind receptive to your point of view is something difficult to teach but which must be acquired to reach the top ranks of trial advocacy.

The voir dire examination is a crucial stage in the case and is an art form in itself. All the complexities of it cannot be covered here, but note should be taken of the fact that there are fewer and fewer practitioners of the form. The need to speed trials and diminish the role of the advocate in the resolution of disputes has caused even more erosion of voir dire as a rhetorical tool. This attack will only serve to hurt the cause of justice and trail advocates should resist it wherever possible.

It has never been a tool in the federal system during my career and in the states system there has been a constant erosion of it. This erosion seems to be the result of many factors not the least of which is a failure by trial lawyers to conduct proper voir dire examinations. As courts have been inundated with cases, there has been a never ending attempt by judges to speed up the trial process. This has usually resulted in the judge's taking away the voir dire function from counsel.

Most judges are sympathetic to the lawyer who wishes to do the voir dire but simply don't have the time to see endless questioning to no apparent purpose. It is my feeling that most voir dire that goes to questions of challenges for cause can be conducted by the judge, if that is necessary, and peremptory challenges can be made with little additional time by counsel. The aspect of voir dire that can only be conducted by counsel is that having to do with the two functions of rhetoric mentioned earlier, establishing the personal character of the speaker, and putting the jury in a certain frame of mind for the purpose of persuasion. These are both peculiar to counsel and not to permit voir dire for this purpose can take away much of the trial lawyer's arsenal.

IMPRESSING THE JURORS WITH YOUR SKILLS

It is important to impress the jurors with your skills. In addition to memorizing their names before addressing them, you can also demonstrate a grasp United States history as it relates to their role as jurors. In this respect I keep near my desk The *Almanac of Liberty* by William O. Douglas. In that excellent book the former Supreme Court Justice relates an event in American history for every day of the year that has special significance for American liberty. On the day of my voir dire it gives me an event that I try to weave into my voir dire that indicates to the jury the importance of their role in a historical sense, but also serves to demonstrate that I see the trial as part of our history and have a good grasp of our history.

It also helps to lead the jury to a conclusion about some important aspect of the case that you will rely on that they feel was not force fed but in which they participated. I find this particularly useful in defending criminal cases where I want the jury to concede that they do not begin the case as neutral observers but in fact begin the case convinced of the defendant's innocence. It goes something like this.

After some preliminary questions that give me a sense of rapport with the jury panel I ask the following question:

"Mr. Winston do you have an opinion as to the guilt or innocence of the defendant as he sits here as this moment?"

Not wishing to show any bias and believing he should be open minded the juror's response is always 'no'. The same question is then put to others with the same response.

At this point I leave the subject and ask some other questions. Then I ask one of the jurors who were left out of the earlier sequence if he has any objection to the court's admonition that the defendant is presumed innocent until proven guilty. I usually question him at some length on this principle and give him examples of why it is important and gain a concession from him that he would insist on that presumption for himself or a loved one should either be on trial.

Having hammered home the concept of presumption of innocence I adopt a sense of appearing to come to a conclusion myself and return to Mr. Winston with the following:

"Mr. Winston I know you've been listening to this very carefully and I feel that having heard all this you may realize now that your earlier answer with respect to having an opinion as to the defendant's guilt or innocence may be different now."

If I'm lucky Mr. Winston, who I selected for this in the first place because he seemed intelligent, will have seen the light and agree with me. If he doesn't I plunge on.

"So you see now that if the law presumes the defendant to be innocent and that presumption stays with him until overcome by proof beyond a reasonable doubt, then you must have an opinion now that as the defendant sits he here is innocent. If for some reason you were required to give a verdict at this moment by the court it would have to be Not Guilty! It would have to be that because the defendant is presumed to be innocent. It is the cornerstone of our system of justice and if you don't agree with that principle then you should let us know and be excused."

By now Mr. Winston is in complete agreement with me, as are the other jurors, and I must say it usually thrills me to see the gradual realization of the point on each of their faces. I go on to make all the jurors individually admit the fact that they have an opinion that the defendant is presumed innocent at that moment and they will continue to hold that view until the prosecution convinces them otherwise beyond a reasonable doubt.

By this device I have developed a rapport with the jurors in the sense we have unraveled a sort of legal conundrum together without preaching to them. They are impressed with my own ability to put this abstract notion into understandable terms, and they have committed themselves to a position of having a strong feeling about the innocence of the defendant and the necessity of being taken 180 degrees by the prosecution to return a verdict of guilty.

Continual Focus On The Jury

A common error of advocates is to forget during the trial that it is the jury they are appealing to. When this happens the advocate misses many opportunities to communicate and relate to it.

Rufus Choate was considered the very best at taking command of a trial and orchestrating his appeal to the jury. Here's how his style was described in *Reminiscences of Rufus Choate:*

> [H]is appeal to the jury began long before his final argument; it began when he first took his seat before them and looked into their eyes. He generally contrived to get his seat as near them as convenient, if possible having his table close to the bar, in front of their seats, and separated from them only by a narrow space for passage. There he sat, calm, contemplative,

> *in the midst of occasional noise and confusion solemnly unruffled; always making some little headway either with the jury, the court, or the witness; never doing a single thing which could by possibility lose him favor; ever doing some little thing to win it; smiling benignantly upon the counsel when a good thing was said; smiling sympathizingly upon the jury when any juryman laughed or made an inquiry; wooing them all the time with his magnetic glances as a lover might woo his mistress; seeming to precise over the whole scene with an air of easy superiority; exercising from the very first moment an indefinable sway and influence upon the minds of all before and around him. His manner to the jury was that of a friend, a friend solicitous to help them through their tedious investigation; never that of an expert combatant, intent of victory, and looking upon them as only instruments for its attainment.*

In order to make an ally of the jury the advocate should act and speak with the jury constantly in mind. Whenever possible the advocate should speak directly to them, and statements and objections should be made in language calculated for the jury to understand.

The Jury should be approached as if the advocate wants each of them to leave the courtroom feeling they would hire him if ever in need, and would enthusiastically recommend him.

Principle Four

Assume The Jury Is Watching You

Advocates will often work quite hard in the early stages of the trial to establish a presence with the jury only to forget that work in the heat of the battle. It is unfortunate that in so doing the advocate may say or do something that the jury, or one of its members, is aware of that will undo all of the hard work that has gone before.

The men and women who make up the jury are resigned to spending the time on a jury and have replaced their resentment with a sense of expectation. They have preconceived notions of what they will be seeing. Most of these expectations are based on false portrayals of what happens in a trial conveyed to them through television and books. Regardless of the source or the validity the expectations are real and must be taken into consideration by the advocate.

If his voir dire has been successful he will have at least blunted the more unrealistic of the expectations. But he will not have eliminated them altogether. In fact, for the most part, he will have replaced them with others more to his liking and will have entered a silent pact with the jurors that he will deliver certain things to them in the course of the trial and in return they will return a verdict in his favor.

The advocate is now faced with twelve men and women who will be required to sit silently with out control of the situation while the lawyers and the judge perform a drama that often utilizes language they cannot understand, and prevents the witnesses from telling them something they desperately want to hear for reasons they cannot comprehend.

Often I have seen lawyers reach this time in the case and give the impression that having seated the jury they may now turn their attention to the case itself as if the job with the jury is finished or at least interrupted until they face them directly again for the closing argument. This approach fails to take into account a wide range of strategy and tactics that should be designed to continue the relationship established with the jury during the selection process.

In particular the advocate may lose sight of the fact that the jury collectively and individually will see everything that goes on in the courtroom and will base its decision consciously or unconsciously on what it observes and not only on what the testimony or exhibits prove.

Thus the advocate must never lose sight of the fact that one or more of the jurors will monitor his every act, gesture, and behavior towards others in the courtroom. The advocate must understand that the form of the trial (the behavior of the participants and the language used) is as important as the substance of the trial (who is telling the truth who is lying).

A minor lapse in attention to form may cause a juror to develop a negative attitude towards you or your case that will sway him against you. This lapse in form may be nothing more than an expression of chagrin or disbelief or despair; it can be no more than a gesture towards a client or spectator that may convey something negative about your case; it could be an offhand comment made in a hallway or elevator that a juror hears; it can be the inconsiderate treatment of someone in the court.

The advocate must never lose the sense that everything he does is for the benefit of the jury and will count for or against him throughout the case. It is best to adopt a pattern of behavior that is always in place during the trial than to attempt a pattern of behavior that is one thing when you believe the jury is watching and another when it is not.

Projecting Confidence

It is important that the advocate show no weakness in his case and behave in a confident manner. He must counsel his clients and witnesses in this regard. It is not enough to put witnesses through a rigorous schooling on their testimony only to have them botch things because of how they behave as spectators, or in the halls, or elsewhere. The presentation of a good case is often thwarted because well meaning supporters of your client conduct themselves in such a way that causes the jury to have a bias in favor of the opposition.

The need to portray confidence in the case requires particular skill when the other side produces some damaging testimony or evidence. The well-prepared advocate will know when this evidence is coming and will caution his client on how to react. He must school his client not to betray any lack of confidence by reaction to testimony or evidence.

The well-prepared advocate will have decided in advance how he will react to the most damaging testimony presented by the other side. What he does will depend on the particulars of the case. He may attempt to divert the attention of the jury away from the evidence by seeking an interruption of the case. He may try to shift the emphasis of what the witness says by showing surprise at an unlikely moment. He may use previously established rapport with one or more jurors to minimize the testimony by expression or gesture. Whatever tactic he employs must be by design and with control.

If the advocate exudes a sense of confidence, behaves in a successful manner, conveys a sense of self confidence, and demonstrates a clear grasp of the issues and control of the situation the jury will inevitably be swayed to some degree to his side.

The advocate must use every tool at his disposal to impress on the jury positive aspects of the case. It is not enough to present evidence and testimony that supports your case. There are inevitably two plausible sides to the controversy or it would not have reached a trial. The issue is which side can present an otherwise plausible version of the past to the jury in the most compelling way.

Throughout the history of the law and its literature, advocates have had to grapple with the means and devices of having and showing at all times confidence in their client and their case.

In *Phinneas Redux* by Anthony Trollope the hero Phinneas Finn has managed to place himself in circumstances which have resulted in a murder charge against him. He is being held in prison pending the outcome of the trial.

Mr. Chaffanbrass is the barrister who will try the case and on the eve of trial the solicitor, Mr. Wickerby, is imploring Chaffanbrass to go and see Finn. Mr. Chaffanbrass has not met Finn and only reluctantly agrees to see him because Finn expects it, but not because it is important to his defense in the case. In fact Chaffanbrass rather feels that a meeting with the client in a murder case before the trial might be more harmful than good. His concern is whether a meeting might compromise his ability to demonstrate to the jury a confidence in the client:

> "I'll see him [Finn] tomorrow.' [says Chaffanbrass]
> "Yes-he is very anxious to speak to you."
> "What's the use of it Wickerby? I hate seeing a client. What comes of it?"
> "Of course he wants to tell his own story."
> "But I don't want to hear his own story. What good will his own story do me: He'll tell me either one of two things. He'll swear he didn't murder the man"
> "That's what he'll say."
> "Which can have no effect upon me one way or the other; or else he'll say that he did,-which would cripple me altogether."
> "He won't say that, Mr. Chaffanbrass."
> "There's no knowing what they'll say. A man will go on swearing by his God that he is innocent, till at last, in a moment of emotion, he breaks down, and

out comes the truth. In such a case as this I do not in the least want to know the truth about the murder."

"That is what the public wants to know."

"That is because the public is ignorant. The public should not wish to know anything of the kind. What we should all wish to get at is the truth of the evidence about the murder,—as to which no positive knowledge is attainable; but because he has been proved to have committed the murder,—as to which proof, though it be enough for hanging, there must always be attached some shadow of doubt. We were delighted to hang Palmer,—but we don't know that he killed Cook. A learned man who knew more about it than we can know seemed to think that he didn't. Now the last man to give us any useful insight into the evidence is the prisoner himself. In nineteen cases out of twenty a man tried for murder in this country committed the murder for which he is tried."

"There really seems to be a doubt in this case."

"I dare say. If there be only nineteen guilty out of twenty, there must be one innocent; and why not Mr. Phineas Finn? But, if it be so, he, burning with the sense of injustice, thinks that everybody should see it as he sees it. He is to be tried, because on investigation, everybody sees it just in a different light. In such case he is unfortunate, but he can't assist me in liberating him from his misfortune. He sees what is patent and clear to him,—that he walked home that night without meddling with any one. But I can't see that, or make others see it, because he sees it."

"His manner of telling you may do something."

"If it does, Mr. Wickerby, it is because I am unfit for my business. If he have the gift of protesting well, I am to think him innocent; and, therefore to think him guilty, if he be unprovided with such eloquence! I will neither believe or disbelieve anything that a client *says to me,—unless he confess his guilt, in which case my services may be but of little avail. Of course I shall see him, as he asks it. We had better meet then,—say at half-past ten." Whereupon Mr. Wickerby wrote to the governor of the prison begging that Phineas Finn might be informed of the visit."*

Principle Five

Cross-Examination Is Measured By Quality Not Quantity

Justice Jackson of the United States Supreme Court once pointed out that the mind will absorb only what the ass will endure. In this day of electronic bites and information being delivered in thirty second increments the advocate must always keep Justice Jackson's statement in mind.

There is the temptation for the advocate to confuse the quantity of cross-examination with the quality of cross-examination. This is because he is not secure in his judgment of what points to emphasize and which to leave alone. It takes an advocate with a great deal of confidence in his own skills to be content to ask a witness just a few questions on cross-examination. Inevitably if the outcome of the case is contrary to the expectations of the client the performance of the lawyer will come under scrutiny. The failure to ask questions will more often be a source of criticism than asking too many. Thus the advocate, rather than be second guessed for being brief in the cross-examination, will cover every possible area of impeachment often to the detriment of his client.

More often than not, a cross-examiner will fail because he goes too far than because he does not go far enough. Most cross-examination situations can extend into infinity. There are always a great many subjects to explore and each answer can lead to another area of inquiry. Pursuing only a few of the dramatic issues that are possible takes some courage on the part of the advocate since the client and others will always wonder if by pursuing other subjects the outcome might have changed. If the advocate has a firm idea of his case and strategy he should be able to articulate to himself and others why he selected and pursued some points and ignored others.

Dismissing a witness without asking any questions is more effective than asking questions. If this is the appropriate course of conduct it should be done in a way that suggests the testimony is of no consequence. The suggestion may be conveyed to the jury with a tone of voice or, a sense that the testimony while interesting has no relevance.

The strategy of a trial is a rather simple matter. Tell the jury what you are going to tell them (voir dire and opening statement), tell it to them (direct and cross-examination), and tell them what you have told them (closing argument). The advocate who has a clear idea of the issues he wishes to hammer home to the jury will have the best chance of being successful in maintaining a high level of quality in his cross-examination regardless of its length.

SHORTER IS GENERALLY BETTER

One judge I know, like all judges, must continually balance the demands of the litigants for a full hearing before the jury, and the great demands on the court's time, and uses an interesting device for limiting lawyers' time for closing argument.

When he and the lawyers reach closing arguments one or both of the lawyers will ask for more time than the judge thinks is necessary. Rather that reject the request out of hand the judge usually asks the lawyer if he knows who Edward Everett was. It is rare that the lawyer does know. The judge then points out to the lawyer the he was the speaker at Gettysburg who spoke for two and one half hours before Abraham Lincoln delivered his twenty minute Gettysburg address. The point is clear and the lawyers admit they can get by with less time.

DANIEL CROSS-EXAMINES SUSANNA'S ACCUSERS

Chapter 13 of the Book of Daniel deals with an episode in which the beautiful Susanna is asked by two town elders to lie down with them. She is told that should she refuse they will say they saw her lying with a stranger. Susanna refused and the two elders accused her of lying with a stranger. They each testified against her and, based on their sworn eyewitness account, she was sentenced to death. Daniel, then a young man, came forth from the crowd and insisted that there be a meaningful cross-examination of the elders. His request was granted.

This account from the bible is rightfully given as an example of the earliest use of cross-examination in the Judeo-Christian tradition. I include it at this particular point, however, because it so beautifully demonstrates the importance of the principle of quality over quantity in cross-examination. Daniel asks only one question and gains an acquittal for Susanna. It also makes use of another important principle of trial tactics: the requirement of asking the court to sequester witness and order them not to discuss their testimony before or after they testify:

> In Babylon there lived a man named Joakim, who married a very beautiful and God-fearing woman, Susanna, the daughter of Hilkiah; her pious parents had trained their daughter according to the law of Moses. Joakim was very rich; he had a garden near his house, and the Jews had recourse to him often because he was the most respected of them all.
> That year, two elders of the people were appointed judges, of whom the Lord said, "Wickedness has come out of Babylon: from the elders who were to govern the people as judges." These men, to whom all brought their cases, frequented the house of Joakim. When the people left at noon, Susanna used to enter her husband's garden for a walk. When the old men saw her enter the garden every day for her walk, they began to lust after her. They suppressed their consciences; they would not allow their eyes to look to heaven, and did not keep in mind just judgments. Though both were enamored of her, they did not tell each other their

trouble for they were ashamed to reveal their lustful desire to have her. Day by day they watched eagerly for her. One day they said to each other, "Let us be off for home, it is time for lunch." So they went out and parted; but both turned back and when they met again, they asked each other the reason. They admitted their lust, and then they agreed to look for an occasion when they could meet her alone.

One day, while they were waiting for the right moment, she entered the garden as usual, with two maids only. She decided to bathe, for the weather was warm, Nobody else was there except the two elders, who had hidden themselves and were watching here. "Bring me oil and soap," she said to the maids, "and shut the garden doors while I bathe." They did as she said; they shut the garden doors and left by the side gate to fetch what she had ordered, unaware that the elders were hidden inside.

As soon as the maids had left, the two old men got up and hurried to her. "Look," they said, "the garden doors are shut, and no one can see us; give in to our desire, and lie with us. If you refuse, we will testify against you that you dismissed your maids because a young man was here with you."

"I am completely trapped," Susanna groaned. "If I yield, it will be my death; if I refuse, I cannot escape your power. Yet it is for me to fall into your power without guilt than to sin before the Lord." Then Susanna shrieked, and the old men also shouted at her, as one of them ran to open the garden doors. When the people in the house heard the cries from the garden, they rushed in by the side gate to see what had happened to her. At the accusations by the old men, the servants felt very much ashamed, for never had any such thing been said about Susanna.

When the people came to her husband Joakim the next day, the two wicked elders also came, dully determined to put Susanna to death. Before all the people they ordered: "Send for Susanna, the daughter of Hilkiah, the wife of Joakim." When she was sent for, she came with her parents, children and all her relatives. Susanna, very delicate and beautiful, was veiled; but those wicked men ordered her to uncover her face so as to sate themselves with her beauty. All her relatives and the onlookers were weeping.

In the midst of the people the two elders rose up and laid their hands on her head. Through her tears she looked up to heaven, for she trusted in the Lord wholeheartedly. The elders made this accusation: "As we were walking in the garden alone, this woman entered with two girls and shut the doors of the garden, dismissing the girls. A young man, who was hidden there, came and lay with her. When we, in a corner of the garden, saw this crime, we ran toward them. We saw them lying together, but the man we could not hold, because he was stronger than we; he opened the doors and ran off. Then we seized this one and asked who the young man was, but she refused to tell us. We testify to this," The assembly believed them, since they were elders and judges of the people and they condemned her to death.

But Susanna cried aloud: "O eternal God, you know what is hidden and are aware of all things before they come to be: you know they have testified falsely against me. Here I am about to die, though I have done none of the things with which these wicked men have charged me."

The Lord heard her prayer. As she was being led to execution, God stirred up the holy spirit of a young boy named Daniel, and he cried aloud: "I will have no part in the death of this woman." All the people turned and asked him, "What is this you are saying?" He stood in their midst and continued "Are you such fools, O Israelites! To condemn a woman of Israel without examination and without clear evidence? Return to court, for they have testified falsely against her."

Then all the people returned in haste. To Daniel the elders said, "Come, sit with us and inform us, since God has given you the prestige of old age." But he replied, "separate these two from one another that I may examine them."

After they were separated one from the other, he called one of them and said: "How you have grown evil with age! Now have your past sins come to term: passing unjust sentences, condemning the innocent, and freeing the guilty, although the Lord says, 'The innocent and the just you shall not put to death.' Now, then, if you were a witness, tell me under what tree you saw them together." "Under a mastic tree," he answered. "Your fine lie has cost you your head," said Daniel; "for the angel of God shall receive the sentence from him and split you in two." Putting him to one side, he ordered the other one to be brought. "Offspring of Canaan, not of Judah," Daniel said to him, "beauty has seduced you, lust has subverted your conscience. This is how you acted with the daughters of Israel, and in their fear they yielded to you; but a daughter of Judah did not tolerate your wickedness. Now then, tell me under what tree you surprised them together." "Under an oak," he said. "Your fine lie has cost you also your head," said Daniel; "for the angel of God waits with a sword to cut you in two so as to make an end of you both."

The whole assembly cried aloud, blessing God who saves those that hope in him. They rose up against the two elders, for by their words Daniel had convicted them of perjury. According to the law of Moses, they inflicted on them the penalty they had plotted to impose on their neighbor: They put them to death. Thus was innocent blood spared that day.

Hilkiah and his wife praised God for their daughter Susanna, as did Joakim her husband and all her relatives, because she was found innocent of any shameful deed. And from that day onward Daniel was greatly esteemed by the people.

Principle Six

A Judge's Slightest Word Or Gesture May Carry More Weight With The Jury Than All The Eloquence You Can Muster

Unconsciously we would all like to believe that the men and women selected for service as judges have been endowed with a special wisdom that either insulates them from prejudices or gives them a special gift that allows them to set aside whatever prejudices they have.

It is unfortunate but true that judges not only have prejudices but that they often use their positions to see that the outcome of a trial reflects those prejudices. It is not important whether these actions stem from malignant or benignant motives. What is important is that prejudice exists to a greater degree than any of us like to believe. Effective advocates recognize this and devise strategies for coping with it.

The danger for the advocate is not so much that all judges possess prejudices as it is that the advocate will fail to recognize them and fail to address them adequately in his trial strategy and in creating an atmosphere beneficial to his side.

The prejudice to I refer to is not necessarily one of those usually consider when this term is used. I refer to something more technical: a prejudgment of facts or circumstances before the court, or a proclivity to reach conclusion with respect to a matter and then manipulate the trial to fit that conclusion. The more blatant prejudices we usually think of, such as racial hatred, or sex discrimination, while insidious, are either well to the bar or appear in such a way as to give rise to appellate relief.

Other kinds of prejudice, and in many ways more onerous, are those that lie beneath the surface of the judge's public face, the depth of which may be not be fully known even to him.

These prejudices may stem from a career as a prosecutor or as a defense lawyer. They may also reflect some deep psychological wound suffered as a child. They may stem from some private moral or religious code. Whatever the source, these prejudices should be recognized and dealt with.

Sometimes these prejudices manifest themselves in unexpected ways. It has been my experience that lawyers who have had careers as criminal defense lawyers before becoming judges are much harsher in criminal cases than lawyers who are appointed to the bench after careers as prosecutors.

A most notable example of this in our legal history is that of Sam Liebowitz. Liebowitz spent his career as a criminal defense lawyer and racked up some very good credentials. He was one of the lawyers in the famous Scotsboro Boys case and won himself a reputation as a defender of the unpopular client and as a great criminal defense lawyer. At the height of his career he accepted a position as judge in the state of New York and quickly earned the name "sentencin" Sam for his singularly harsh sentences in criminal defense cases.

JURORS TAKE THEIR CLUES FROM THE JUDGE

If the judge has any prejudices they may be subtly (or not so subtly) conveyed to the jurors. If they are not overcome or neutralized they can have such a negative effect on the case as to undo all the advocate's work.

When jurors enter a courtroom situation they instinctively look to the judge for guidance. This is even more apparent in the federal system where jurors tend to be more isolated from the general hubbub and have no interaction with the advocate until opening statement. This is natural. The judge is supposed to be learned, impartial, and free of prejudice. The jurors understand that the lawyers are there to promote a particular point of view and are by definition partial to one side. The judge, on the other hand, is perceived as the referee whose mistress is the cause of truth and fairness and as the one who will guide the jurors through the fog of deceit they can expect from the lawyers.

In preparing his total case, the advocate must be aware of the particular prejudices (some may prefer to call them idiosyncrasies) of the judge before whom he is trying the case. He must contrive a strategy that will take them into consideration and try and deflect them where they are harmful to his point of view, exploit them where they are beneficial, or, at the very least, neutralize them.

JUDGES CAN MANIPULATE THE CASE WITHOUT APPEARING TO DO SO ON THE RECORD

The manipulation of the trial by a judge can occur in a variety of ways, some subtle and others more flagrant. Generally, more flagrant behavior, the easier to combat. When the behavior is flagrant, the wily advocate can turn the bias to his own advantage. He can play on it to create an "us against them" atmosphere with the jury (i.e., the advocate and the jury against the opposition and the judge). He can intentionally exacerbate the prejudice in such a way as to cause reversible error or to incense the jury's sense of fair play.

It is the subtle forms of prejudice give the advocate the most difficulty. Sometimes a prejudiced judge will hide behind the fact that a record of the proceedings will be written and therefore not reflect his actions or tone of voice.

Many years ago I appeared frequently before a judge whose prejudices were well known to the bar. In fact this judge was reversed on a regular basis by the Supreme Court for his behavior. I once asked him if it bothered him to be reversed so often by the higher court. "Hell no!" he replied. "I reverse those bastards more than they ever reverse me." In spite of this somewhat insouciant response, he did go out of his way to get the verdicts he wanted in ways unlikely to be detected by the higher court.

This particular judge was prejudiced on the basis of race, sex, economic position, and tended to be completely in favor of the prosecution. While the prosecution was presenting its case the judge would say, "All right counsel, call your next witness" in a charming, benevolent tone of voice suggesting that he was anxiously awaiting the witness for the prosecution's testimony. The witness would enter the courtroom and the judge would smile at the witness and say "Take a seat in the witness box." This command would be offered in a paternal tone of voice. It almost seemed as if the judge would rise up in his chair and usher the witness to the box! During the witness' testimony the judge would turn slightly towards the witness, but not so much as to prevent the jury from seeing his expression and nod his head approvingly.

Everything changed when it was time for witnesses for the defense to be called. The judge would use exactly the same words so that the written transcript would appear identical. The difference was in the tone of voice. He said "All right call your next witness" in a tone that implied the jury's time was being wasted and that he was disgusted in advance with anything the witness would say. He said "Take a seat in the witness box" in a tone that unmistakably conveyed to the jury the fact that he didn't think the oath that was about to be administered would have much effect. And, during the examination, he would turn away from the witness and assume expressions of disbelief clearly visible to the jury.

The judge's motivation was clear: when the record on appeal was prepared, it would appear that the treatment given to the opposing sides was as evenhanded as could be when in fact the judge gave the jury every indication that one side was to be believed and the other was not.

Another technique I have seen judges perform with varying degrees of success is what I call "rehabilitation through condemnation". In this situation, the judge fixes the holes in one side's case in such a way that the record will appear to suggest that it is the party the judge helped—not the appealing party—that should be complaining about its treatment at the hands of the court.

The best use I ever saw of this technique was by a federal district court judge. In that case, I was defending a bookmaking charge against my clients. The case was being prosecuted by an attorney from the Department of Justice organized crime task force. During the trial the attorney sought to introduce some records seized from the defendant. It was clear that the prosecutor did not understand all the technical requirements for the foundation necessary to admitting the records.

The prosecutor would lay what he thought was an adequate foundation and then move the documents admission. I would object on the basis of inadequate foundation and the judge would agree with me. The prosecutor would start over and try and correct the error. Again I would object, and again I would be sustained. Finally it appeared that the prosecutor was simply unable to figure out what he was doing wrong and was on the verge of giving up on trying to admit the documents which were fundamental to winning the case. Not wishing that to happen and being fearful of giving any direct help to the attorney, the judge handled the situation in this way.

Judge: "I think this may be a good time to recess. Bailiff, take the jury out of the courtroom." When the door had closed behind the jury, he vented his anger in the following way:

"Mr. Prosecutor. It astonishes me that the Department of Justice would have the audacity to send someone such as yourself into this jurisdiction to try a case of this magnitude. I don't have any idea where you attended law school but they obviously failed miserably in preparing you for the bar. I have lawyers appearing before me while the ink on their license is still wet that can do a better job than you!" By this point the lawyer was flushed with embarrassment and opposing counsel (who had not seen this technique before) were relishing the prosecutor's discomfort. And to think this tongue lashing is coming from an judge with a reputation for being on the side of the prosecution! Maybe he isn't so bad after all. The tirade continued.

"If I had a law clerk just out of school that lacked such a fundamental understanding of such basic legal procedure I would recommend he take up another profession." Now came the crucial part. "It is beyond me that a lawyer in your position would not know that the way to lay a proper foundation in a situation like this is to . . . ." Here he would carefully set forth the steps necessary to lay the foundation for the introduction of the documents in question. He would angrily say, "I'm tired of you ineptness. I'm recessing for the evening. Please try and show a little more skill tomorrow." Of course, armed with this new information the prosecutor appeared the next day and breezed through the introduction of the documents. The judge was not a fool. In the event of a conviction, the record on appeal would show an injudicious diatribe towards counsel for the prosecution for which the appellate court might gently chastise. The appellate court would also be likely to point out that if anybody had a basis for complaint it would be the attorney receiving the tongue-lashing.

THERE ARE WAYS TO RESIS JUDICIAL MANIPULATION OF THE JURY

For the most part, a record on appeal that consists of a written transcript will not reflect a judge's tone of voice or the look of incredulity on his face during certain testimony. It is the brave advocate indeed who will dare to say "let the record reflect that the judge's comments were delivered in a sarcastic or incredulous tone."

The more subtle the manipulation, the more difficult the task. The direct approach is to inform the judge of your perception that he is manipulating the case and ask him to stop. Where the judge is more flagrant, one technique is to play to the prejudice in such a way that it will become apparent to all—including the appellate court—that he is in fact biased.

If the bias is towards the advocate because of the advocate's reputation, the advocate can quite often blunt it by displaying professional behavior, acting like a gentleman, and, in effect, charming the judge away from a preconceived notion.

In sum, juries will always look to the judge for guidance, and if you cannot neutralize the biased judge your battle will be an uphill one.

Principle Seven

The Closing Argument Should Be Formulated At The Outset Of The Case

The first thing an experienced advocate does in preparing for trial is to compose his closing argument based on the jury instructions he expects will be given. He then works backwards through cross-examination, direct examination, opening statement, and finally voir dire.

Many advocates assume that formulating the closing argument or summation should wait until most of the evidence has been presented. In a trial there is usually a period of time after the evidence has been presented and before the case is argued to the jury and the judge's final instructions are given. Many advocates rely on this time to formulate a closing argument to fit the evidence that has been presented.

This technique often leads to a rambling, incoherent, unfocused summation. The better course of action is to think of the closing argument as the posing of questions to the jury that are reflected in the court's instructions of the law and are answered to your advantage by the evidence. Consider the following summation:

"Ladies and gentlemen of the jury: Before you can convict the defendant, you must find that he intended to commit the crime of securities fraud. For instance, did he know that the information contained in the prospectus was a lie? This is one of the questions to which you will have to answer yes before you can convict him. How do you answer the question? You must review the evidence and I propose we do that together."

The advocate should have formulated this summation before the case began. He also should have directed the case in such a way that when he poses this question in his summation there will have been presented to the jury many points (emphasized in a variety of way) that will lead them to answer the question in your favor.

If the advocate begins to prepare the closing at the earliest possible moment in the case, and distills and filters and revises it throughout the trial, then he will sound and appear in complete control when delivering his summation and will be able to give the jury a cogent structured argument which will seem natural.

The first interview with the client should be the time when the advocate begins formulating his closing argument. Having at least the outline of a closing argument in mind forces the advocate to focus his thoughts on the most important questions of the case. In any complex litigation, the advocate who can maintain his focus on narrow and simple issues will have a distinct advantage in keeping the jury on his side all the way to verdict.

DEFINITION AND FOCUS

Advocates who do not have a clear idea of their summation will often confuse movement for direction and activity for action. This will have a direct bearing on the quality of their cross-examination. Often, a witness will present opportunities in the direct examination that the advocate will see as a point on which the witness can be challenged. The vulnerability of the witness is not the only test in deciding whether or not to pursue a point. If exploiting the weakness will have no bearing on the case or the credibility of the witness then pursuing that point may lead the advocate into a thicket that spells disaster. Unless the advocate has a clear idea of the issues he is concentrating on he will not be able to make those decisions necessary to conducting cross-examination in an informed way.

Being able to define your case, whether it be intent, knowledge, opportunity or lack thereof, alibi, or identification, in several sentences will aid you in conducting succinct and straightforward cross-examination. Knowing the precise nature of the defense will allow the jury to place what they hear in bits and pieces into some coherent framework. The continuing act of preparing the closing argument will act as a constant exercise in redefining for the advocate the strong and weak points of the case. As all advocates know, a case often takes twists and turns that are unpredictable and unavoidable. The successful advocate possesses the ingenuity and creativity to cope with these unexpected events and either neutralize them or turn them to his advantage. A witness may change his story. An event portrayed to you by the client may prove to be false. Something about one of your witnesses may come to light that has been withheld from you and which severely effects the credibility of the witness. Obviously if a closing argument has been formulated at the outset of the case it must undergo change to accommodate this unexpected turn of events. But the change in strategy or tactics required will be much easier to make if the overall framework of the argument is in place.

THE EVIDENCE PROVIDES THE ANSWER, SUMMATION THE QUESTIONS

If the advocate waits until the end of the evidence to formulate his closing argument, he has waited too long and any success in the case will be in spite of the closing argument, not because of it. This approach is akin to assuming that the case as it unfolds will present the questions and the summation will provide the answers. The opposite is true. The closing argument provides questions for the jury the answers to which have been provided by your presentation of the case. In other words, the advocate should know at the outset of the case what he wants the closing argument to be and with this in mind should structure the case and his cross-examination, to serve this end.

The advocate should ask himself what answers he wishes to give the jury that explain the past in a way consistent with his client's version. Having these answers in mind provides him with a clear road map of what is important in his case, what is extraneous, where his cross-examination should be directed, and what he can eliminate to keep the jury focused on the issues as he perceives them.

The advocate should keep in mind the story of Gertrude Stein on her deathbed. Stein was known by her friends to be dying and they along with her biographer and companion, Alice B. Toklas, were at the bedside to lend aide and comfort in her last moments. Stein looked at her followers and said:

"What is the answer? What is the answer?"

The group looked at each in puzzlement and with some embarrassment. None of them knew the answer and yet each felt that after being with Stein all these years they should. Stein asked again:

"What is the answer? What is the answer?"

Again, looks of puzzlement and despair over not knowing the answer. Finally Stein looked around once more and said. "What is the question?"

WITNESS PREPARATION, COACHING AND SUBORNATION OF PERJURY

One of the pitfalls of advocacy is to succumb to the temptation of seeking facts to support the conclusion. This can happen in a variety of ways some more onerous than others. The advocate must constantly ask himself when witness preparation turns into coaching which, in turn, can become subornation of perjury.

We saw earlier an example from Anthony Trollope where Mr. Chaffanbrass expressed a desire not to have to face the problem of what the defendant might say by simply avoiding talking to him. Advocates today still use a variation of this. They prepare the defendant for the case by explaining the evidence against him and informing him of a variety of explanations of his behavior that would be inconsistent with guilt. An example is the statement to the defendant that if he can prove he was somewhere other than the crime scene he would have an alibi, and in order to prove an alibi he would need a credible witness to support his story. Having thus planted the information the advocate then waits to hear what the defendant has to say on the subject. If the defendant should appear in a day or so with a story of being somewhere other than the scene of the crime and with a list of witnesses to support the story, the advocate may feel he can present the defense with a clear conscience.

Balancing ethical requirements of the profession while serving as the advocate for the client is a difficult affair. It presents some narrow boundaries that every lawyer must come to grips with in his own way. The young lawyer should be careful to read the disciplinary opinions on the subject and seek advice from older more experienced lawyers. In my opinion the canons of ethics provide a minimum standard of behavior below which the advocate cannot go, but do not dictate that the advocate cannot set for himself a higher standard. Each lawyer must ultimately search his own conscience. As difficult and as somber as it sounds, the problem and the way lawyers have handled it provides some of the more clever anecdotes in the lore of the law.

My friend, Louis L'Amour, the great western writer, shared with me a passion for stories about lawyers, especially lawyers who practiced in the American west. Louis told me the following anecdote about a frontier lawyer who performed extraordinary feats but who is largely forgotten. He was Moman Pruitt from Oklahoma. One day Pruitt received a telegram from a person charged with murder. The telegram went like this:

> *"How much will you charge to defend me on a murder charge?"*
>
> *Pruitt's response: $5,000 if you provide the witnesses; $10,000 if I provide them."*

Principle Eight

Avoid Unnecessary Note Taking

Lord Russell, one of England's great barristers, was trying a case and with a new barrister just beginning his career. Russell, who never missed a nuance in the case, happened to look at the young associate and saw that he was taking detailed notes on all that was being said. Russell quickly penned a note and passed it to the associate. "What are you doing?" Russell's note asked. "Taking notes," was the ingenuous reply. Russell quickly scribbled on the paper. "Watch the case!"

A case cannot be tried effectively if the advocate is not able to observe everything that is going on. The judge, the witnesses, the jurors, the court clerks, the bailiffs, and opposing counsel will all give the advocate helpful clues through body language: the way they sit, their facial expressions, and, their movements. These clues will indicate which testimony is telling and which has been missed, whether your points are hitting home, what points the other side has scored, and whether there is some confusion on the part of the witness or the other side. The faces of the jurors will give a good indication of what is being accepted or rejected. In short much of the case is to be garnered from watching all that is going on. Any time spent writing notes is time away from observation.

The advocate must have some device for remembering (1) what witnesses have testified to and (2) what takes place during the case that will require comment at a later time. But to be effective he must develop techniques that will permit him to keep note taking to a minimum.

Extracting The Critical Points

In these days of long trials the demands upon the advocate to render complex issues into matter-of-fact experiences a jury can understand have become overwhelming. It is not unusual to see criminal cases, especially so-called white collar crimes, in which there are hundreds of thousands of documents-cases in which an advocate would have to spend every minute of a 40 hour work week for several years just reading the material presented to him. Of course, this kind of time is never available. Even with the year or so that the advocate may have to prepare himself, he still must face the fact that the case will be decided by a jury with at most a few weeks to digest the complex legal and factual issues which the government and defense have had months or even years to analyze.

The advocate's task is to boil the case down to a few special points that jurors (whose experience has not prepared them for the complexities of the case) can understand. If the advocate becomes bogged down in minutiae and is unable to present information cogently, the jury will find it difficult to do so also.

In essence, the advocate's job entails taking even the most complex case and reducing it to a brief essay that he can repeat over and over to the jury. This essay must be supported by the evidence that supports his client's interests. Use of techniques that will help accomplish this goal during trial is imperative. The fact that an advocate has assembled several thousand documents of his own and has associates wheel them into court each day does not mean that he can use the information in a way that will impress the jury. He can bring the jury to his side only if he has made the information into a cohesive whole. Without this, all the information stored in computers or file drawers will be of no avail. The advocate will not win the jury by proving that his documents weigh more than the opposition's.

Use A Back-Up Note Taker

As a way of keeping track of the case, the advocate should have trusted members of his staff take notes to which he can refer from time to time. (This is often done by a secretary or paralegal.) Notes taken by staff members should serve the same purpose as those taken by the advocate. Relying on someone else to take notes allows the advocate to concentrate his own efforts on watching the case.

Developing Better Memory

When the advocate cannot afford to have someone in the courtroom throughout the trial to help him, he should develop techniques for note taking that will have a minimum impact on his ability to watch the case. He should learn to make notes of one or two words that will serve to trigger his memory. He should wait until a recess or the evening break to go back and expand on the notes. But the most important quality the advocate should possess in this respect is a good memory. With the information explosion and the retrieval systems we have now, it has become unusual to cultivate a good memory. This is unfortunate in every walk of life and potentially disastrous for the trial lawyer.

The flow of cross-examination is much more effective if the advocate knows what points he wishes to make, and can extract the points from the witness without unnecessary fumbling through documents. If his examination flows smoothly, he will be able to keep the witness off stride and maintain the interest of the jury.

A show of good memory may help convince the jury of the advocate's character and ability. This can be done in a rather simply and easily early in the trial. I make it a point of memorizing the names of the jury members before I am called upon to address them in voir dire. When I first speak to them I make sure I am not carrying notes and stand beside the lectern so that they are aware that I am not using a written list. I then try and pose a question to each of them at random using their names. It is a simple device but one that I believe shows the jury that (1) I cared enough about them to learn their names and (2) that I had the ability to do so in what must seem to them a very short time. This small exercise may work to my advantage when the jurors are discussing their decision and questions arise regarding how to resolve a conflict between sides with respect to certain testimony. The jurors will be able to say that my memory is better on the subject because I had demonstrated a good memory at the very outset of the trial when I learned each of their names so rapidly.

Natural Versus Artificial Memory

The idea that people either have or do not have a good memory by virtue of some gene pool is only half true. There is "natural" memory and "artificial" memory. "Natural" memory is the ability to recall events that comes naturally and exists to a greater or lesser degree in all people. "Artificial" memory on the other hand, is the ability to remember things that can be learned and developed through memory-strengthening exercises. Artificial memory played a significant role in the history of man until the advent of the printing press and has diminished proportionally as our ability to store and retrieve information in machines has increased. The resulting deemphasis on memory as a necessary part of our learning experience misses the point that information stored in a computer or written in books has not necessarily been *learned*. All we know is that the information exists and where we can to find it. We haven't actually learned the information.

To convey information to jury members so that they will know and agree with it at the end of the case the advocate must himself know that information. That is, he must have it stored in his memory. To do that, he must train his memory.

This idea is not new to the field of law. Before the advent of the printing press law was learned by memory. Indeed, the most pressing principle was that law that has existed "since the memory of man runneth not to the contrary"—a principle that was still being enunciated by Blackstone in his commentaries in 1765.

The importance of a good memory goes back at least to the early Greeks who believed that Mnemosyne-the Goddess of Memory—was mother to the nine Muses. This notion that, in the words of Aeschylus, "Memory is the mother of all wisdom," was carried down through history until recent times. Saint Thomas

Aquinas made memory a part of prudence which, along with justice, fortitude, temperance, faith, hope, and charity, is one of the cardinal virtues.

Classical Mnemonic Techinques and Memory Devices

Given the importance attached to memory, earlier thinkers created special mnemonic techniques. Simonides (c. 556-468 B.C.E.) developed a technique that Cicero described as a system of constructing a mental image of a temple, palace, or other large building. A person would visit a known place such as a temple. He would place firmly in his mind the various rooms and wings of the location and then invest this location in his mind with ideas he wished to remember. The person wishing to remember those items would conjure up the location in his mind. The reference would then trigger his recollection of the desired information. Thus a trial lawyer might erect a palace in his mind and construct wings for each of the phases of the trial. Each of the wings would contain rooms into which he would mentally place various topics (a particular witness, for example). On the walls of the room he might put pictures representing ideas he wishes to confront the witness with. (Interestingly, use of these places as memory devices has given us the word topic. The word topic comes to us from the Greek *topo* meaning place.)

Peter of Ravenna, the author of a 16th century text on memory, boasted that using this system he could repeat verbatim the whole canon law, two hundred speeches of Cicero, and twenty thousand points of law. Matteo Ricci, a Jesuit priest in late 16th century China devised a scheme for the emperor's family that again employed the idea of a memory palace that could be as large as one desired and possess as many rooms as necessary for the subject to be memorized. All of these systems recognize the fact that information cannot be integrated into the entire fabric of one's thought process until it becomes part of one's memory.

Knowing that Hamlet spoke on the subject of suicide in one

of the great soliloquies of all time and knowing that this soliloquy can be found in Act 3, Scene 1 of that play is a much different thing than committing the speech to memory. Only when it is part of the memory and can be pulled up at will can its full meaning be applied.

The same holds true with facts and ideas that are part of the trial. Searching a document to find that a witness made a contradictory statement on page 158 of a deposition is not the same as having that knowledge in your memory. Sending a runner to the computer outside the courtroom to search for documents, as I have seen some advocates do, is not the same as the advocate having the information in his memory.

Part Two
Plotting The Strategy

Principle One

Should You Cross-Examine At All?

Cross-examination of a witness has been described as driving a flock of sheep down a fenced path which has numerous open side gates. The advocate must arrive at the end of the path with all the sheep in his possession and allow none of them to escape through one of the side gates. It is a difficult task and one that should be undertaken only if there is no other alternative.

It is the foolish advocate who rushes into cross-examination without first convincing himself that there is no other way to deal with the testimony of a witness. The wise advocate must always keep in mind the fact there are a great many things that can result from cross-examination and most of them are bad.

The advocate must know precisely what his case is and ask himself whether the witness has testified to anything that really affects the case, or whether anything beneficial can be gained from the witness? If the answer is no then the decision is automatic. Simply say "No questions."

If the witness has hurt your case, you must determine whether cross-examination is the best way to deal with it. There are several choices other than cross-examination. The advocate can leave the issue alone and deal with it in his argument; he can wait and rebut the matter with another witness; he can answer it through silent cross-examination. If any of these possibilities are likely to succeed, the advocate should use them and forswear the cross-examination.

Steuer's Two Rules

Max Steuer, a well-known New York trial lawyer during the first half of this century, had two rules that he professed with respect to when one should cross-examine: (1) never cross-examine if you can handle the witness' testimony in another way, and (2) never cross-examine without something to cross-examine on.

Knowing that the pitfalls are substantial, the great cross-examiner always avoids cross-examination if possible. Their first analysis of the witness is not whether the witness is vulnerable on some point, or has lied on some point, or what will be the best approach to the witness in the cross-examination. The first analysis is: Is there any other way to rebut and cast doubt on the damaging parts of this witness' testimony without cross-examination?

Steuer believed that he could often deal more effectively with testimony in argument than through direct confrontation. An example given of this is the case in which a witness testifies to certain damaging events which involve the recollection of the time that an event occurred. It is a fact that this witness had many transactions surrounding this event and their recollection of the precise time may seem strange when there were similar transactions involving others both before and after the one testified to. Steuer took the position that, if he went into the subject on cross-examination there was a strong likelihood the witness would have an explanation that would salvage the situation and further hurt the client. On the other hand, he believed that, if the matter was left alone with the witness, the jury themselves might find it unbelievable, and in any event, he stood a better chance of using it to his advantage by waiting until closing argument to point out the error. Then it would be too late for the opposition to allow the witness to offer an explanation.

The advocate must consider whether the best way to point out the errors of the opposition witnesses is through direct examination of your own witness rather than opening new doors on cross-examination. Cross-examination may remind the other side of something omitted by them on direct examination and give them the opportunity to bring it out on redirect examination.

Steuer's second rule that you shouldn't cross-examine unless you have something to cross-examine about seems obvious but is frequently forgotten. There is a natural compunction on the part of the inexperienced to "give it a go" with the witness without having a clear idea of what the goals are. This stems in part from a failure to have clearly formulated a case strategy and to succumb to a false ego and the belief that counsel can be a match for any witness. This tactic only works in spite of itself.

Factors To Consider

When deciding of whether or not to cross-examine the advocate must consider the following:

1. Was the testimony so harmful as to demand that it be refuted through this witness? Is it the testimony or the witness that is harmful? The answer to this question may not only depend on the testimony itself but on who the witness is, their relationship to the case, the impression made on the jury, and the point at which they testify in the case.

   If a determination is made that the testimony itself can be best dealt with in another way then the decision should be made whether the witness is so important or effective that, when given a choice between your alternative explanation and the one of this witness the jury may decide, based on the character or position of this witness, that they must accept his version. If this seems to be the situation, then the advocate may be required to use cross-examination to impeach the witness rather than the testimony.

2. Another factor that may come into play is whether the witness, although damaging, is presented at such an early stage in the trial that his impact on the jury is likely to diminish as the trial drags on.

3. You need to know what points you wish to make, and whether you have a reasonable expectation of doing so with a particular witness? This issue cannot be resolved if the advocate does not have a clear picture of what he expects to accomplish with the witness and how it fits into the overall case. The advocate should know what point he reasonably expects to make with the witness and it must be a point he can refer to in closing argument as being in favor of his client.

4. Is there a reason to believe the witness is untruthful? Do you have any evidence or impeaching material that suggests the witness is lying? If so, is cross-examination the most efficacious way of exposing the lie? Remember that confronting a witness with a lie gives that witness an opportunity to offer an explanation consistent with truth. If, however, you do it by other means it will be much more difficult for the opposition to answer.

   An example of this situation may be a witness who has testified to events that involve a train trip, on a Wednesday, on a specific rail line. Assume that the advocate has evidence that the train did not operate on Wednesday. If he cross-examines the witness on this fact and confronts him with the inconsistency, the witness may simply say, "I must have been mistaken. Perhaps it was the following week or the previous week. Or the previous day." It is unlikely the jury will cast doubt on the other events testified to by the witness in light of this common sense explanation. On the other hand, if you let the matter alone and produce a railroad official later in your case that testifies the train did not run on that day, it will give you much more of an argument with the jury. The argument is that if the witness was incorrect or untruthful about the train how can the balance of the testimony be relied on by the jury.

5. Another issue the advocate must take into consideration is whether the jury really needs to hear the witness cross-examined for his testimony to be discredited? The answer

can be determined by watching the jury carefully during the direct examination. Jurors will often show disbelief, agreement or puzzlement with the witness by their facial expression and body language. This must be analyzed and taken into consideration. If clarifying the matter will be beneficial to your side, then you should do it.

Reading a jury is a difficult and delicate matter continuing throughout the trial. The wise advocate can determine during direct examination which points seem to make the most impact and which are received with skepticism. Often he will perceive different reactions from jurors. Taking note of specific reactions of individual jurors throughout the trial will help you decide much about your cross-examination strategy.

SILENT CROSS-EXAMINATION

Silent cross-examination is another possibility the advocate should consider. It is the ability to dismiss a witness without questions in such a way as to convey to the jury volumes about the testimony he has given.

Walter Gerash, a noted Denver trial lawyer, is the best I have ever watched at dismissing a witness without a question and in so doing convey to the jury that nothing the witness could possibly say is worth listening to, or that nothing said in the direct testimony is harmful. He will stand and look intensely at the witness with scorn or derision on his face for some time and then as if to say "what's the point you'll probably continue your lies if I take the trouble to question you" he waves him off the stand. Other times he will look inquiringly in the direction of the prosecution as if to say "why did you waste our time with this witness? He hasn't told us anything helpful" and then, as if doing the jury a favor he dismisses the witness.

How the dismissal takes place often serves as a form of cross-examination. If at all possible the dismissal should convey to the jury a feeling that benefits to your case. Perhaps that the witness is merely there to divert the jurors attention from the real issue. This can be done by conferring with you client, looking inquiringly at the client, and then dismissing the witness.

Another technique is to rise as if you are going to question, look pensive for a moment, then look at your client as if to say "what's the point?" and then dismiss the witness.

The decision to cross-examine must be given careful consideration regardless of what form is to be used. A decision to cross-examine should not be automatic. The advocate must always be aware that the decision to cross-examine can be every bit as harmful as a decision not to cross-examine.

Principle Two

Stipulate To Testimony And Evidence Wherever Possible

It is necessary to keep the jury focused on the important issues in the case and to eliminate any possibility of distraction. Stipulation as to matters that are not in contention will serve this purpose well and will help you in your relationship with the judge.

By preparing your closing argument first you'll be able to tell which issues are germane to the case and which are extraneous and can be stipulated to.

This reverse engineering is required to give the case the coherence and the necessary structure to win the jury to your point of view and keep them there until they render a verdict in your favor. Preparing in this way will allow the presentation of a case to be appealing and advantageous, and will give the advocate a clear understanding of what the case is really about and how he will proceed. It means that you must keep the issues as clear and simple as possible and avoid the possibility of the jury's being seduced by some extraneous issue. It is also important that the jury perceives your side as being interested in the fair and clear presentation of the case.

Compiling Too Much Information

Recent trials have taken a turn which most participants deplore: opponents are being worn down emotionally, physically, and economically through pretrial discovery and depositions. It makes litigation costly and inefficient.

Such techniques are carried out by a new breed of lawyer who do not understand the art of the trial. These litigators require a client with substantial resources which are used to destroy the opposition before the case ever reaches the trial. Unfortunately, clients have been willing to allow this situation to continue and have equated the assembly of vast quantities of documents with a cogent and well—reasoned trial strategy.

When the case finally goes to trial, the litigator is hopelessly immersed in so much information that he cannot make a cogent summary of it. He relies on overwhelming the jury with so much information that they will vote for his side because he has literally tipped the scales of justice by submitting more paper than the opposition.

The advocate who can resist this confusion of quality over quantity and can persuade the jury of the basic issues in the case will win. He knows how to simplify the issues and separate the wheat from the chaff, and keep the jury focused on the points that will ultimately result in a winning verdict.

STIPULATION VERSUS OBJECTION

Making an objection at every conceivable moment only dilutes an effective weapon in the advocate's arsenal. The wise advocate will endeavor to keep the jury focused on his case by not objecting to evidence and testimony at every possible occasion. The jury and the judge will appreciate his desire to focus their attention on what is important. The advocate will gain the advantage of letting the judge know when to pay close attention and when to be free to think of the hundred other things that must constantly be dealt with. If the advocate fights about every minor thing in the case, the judge will never know what is important and what is not.

By stipulating to evidence whenever possible, you will avoid the appearance of being obstructionist and of trying to confuse the jury. If you object to evidence on technical grounds and are overruled, it may have an adverse effect on the jury. You may appear to be an obstructionist.

A worthwhile tactic is to minimize the impact of evidence or testimony by casually stipulating to its introduction as if to say this information is of little consequence and if the other side wants to waste our time with it alright but let's do it as quickly as possible.

IMPACT OF OPPONENTS STIPULATION

Sometimes, however, even the offer to stipulate is rejected and the results can be devastating. An example of this took place in Denver Federal District Court where the judge, known for his impatience with his time being wasted and with counsel that wasted it, punished the wrong lawyer.

It was a case in which one side called another lawyer as an expert witness in the evaluation of personal injury cases. The side calling him began to have the lawyer recite his credentials and the opposing counsel wisely offered to stipulate that the witness was an expert in the field. The lawyer calling the witness said, as is often the case, that he felt it necessary for the jury to know the expert's background.

The judge, apparently thinking this to be a waste of his time said. "Counselor, everyone knows that this witness is the leading expert in this field in the state of Colorado. It isn't necessary to waste our time going through it. Get on with the case." Realizing that this outburst by the judge had the effect of telling the jury that they should believe the witness the opposition wisely settled the case.

REFUSAL TO CROSS-EXAMINE AS STIPULATION

Stipulating to testimony may take another form. You can decide not to cross-examine when the opposition has assumed you will and has relied on it to get certain information to the jury that is damaging to your case. An example of this involves William Howe of Howe and Hummel fame.

Howe was defending a criminal case with a defense of insanity. He hired Dr. Allan McLane Hamilton to examine the defendant. Hamilton conducted an exhaustive examination of the defendant and prepared himself well for the court appearance. His credentials were impeccable and impressive. Howe decided that the best tactic would be to allow this information to be brought out on cross-examination thus giving it more impact. He was sure that counsel or the other side would not be able to resist the cross-examination. He called the doctor and the examination went thus:

Q (by Howe) State your name.
A. Dr. Allan McLane Hamilton.
Q. Dr. Hamilton you have examined the prisoner at the Bar, have you not?
A. Is he, in your opinion, sane or insane?
Q. Insane.
  (By Howe) You may cross-examine.
  (By defense counsel) We have no questions.
  (By Howe) What? Not ask the famous Dr. Hamilton a question? Well, I will.

Realizing the trap Howe began to ask the witness about his credentials. Defense counsel objected that since there had been no cross-examination Howe had no right to re-direct and was sustained. Dr. Hamilton's testimony was reduced to little or nothing. What defense counsel did here was in effect stipulate to the testimony of the doctor, and thus prevent Howe from admitting into evidence the important facts of his qualifications and the basis for his opinion.

Principle Three

Know What You Seek To Accomplish In Your Cross-Examination

No great cross-examiner prepares a list of questions for his cross-examination and then blindly adheres to it regardless of the actual situation. The advocate must have the flexibility and quickness of mind to adjust to the situation.

The cross-examiner must be prepared in all the aspects of the case, and have a good understanding of what the opposition intends to do. This knowledge is arrived at by deposing witnesses, reading their statements, conducting investigations, consulting with experts and acquiring or familiarizing himself with any relevant experts.

He has formulated in his own mind the case what he intends to have the jury hear and he has a clear idea of what he expects to accomplish with each witness. He has prepared the jury instructions he intends to ask the court to give, and he has a closing argument firmly in mind. Before the first witness is called he has conducted the voir dire, established his own character with the jury, and put them in a frame of mind that will be receptive to his case.

It is in this overall framework that the skills of cross-examination come to bear. If everything goes as he has planned, the witness for the opposition will testify as planned. When he asks his well-thought out questions on cross-examination, the witness will cooperate and answer just as the advocate wishes.

It is in this overall framework that the skills of cross-examination come to bear. If everything goes as expected, the witness for the opposition will testify as planned. When the cross-examiner asks his well-thought-out questions, the witness will cooperate and answer just as the advocate wishes.

In the vast majority of cases, however, this scenario is fiction. It only happens when there is an omniscient narrator controlling the events and the characters behave in a controlled way. In the real world, unexpected events occur.

It is for these reasons that the skill of cross-examination is so difficult and so rare. Spontaneous innovation is in constant demand and a wrong decision can destroy the case.

Consequences Of A Failure To Prepare

Often, the advocate is faced with an unexpected situation in questioning a witness and must make a sudden decision whether to continue the line of questioning or to abandon it. Many elements enter into the decision: the drama of the situation; a sense of whether the jury is on your side; the chances of reversing the fortune with additional questions.

Charles Spencer conducted a trial against Edwin James involving a soldier's claim for $1800, money loaned to a friend after the Civil War. Defense counsel James cross-examined the plaintiff:

Q. *You loaned him $1800?*
A. *I did, sir.*
Q. *When, sir?*
A. *In 1866.*
Q. *Where did you get it?*
A. *I earned it, sir (meekly).*
Q. *When did you earn it?*
A. *During the war, sir (meekly.*
Q. *What was your occupation during the war?*
A. *(modestly) Fighting, sir.*

The cross-examiner had to make a spontaneous decision when faced with this unexpected disclosure that the witness was a veteran.

He knew that so recently after the war the jury would have sympathy for the man and less for the debtor. He decided to withdraw from that subject and hope he could deflect the damage in some other way.

The verdict went against him and the following day he commented to Spencer that "it was that speech of yours (Spencer's) that did it, and it was the fault of my cross-examination. Otherwise, you would have known nothing about his war record."

"Ah," said Spencer, "the mistake that you made was that you didn't find out that my client was a Confederate soldier, or you could have changed the whole verdict yourself."

There are some aspects of this story that are incredible to the modern lawyer. It appears from the conversation after the verdict that neither attorney knew that the plaintiff was a veteran. Without analyzing that aspect of the situation there is a valid inquiry of what options were open to James when this information was given. The damage was done; and, unless he had some witness or evidence that would otherwise contradict, his only hope of salvaging something was to continue with the witness. There was little harm to be done in probing the issue. Certainly a question with respect to which side the witness had been on would have been a safe area of inquiry. This is a case where the cross-examiner was not prepared and lost the case though his neglect and ineptitude.

By the time the first witness is called in a case and the advocate is faced with the imminent prospect of cross-examination, he must have a clear idea of what the case is about and what he hopes to achieve with each witness. He should have a notebook indexed with respect to the witnesses and containing information about what the witnesses are expected to testify to and where the testimony fits into the case. Such information will allow him to make decisions regarding improvisation on new matters with the greatest chance of success.

All too often juries see advocates begin their cross-examination without a clear road map and destination in mind. If the advocate can't stay on the straight road to the ultimate destination, it is unlikely the jury will do so.

Principle Four

Always Observe The Witness During Direct Examination

While the subject matter of cross-examination can be formulated as part of the overall strategy of a case, the decision regarding the manner in which the witness will be cross-examined usually must wait until the witness is in the court room testifying.

Even if the lawyer has had the opportunity to depose the witness before trial, he must be careful not to decide on the manner of cross-examination based on that experience, since the way in which a witness handles himself in a deposition may vary greatly from the way that he testifies in the courtroom.

The advocate has a wide variety of techniques to use. Should the approach be aggressive or subtle? Direct or obtuse? Fast or slow? Is there reason to believe the witness is unsure of a point? Lying about an issue? Merely confused? Passively vindictive? The answers to these questions and the information needed to decide on the style of cross-examination are given by a close observation of the witness in the courtroom before and after his direct testimony.

What the witness *says* in the courtroom will only provide the advocate with one part of all the information he must rely on in deciding what his approach should be. The decision must also take into consideration everything the witness' non-verbal performance on the stand and the effect it has on the judge, jurors, and spectators.

The advocate must decide how to cross-examine in a brief period of time and must be able to change tactics if the manner first adopted proves ineffective.

WITNESSES

The advocate should begin his observation of the witness from the moment the witness enters the courtroom. Witnesses are particularly vulnerable at that moment. These observations can disclose a great deal about the witness. Often a witness will bring a friend or family member to court for support. Sometimes the opposition will have someone in court from who has established a relationship with the witness and is there to coach him by nodding approval or helping in some other way. If you recognize the setup, you can use it to your advantage by blocking the witness' view of the person he's relying on for help. It can have a devastating effect. I have had situations where the witness has begun to lean to his right or his left in an attempt to see past me and get his signals or support from someone in the courtroom. This is never wasted on the jury. In some cases I have stopped the cross and have turned from the witness and faced the other person and asked the witness "Would it help if we stopped for a moment so you can consult with the gentlemen in the third row?"

This behavior by a witness can be turned to your advantage even though you have been unable to shake the substance of the testimony. If the jury feels the witness has been coached to such a degree they instinctively discount the testimony.

The advocate should not rely solely on his interpretation of the witnesses non-verbal behavior. Recognizing points of vulnerability in the witness can also be gained by observing other participants as the witness testifies.

JUDGES

Judges are a good source of information in this respect. They are trained not to display their feelings in a case and the best ones are very careful not to. When they do exhibit some feeling, they do so in a way that they hope will not be obvious to the participants. The advocate must realize that, when a judge shows some emotion, it is usually after some serious provocation and thus will tell the advocate more than if it came from some other source. You can be sure that is a judge reacts negatively or positively to some evidence, the jury surely will. This is one of the reasons why a judge who deliberately sets out to manipulate a jury can be so effective.

Jurors

Jurors are a good source of information for how to attack a witness. Often a juror will display some emotion during the testimony that will provide important information about how to cross-examine the witness. Surprise at something the witness says, or incredulity will often register on one of the faces regardless of efforts to remain stoic. The advocate must also monitor the jury for clues to their feelings which may be displayed in the juror's attempt to mask his true feeling.

Opposition Counsel, Staff, And Spectators

The opposition is also a good source of information with respect to what manner of cross-examination will best succeed. The lawyer for the other side will often betray the fact that the witness has surprised him by changing the testimony or its emphasis. He then betrays his frustration with the witness by the tone of his voice or looks of despair. A more fertile ground for information may come from the other members of the opposition team. Often, because they are not directly involved in the case at that moment, or because they don't believe anyone is watching, they will betray a weakness.

Because spectators can be more open in their reaction to testimony they can often be a good source of information. When I am trying a case I often seek out spectators during a recess and inquire about specific incidents in the trial to get their reaction.

Principle Five

Each Objection Should Be A Statement To The Jury

Cross-examination consists of the words and actions employed by the advocate to male the jury doubt the witnesses and the testimony presented by the opposition. Every statement made by the advocate should be designed to persuade the jury of your point of view.

The use of objections as a means of persuading the jury is often overlooked.

The exclusion of inadmissible or prejudicial testimony or evidence is the primary reason for the objection; but how the objection is made, and how frequently it is interposed can play a large role in the case. Objections for the sake of demonstrating a keen grasp of the technical rules of evidence is self-defeating. The jury will be lost and resent the interruption.

The jury must be included in the entire case. Conversations in open court between counsel and the judge that resort to legal language tend to put the jury off. Jurors have only a vague notion of the technical meaning of words such as "hearsay", "relevancy", and "no foundation". They have even less understanding when someone says "objection Rule 801".

The statement of an objection is an opportunity to prevent the admission of inadmissible evidence and is also an opportunity for counsel to inform the jury of why it is inadmissible and why fair play dictates that you object to it. It is foolish to allow the jury to think you are objecting because something is harmful to your

115

case when the proper reason will help them understand what you are doing. Objections should be made in such a way as to include a common sense explanation for the jury.

How To Object

The advocate should make the objection as if he were speaking directly to the jury instead of the judge. It may help to practice stating the objection in language they will understand. Something like this: "The jury is not permitted to hear this information because it was made outside of court and was not under oath. Also, since my client will not be able to cross-examine the statement, it is unfair to him to have it presented to the jury untested." Most courts will not let you go that far, but you should say as much of it as the court will allow.

Juries do not always understand that objections based on hearsay, relevancy, or calls for a conclusion, etc., are based on fundamental considerations of fairness. Without a reasonable explanation, juries may believe that objections are only offered to confuse the issues.

Objections cleverly stated can educate a jury to your point of view or distract it from damaging testimony. If a witness is in the midst of some particularly damaging piece of testimony, a well-thought out and well-timed objection can distract the witness and the opposition from the point and severely disrupt the pace of the testimony. Objections expressing a point of view can be made with telling effect when the basis for the objections is relevancy. "Your Honor, the issue in this case is whether the defendant shot the deceased not whether it took one or two bullets to do the job. The question is irrelevant to the issue before the jury."

Objections can offer to the jury a plausible alternative to an answer given by the witness. "Your Honor, this witness could not have seen the events he just described; the evidence shows that there was insufficient lighting to see." Objections such a these are often overruled but will serve a purpose.

Objections can serve to upset the pace and rhythm of opposing counsel, and may be used to suggest that opposing counsel is being unfair in asking questions that seek to inject testimony that would otherwise be inadmissible. Objections can be used to remind the jury of the theory of your case and prepare them for your closing argument.

Objecting to a conclusion by the witness might be expressed along the following lines. "Your Honor, what counsel has asked calls for a conclusion by the witness and not fact. This invades the province of the jury and should not be allowed."

Relevancy objections might be stated as follows: "Your Honor, the issue before this court is whether or not the defendant committed the crime and not whether he drinks too much. The question is not relevant to the issue in this case."

Stating the objections in these ways should serve to give the jury a reasonable explanation of the underlying principles and explain why the question is improper. If the objecting is done skillfully, it will appear that, rather than keeping something from the jury, you are really protecting its right to hear everything that is relevant in the correct way.

Improper Objections

The advocate must use this strategy keeping in mind that objections should not be used for an improper purpose or without proper regard for legal ethics. Placing before the jury statements by counsel that inflame the jury or are otherwise inadmissible is an example. Aside from the ethical considerations doing so will cause the judge to become more active in the case. The judge may seek to prevent such behavior by restricting the way that objections are made and deprive counsel of a useful tool.

Plain English Versus "Legalese"

Because it is important to engage the jury in the entire case, counsel should be careful not to exclude them by making statements in their presence which they will not understand. Jurors resent it when counsel make objections which are understood by the court and opposing counsel but which are considered "legalese" everyone else. As a result of this formal language, the jury is left wondering what counsel tried to keep out of evidence by making the objection, leading them to speculate that counsel has such a week case he doesn't want them to hear everything.

This result can be avoided by stating the objection in a way that conveys to the jury a logical reason for the inadmissibility of the evidence. The rule you invoke exists to protect the interest of your client, and the jury should be made to understand that you are not objecting frivolously.

Let's assume that the identification of your client is a serious matter in your case. The prosecutor is questioning a witness about identification.

QUESTION BY THE PROSECUTOR: *"Who else was present when the shooting occurred?"*
A. *"Mr. Smith, one of the owners of the store."*
QUESTION BY THE PROSECUTOR: *"And did Mr. Smith tell you who he saw at the time the crime was being committed?"*
RESPONSE BY DEFENSE: *"Your Honor, asking this witness to testify as to what someone else said is hearsay and will not be subject to cross-examination unless Mr. Smith is called to the stand in which case we should wait until then for his testimony.*
BY THE PROSECUTOR: *Your Honor, this is not being offered for the truth of the statement and is not hearsay.*
BY THE DEFENSE: *We further object because the opportunity for Mr. Smith to see what happened was impossible because of the light at the time. In any event, there is no testimony that Mr. Smith has good vision or hearing."*

In this case, the improper question by the prosecutor can be turned to your benefit and suggest to the jury that there is a real issue of identification and the prosecutor has attempted to prove it through hearsay testimony. It will also serve to suggest that the real witness may have physical problems that would call the testimony into question.

Principle Six

Never Object To Your Own Questions

Oscar Wilde once pointed out that there are no indiscreet questions, only indiscreet answers, advice that he failed to follow in his own trial when subjected to one of the most brilliant cross-examinations in the history of trial law. This is good advice for the advocate in many ways.

There are questions that any good trial lawyer knows to be inappropriate. Asking these questions may result in a mistrial which, if found to be deliberately provoked, may further result in disciplinary action against the lawyer. There are others that are so blatantly improper that the lawyer asking them will deservedly receive the calumny of the court and the profession.

However, the advocate should not refrain from asking a question because the advocate believes it violates some rule of evidence, such as being leading or calling for a hearsay response. The lawyer should remember that objecting to questions that may be inappropriate is the task of the other side. The advocate should never censor his own questions by applying the rules of evidence for the opposition.

When the advocate fails to ask a question because it violates some rule, he may be giving up a point that, may have been overlooked by the other side through inattention or ignorance.

No advocate should not perform the job of the opposition. The rules of evidence are of such flexibility of interpretation to the trial judge that cases are rarely reversed on these grounds. What the advocate may regard as objectionable material, such as hearsay, conclusions or opinions, may not be considered such by the other side or the judge.

Before a question can be disallowed, someone has to object to it. The advocate must remember that questions in and of themselves are not objectionable. What makes a question objectionable and, therefore, does not permit the witness to respond, is threefold. First, some rule of law must say it is objectionable. Second, the opposition must assert an objection. And third, the judge must find the question is objectionable.

If the advocate decides that he will not ask a question because it is objectionable, he assumes too much and deprives himself as a great deal of benefit or possible benefit. He must remember that rulings on evidentiary questions vary from judge to judge, and that before the court will disallow an answer the judge must agree with the grounds for the objection stated by the opposition. of evidence are in no way exact: they are vague and their interpretation changes from judge to judge. The advocate must remember that before the court will disallow an answer the judge must agree with the grounds for the objection stated by the opposition. Thus the advocate owes it to himself and his client to ask the question and leave it to the opposition and the judge to tell him it cannot be asked or answered.

STRATEGIC VALUE OF A DISALLOWED QUESTION

Objecting to one's own questions also fails to take into account the fact that a question asked but not allowed may have a beneficial role in the strategy of cross-examination. The advocate must be cautioned, however, that every tactic he uses in the trial must conform to ethical requirements.

Asking the question may serve a purpose other than eliciting the answer. It may call the juries' attention to something that you feel has been forgotten or overlooked or for which the significance has not registered. For instance a witness may be asked if he is aware that another witness testified to a certain fact which is beneficial to your side. This question may be objectionable for several reasons but even if it is sustained, the asking of it will remind the jury of what the previous witness may have said. When asking a question that may draw a sustainable objection it is wise to frame the question in such a way that it has the appearance of legitimacy until the last possible moment. A question such as "Isn't it true that Mr. Smith told you the defendant was innocent?" will draw the objection as soon as you have said 'Mr. Smith told you'. The better phrasing is "You know the defendant is innocent because Mr. Smith told you. Isn't that true?" In this way, the opposition is not alerted to the reason it may be objectionable, (hearsay) until after the important information has been put before the jury. The opposition objects, the judge sustains and directs the jury to disregard it, but, as Justice Jackson told us, telling a jury to disregard that which they have already heard is like unringing a bell.

Principle Seven

Do Not Allow The Witness To Repeat On Cross-Examination Everything He Said On Direct Examination

The spectacle of an advocate cross-examining a witness by asking him the same questions asked on direct in the hope that he will change his mind is one that happens with alarming frequency. This kind of cross-examination serves only to take the witness through the direct examination once again and give it more credence because it came during the cross-examination.

This error of allowing the witness to repeat everything testified to on direct often is the product of inexperience. While harmful, tedious, and time wasting, it may not do any more damage to the case than was done by the direct testimony. If this is the case the advocate can consider himself lucky. There are many cases, however, where this error will do more than allow the reiteration of points made on direct. It will enable the witness to add to the direct testimony, bolstering it in the juror's minds.

Compounding The Damage

For some perverse reason, lawyers who make this mistake tend to do it at the worst possible juncture and with the opposition witness likely to inflict the greatest on their cases. This is the witness who has already made a great impression with the jury. It is usually the witness who is well spoken, artful in his presentation, and enjoys the game. Indeed this witness is often the opposition's professional witness or expert. The really good ones will set false trails during the direct examination then wait for the unwary advocate to follow the path a short way before the trap is sprung.

These witnesses have not only studied the subject about which they intend to testify, they have also studied the subject of how to be a witness. They enjoy the game and enjoy matching wits with the lawyer. They know precisely how to seize every opening presented to them for the purpose of elaborating on the direct testimony by the unartful cross-examiner.

These witnesses will often show hesitancy during direct suggesting to the unwary advocate they have a weak memory on the matters being testified to. When the advocate then proceeds to probe this point, the witness inevitably will say something outrageously damaging.

This witness rather than gratuitously giving more than a "yes" or "no" answer will turn to the judge in the most ingenuous manner and politely say. "Your Honor may I explain that?" The judge will often say yes. The advocate has lost control and the jury believes that the judge thinks the matter is important.

Thus, after having begun the cross-examination in hopes of finding some weakness in the witness's armor the advocate finishes with doing nothing more than permitting the witness to drive whatever nails were loose even deeper into the coffin.

Lawyers commit this error is because of lack of experience, not having clear idea of what they seek to accomplish through cross-examination or a failure to prepare and understand their case. The advocate's ego may feed into an unshakable belief that he can and should discredit every witness regardless of the witness's truthfulness, honesty and ability to withstand cross-examination. A witness has hurt the case on direct examination with all or part of his testimony; and the lawyer cannot bring himself to accept the fact that he will not be able to shake him. Rather than dismiss the witness, the advocate launches an attack, the result of which is to impress the jury all the more with the testimony.

A Set-Up Versus Mere Repetition

The mistake of allowing a witness to simply repeat his testimony on direct should not be confused with the strategy of forcing the witness, through repetition, to commit to a position from which he will be able to extricate himself when faced with a contradiction.

This usually happens when the advocate has good impeaching material and the reason for the repetition is to make the witness commit himself so solidly and in so many ways that when confronted with the contradiction they will not be able to fashion a reason for the discrepancy without appearing at best foolish and at worse a liar.

This strategy should be in every advocate's arsenal, and some of the most dramatic examples in legal history have used this technique.

When Refusal To Cross-Examine Is Tactically Impossible

Following the principles contained in this book will help prevent the advocate during cross-examination from merely taking the witness through his direct testimony once again Recognizing the professional witness and the traps that they may set is also something that can be readily mastered. The more difficult task is being faced with the witness who is self-assured, artful, and waiting to take on the advocate and knowing that some damage must be done to the witness if the advocate hopes to win the case.

It is not always possible, when faced with this situation, to dismiss a witness without cross-examination. While this is the more desirable approach, often the testimony is so damaging that one must cross-examine or lose the case. It is in this situation that all the skills of the cross-examiner must come to bear. This is the role of the art of cross-examination; and the truly great lawyers are great because they are able, through ingenuity, to extract from even the most damaging witness some concession that is helpful to their side.

This witness should never be taken head on. His strengths should be your strengths. If he has made an impression on the jury as being honest, then some small concession should be extracted from him that can be used in argument to support another proposition that can be helpful to your case. His testimony should be contrasted with that of a witness who had a better vantage point. They may be faced with having to contradict a witness who they do not wish to contradict such as a fellow police officer. Professional witnesses are reluctant to do this, this reluctance stems from some sense of brotherhood that can often be exploited with a witness.

Principle Eight

Victories Achieved On Cross-Examination May Be Lost On The Jury

The advocate must always be aware of the danger of making a point during his cross-examination that is not understood by the jury. This problem can arise for a variety reasons. Often the advocate believes that, because he is aware that he has made a telling point with a witness, the jury will understand it as well. He may fail to appreciate the fact that he understands the case so well that he recognizes every nuance while the jury, having just come into the case, does not have sufficient understanding of the matter to recognize a valid point. Be ever alert to the reaction of the jury and drive home the point until you are sure that each juror recognizes its significance.

Timing And Balance

Timing can be an important factor. A point may be made with a witness when the jury is distracted by some incidental event in the courtroom. The opposition realizing the point is about to be made, may distract the jury at the crucial time and dilute its attention.

The time of day can be a factor. Is it late and the jury is tired? Is it just before lunch and they are hungry or just after lunch and they are dosing a little bit? Does it come at the end of an otherwise dull series of questions and the frame of mind of the jury is to expect another dull question?

The obverse of this coin is that the advocate, in his cross-examination must be subtle in the way that he leads the witness to a trap but not so subtle that he leaves the jury behind. If you don't show your hand to the witness and the opposition and thereby give them a chance to anticipate the point then you can be reasonably sure that the jury will not see it coming either. You must balance keeping the witness ignorant of what is coming with making sure that the jury understands once the trap is sprung.

DRAMATIC DEVICES

A trial is a drama and the jury is the observer. Dramatic devices are commonly used by the playwrights and actors to increase the impact of a drama on the audience. The advocate who can utilize the dramatic device best will stand the best chance of success. Each event in the trial becomes a drama within a drama. Each cross-examination has the elements of drama and must be considered in this light.

No aspect of what helps the drama along should be over looked. What one says and does on cross-examination may be adversely affected by the way one is dressed.

Jake Ehrlich thought dress was important because it drew the attention of the jury to him and gave him an initial edge. Earl Rogers shared the view. He used to say "True, clothes do not make the man nor the woman, but they are the first thing you see. Why handicap yourself?"

Ehrlich went so far as to change his white shirt every day at noon during a trial so as to remain looking fresh. Clarence Darrow, on the other hand, affected a rumpled look that he hoped would proclaim him as part of the working man. In both cases, these great trial lawyers understood the need to use their dress as part of their repertoire.

Setting The Trap; Catching The Quarry

When the advocate is cross-examining a witness, he must control the action and the pace in such a way as to produce a climax with impact. How this is effected will depend greatly on the type of cross-examination being used.

Let's assume the device in question is that of having one damning piece of evidence with which to confront the witness and that the examiner's approach is to take the witness through a long serious of questions which seem to be repetitious but which are designed to force the witness to commit himself to a position from which it will be impossible to extricate himself when the crucial confrontation occurs. This kind of questioning is inherently boring. It is designed to be so. It is designed to lull the witness and the opposition into a false sense of security. Needless to say, the jury will be bored as well.

Before the advocate can expect to enjoy the full impact of confronting the witness with the contradiction, he must break this spell. He must give the proceedings a sense of rising action and focus the attention of the jury on the moment. He can achieve this in several ways: by changing the volume and inflection of his voice; by asking the judge for moment and looking through some documents, thus breaking the action and refocusing the jury; or by beginning the attack on the witness by looking at the jury and, through eye contact and judicious pauses, alerting them to the fact that something is about to happen.

After the initial point is made the advocate must not let up. It is not enough to merely ensnare the quarry; rather, the quarry must be held in the trap and allowed to squirm for a sufficient time to make a forceful, and hopelessly devastating, impact on the jury. A danger arises, however, that counsel must be sensitive to: allowing the quarry to squirm may present the witness with an opportunity to escape. thus, your trap must be designed to close even tighter once the squirming starts.

Knowing When To Break Off

This quite naturally raises the question of how to know when enough is enough. If you go too far, the jury may consider you cruel and turn its sympathies to the witness; if you don't go far enough, the full impact of the situation may be lost on the jury. Experience will often be a key to sensing this delicate balance.

This is another example of why watching the case is so important. While setting the trap, the advocate should be aware of the reaction of the individual jurors and should monitor it as the trap is sprung.

If the advocate has been successful in developing a good rapport with the jury in the early stages of the case, he should be able to draw some guidance from them during this period of time. He should, by now, have a good idea of which jurors are on his side, which are committed to the opposition and which are neutral. The reactions of each will indicate whether they are following the line of attack, and their reactions will be especially useful when the trap is sprung. The lawyer should, at that point, know very well what the reaction to the strategy is on the part of most if not all of the jurors and should then be able to gauge how far he must drive the point home.

PRINCIPLE NINE

If You Aren't Prepared For The Answer Don't Ask The Question

Every lawyer, when asked for a rule of cross-examination, will answer that you should never ask a question if you don't know the answer. Put into practice, this rule would result in a great many necessary questions not being asked. This so called rule is a luxury in which few trial lawyers can indulge themselves. It is not always possible to be certain of a witness' answer before asking a question, and limiting the cross-examination to questions for which you have an answer will result in an ineffectual cross-examination.

The more appropriate rule is that the cross-examiner should never ask a critical question if he is not prepared to deal effectively with whatever answer he receives. No matter how much pre-trial preparation the advocate engages in there will always be surprises in the trial itself. This can happen in a variety of ways; a witness may disclose something on direct examination that introduces a new subject into the case, it may occur during cross-examination when, in response to a question, the witness suggests something not previously known to the lawyer, it may arise when a witness contradicts something a previous witness has said. Any of these situations present the possibility of discovering something through cross-examination that will help your case. The danger is that the information you are seeking may turn out to be harmful to your case. The problem for the cross-examiner is how to explore new matters in a way that will allow him to discover whether the information is beneficial or harmful without suffering serious damage. The goals are (1) to discover where the new material may lead in such a way that if it is harmful you can abandon the line of questions before the jury is aware of the full impact, and, (2) put the witness in a position that if the answer to the critical question is not the one you want you will be able to impeach him with his answers to previous foundation questions.

HOW TO PROBE WITHOUT GETTING BURNED

There are several methods for achieving these goals:

- Crucial questions should only be asked upon a foundation of other questions. The lawyer should have a very good idea of the answer to a crucial question long before the jury or the opposition knows it.

    * If it appears to the advocate that the answer to the ultimate question is one he doesn't like, he can change the topic before the jury is fully aware of the damaging material.
    * Eliciting favorable answers to tangential questions will allow the advocate some basis for impeachment in the event he has misjudged the situation and the witness gives an answer to a crucial question which is at odds with the previous answers.

- The witness must be placed such a position that an undesired answer to a critical question will make him appear foolish and contradictory in the eyes of the jurors.
- The witness' answers to foundation questions should give the cross-examiner sufficient information to decide what the likely answer to a crucial question will be. If the answer

is likely to be one he doesn't want the jury to hear, he can leave the subject altogether. If, on the other hand, the advocate feels the witness must answer the question in a desired way, he should ask it. If the witness gives an unexpected answer the advocate will be in a position to impeach the witness with answers to the previous questions.

FAILING TO LAY A PROPER FOUNDATION

There is an example from Samuel Liebowitz of poor cross-examination that illustrates the common mistake the advocate makes in failing to lay a proper foundation before asking a crucial question. It is instructive of what not to do, and gives a basis for exploring what might have been done.

A man is charged with the holdup of a passenger on the mezzanine of a subway station. Defense counsel questioned the victim:

> *What was the condition of the light on the mezzanine?*
> *Very dim, responded the witness.*
> *The lawyer rubbed his palms together and instead of letting well enough alone plunged ahead.*
> *Now, Mr. Witness, he thundered, inasmuch as it was so dim, where you say the holdup took place, how can you swear positively that my client is the robber?*
> *Why, Counselor, the platform may have been dimly lighted but your client and I were right under an electric light when he stuck the gun into my face and told me that he would blow my head off if I didn't give him my wallet!*

This devastating response by the witness could have been discovered by the lawyer and avoided or impeached through preliminary questions asked before the crucial one of identity.

A lawyer having visited the scene of a crime, should have put several questions to the witness regarding the familiarity of the witness with the platform. These questions should have established how often the witness had been on that platform, was it part of a daily commute, or a first time situation? What time of the day did the event occur and how many other people were present?

The witness should have been asked to describe the location in detail. How good his ability to recall all the details of the lighting would have given some indication of his memory and of his answer to any question that might have been asked regarding his ability to identify the defendant. The questions might also have laid a foundation for impeachment by committing the witness to a situation of poor lighting.

The witness should have been asked a series questions regarding his movements on the platform before the holdup and required to give his exact location when the holdup took place.

The result of these answers would have informed the lawyer whether the witness was in a position to see the defendant well or whether the lighting was inadequate. If his answers indicated that he was in a position to see the assailant very well, then the question of identification should not have been posed. In that case, the lawyer could have relied on other inferences in the case to suggest that the lighting was poor or point out that some portions of the platform were poorly lighted by using another witness.

On the other hand, if the answers had indicated that the assault took place on a poorly lighted location, then the witness should have been asked questions in the form of statements such as isn't it true that the lighting where you were standing at the time of the assault was such that you could not get a good look at the defendant? If the witness answers no then he could have been impeached with his prior answers as to the location of lighting, his location during the assault, and his familiarity with the location.

Part Three
Selecting The Tactics

Principle One

Tactics In Cross-Examination Must Be Based On The Entire Case

The tactics any advocate will use against a particular witness on cross-examination must be considered and refined while the witness is testifying on direct and will require intuitive decision making on the spur of the moment. Sometimes these decisions made in the heat of battle will determine the outcome of the case.

Not every eventuality can be anticipated in advance. Often a new situation will develop during the examination that takes the advocate by surprise. Deciding whether to pursue the matter, and how far to pursue it, requires quick wits and a firm grasp of the case. For the most part, the intuitive decision making process depends on a firm understanding of some fundamental rules.

An experienced lawyer once scored rather a remarkable victory by pursuing an issue that had not come up in the case and which appeared to be fraught with dangerous traps. After the case an observer approached the lawyer and congratulated him and also opined that he had been quite lucky in his cross-examination of the witness. "Yes," replied the lawyer, "its remarkable how lucky one becomes with practice."

Some Basic Rules

There are fundamental tactical rules that every advocate should follow in deciding what to pursue on cross-examination and how to pursue it in the actual heat of battle.

- Always keep in mind what the jury is reacting to in the testimony and wherever possible pursue matters be aware of what points are scoring with the jury, and should take from the jury clues with respect to pursuing new subjects.
- The advocate should conduct even the weakest cross-examination without hesitation and wherever possible pursue matters in a way that appeals to the jury.
- Conduct even the weakest cross-examination without hesitation and convey a sense of confidence. This confidence can be helped along by conducting the examination without notes and with a firm purpose in mind. * the advocate should resist the temptation show the witness up by pouncing on small errors in the testimony.
- Avoid lengthy cross-examination wherever possible.
- Respond quickly to a harmful answer thus deflecting the attention of the jury away from the damaging matter as much as possible.
- Keep in mind: (1) that witnesses may be used to an advantageous purpose even though their direct testimony is not vulnerable to cross-examination. (2) That cross-examination can be an opportunity to make statements to the jury in the form of questions, and (3) that cross-examination can be used to repeat favorable testimony made by other witnesses.
- It is not enough to expose a weakness or lie in the witnesses direct testimony. The matter must be driven home and put into such a light with the jury that no amount of rehabilitation by the opposition will salvage it.

Keep To The Theme Of Your Case

The theme of the case should have be stated on voir dire examination and repeated in the opening statement. Cross-examination is the opportunity to state and restate the theme and to drive the message home. It is important not to allow yourself to forget the theme by pursuing other matters in the cross-examination simply because they are attractive subjects and will provide you an opportunity to show your skills. Any matter not germane to the overall theme of the case should be ignored.

Tactics used to pursue a particular witness must not be formulated on the basis of what the weak points of his testimony were. A witness may exhibit several weaknesses in his testimony that have no relationship to the case you have decided upon.

Don't Show Off

It is always tempting to show how clever a cross-examiner you are by showing up a witness before the jury. Unfortunately, there are risks to this kind of behavior that usually outweigh any possible good.

I remember observing one situation in which the defendant in a criminal case was charged with murder. His defense was that he had an alibi. In the opening statement, the defense counsel made it clear that he was not disputing the fact that the victim had been shot and killed. He was taking the position that the defendant was elsewhere when the shooting occurred and could not possibly have been the assailant.

As part of the state's case they called a ballistics expert who had conducted tests on the weapon recovered from the scene and the spent bullet recovered from the body. Usually an expert in the field can give an opinion, based on the test, as to whether the bullet recovered from the scene and the one fired by the expert came from the same gun.

Counsel for the defendant apparently believed there was a weakness in the ballistic expert's testimony and decided to challenge his credibility and the credibility of the test results. He overlooked the fact that the witness was an expert who had conducted thousands of these tests and testified in hundreds of cases. Indeed, this individual was not only an expert but also a professional witness, a deadly combination for even the best trial lawyer to attack.

As the cross-examination proceeded, the expert made several points that gave the impression that counsel was not well informed.

The hapless cross-examiner could not find an effective way to extricate himself. His frustration grew and the jury's sympathy for him began to erode seriously. He finally obtained some minor concession from the witness and then sat down.

The cross-examination had a negative on defense counsel's side to in many ways. He tried to shake a witness and failed. This is always harmful to the case, because the jury instinctively believes the advocate has something to prove when he cross-examines. He also raised a false issue in the case by spending so much time on trying to show the weapon didn't fire the fatal bullet. There was no need to cause this problem. His defense was that his client knew nothing about the killing and was not present at the time. Even if he had damaged the expert's findings, it would have had no impact on the case.

Counsel believed he had an opportunity to damage the expert or he would not have undertaken the cross-examination. What he failed to consider was how would the success fit into his closing argument. Had he made that analysis he would have shown that the risks inherent in the cross-examination were needless. This is no to say that he should have dismissed the witness without any questions.

QUESTIONS NOT CHALLENGING TESTIMONY ON DIRECT

Often declining to ask any questions will give the jury the impression that the prosecutions case is airtight, and that you are just going through the motions in your defense. Where an alibi defense is involved, for example, there will be a great many witnesses testifying to events not relevant to defense counsel's main theme. Unfortunately, several of these witnesses may testify in a row, and simply dismissing them without questions may itself have a negative impact.

Some questions should be asked but not necessarily about the direct examination. Here is a chance to reiterate your defense without risk. The examination of the ballistics expert might have proceeded along these lines.

Q. Mr. Expert, is it fair to call your field of expertise a science?
A. Yes.
Q. By a science do you mean a discipline which has rules which if applied correctly will result in a conclusion that every expert will be able to reach?
A. Yes.
Q. In other words you would agree that another person with your credentials and experience in examining these bullets would come to the same conclusion as you have?
A. Yes
Q. And this is because what you do is objective as opposed to subjective?
A. Yes.
Q. By subjective you would mean the use of emotion, guesswork, or something not scientific and may vary from person to person?
A. Yes.
Q. In other words, Mr. Expert, while you can testify, based on the tests you have described, that these two bullets came from the same gun you cannot testify that these tests tell you the defendant pulled the trigger of the gun when it was fired at the deceased?
A. No.
Q. You don't know from these tests where the defendant was at the time of the shooting?
A. No.

In the case where there had been no tests on the defendant to determine if he had fired a weapon recently you may go one step further.

Q. Incidentally, Mr. Expert, there are tests, are there not, to determine whether or not a person has fired a weapon recently?
A. Yes.
Q. Did you conduct such a test on the defendant?
A. No.

Q. To your knowledge did any one else conduct such a test?
A. No.

In this way the advocate has reminded the jury of the theme of the case (alibi), and sown seeds of doubt about the fact that the police had at their disposal the means to test whether the defendant had fired a gun, and that it would have been prudent to do so. Also that the test may not have been conducted because it would have pointed to defendant's innocence.

Extracting Minor Concessions For Later Use

The advocate should guard against deciding that a witness will testify to items that are not germane to the defense and therefore not pay strict attention to the testimony. Keep in mind the fact that testing the truth of the statement on direct testimony is only one reason for cross-examination. Often, the advocate can extract some seemingly minor concession from a witness that can be used with another witness who is crucial. This tactic is often used with when one expert is not important to your defense and another may be. In this case it may be possible to have the non-important expert agree to an opinion which may be used later on against another witness to sow seeds of contradiction between the two. Even if the point involved is minor, the jury will consider that you have shown a weakness in the opponent's case.

Watching For Clues

It is important to watch the witness closely on direct examination for clues that may indicate weakness with respect to matters that are crucial to your case. Does he hesitate when dealing with a question which bears on a point you hope to make? Does he show nervousness over some point about which he should be confident? His demeanor and reactions will tell you a great deal about his vulnerability, but that vulnerability must be considered carefully when deciding on the tactics to employed. A witness may exhibit weaknesses in areas that have nothing to do with the goals you have set for your case. Attempts you mount to exploit them may damage your opponent's case, serve to rehabilitate the witness, or create sympathy for him with the jury.

Say for example, that you have built your case around the fact that a crime of murder was indeed committed but that your client is not the one responsible. The state produces a witness to establish cause of death without suggesting that your client was the person responsible. The witness, in turn, shows vulnerability with respect to his procedures or conclusions. You must then weigh carefully whether it is important to show the witness is sloppy or that his conclusions are technically incorrect. If you don't intend to dispute the specific cause of death on your argument, will it serve any purpose to show the witness lacks credibility? The answer depends on whether or not you seek to attack the case: (1) because there is no evidence pointing to your client or (2) because your client has an alibi or (3) you are relying on the poor investigation in general. In the latter case, you may want to cross-examine to point out the poor work. You can argue later on that because the investigation was flawed, the state's identification of your client is unreliable.

Principle Two

Knowing The Reaction Of The Jury Is Vital To Cross-Examination

Often the advocate believes he is scoring points against the witness when a simple glance at the jury will disclose they do not understand the significance of the line of questioning. Moreover, the jury may disapprove of the method being employed against the witness even though the advocate feels he is doing quite well. The sympathy of the jury may remain with the witness and the advocate not realize it. It may be the jury needs some point clarified and the advocate by not monitoring fails to notice and releases the witness prematurely. It may be that one or more jurors are distracted at a crucial time and the point must be repeated. If the advocate is not aware of this a point scored will go for naught.

If the advocate has done his work properly during those stages of the trial leading up to the cross-examination, he will have established a rapport with some or all of the jurors which will serve to give him guidance in his cross-examination. Jurors inevitably tell you something about the case. Some fall in love with the attorney for the other side and dwell on every word and action. Others fall in love with you. You have to discern which is which. And having decided which is which maintain the relationship with the one and convert the other.

It is never wise to treat the jury as a non participating observer in the case. From the inception of the trial the good advocate has sought to sell his own character to the jury and to put the jury in a frame of mind that is sympathetic to his case. To go to all this trouble and then not reap the rewards is foolish.

Jurors are thrown into a difficult situation in which the natural reaction is nervousness. They are told they must adopt a set of rules that they often do not understand or which they regard as contrary to their long held feelings and emotions. In their everyday lives jurors evaluate situations and make decisions without applying the rigid standards the law may impose. In real life, for example, people accept hearsay as a basis for a decision, or fail the sift the relevant from the irrelevant. The idea that someone who is charged with a crime is presumed innocent often runs contrary to the instinct. The more normal response is 'if the defendant hasn't done something wrong why is he here?"

It is very difficult for jurors to accept all the rules of fairness we as lawyers have fashioned over the years. But they will try and in trying they will often convey to the lawyer what it is they're struggling with. What jurors believe, feel, and intuit often shows on their faces. Whether they agree with a tactic or whether they take notice of your point their feelings will always show.

Jurors may inform the lawyer that they will have no difficulty applying the notion of presumption of innocence when in fact the keen observer will recognize that there is a great deal of unspoken reservation on this point. An alert advocate will recognize the problem and monitor the jury continually, striving for a way to overcome this deep-seated prejudice.

It is impossible for a human being to spend several weeks in a courtroom without giving the observer some clue to their feelings. Some jurors never realize they are giving information away to the observant advocate, while others cannot resist giving some sign— not keeping a secret, as it were.

The advocate should be aware of the needs of the individual jurors and not be inhibited about addressing those needs. It may be important to point out that a juror is having apparent difficulty hearing the witness, or to even ask the juror if they did hear the answer to a question. This kind of action not only ensures that the juror heard the response and makes them realize you are aware of their participation in the case it also serves to reiterate and emphasize a particular point.

PRINCIPLE THREE

There Should Be No Hesitation In Your Cross-Examination

It is important in any case to establish a rhythm and flow. Conveying a sense of being in control of the situation and of not being confused by anything the opposition does is a subtle technique that will make the jury have confidence in you and your case.

Nowhere in the trial does this have more impact than on cross-examination. As soon as the opposition says "your witness" or "no further questions" you should be ready to begin the cross-examination. All you do in this respect should convey a sense of control and confidence. It should appear to the jury that the witness has done absolutely no harm to your case and that you can't wait to point this fact out to the jury.

There should be no conferences with co-counsel or the client before rising and beginning the cross. If the witness has said something that catches you off guard or is otherwise disconcerting you should still begin the cross without hesitation. If the note the opposition finished on requires some consultation with the client or co-counsel you should nevertheless begin the cross immediately with a remote or unimportant subject and wait for a good moment to interrupt the examination to hold the conference. Remaining at counsel table for even a short period of time before commencing the cross-examination can convey a notion of confusion or weakness

I find it useful in many cases to begin the examination while I am rising from my seat to go to the podium. I think it helps to convey to the jury that I can't wait to show the witness up for the charlatan he is. The implicit suggestion is that the sooner all the facts are before them, the sooner they can find in my favor and return to their private lives.

It is often useful to begin the cross-examination with a subject of minor importance that will not require the use of any notes. Rise from your chair and leave your notebook on the table as near the podium as possible. Begin the cross-examination immediately and make certain the jury can see that you are doing so without reference to notes. After giving the jurors an opportunity to focus on the cross-examination itself and on the witness you can unobtrusively place the notebook on the podium for reference. The jury has been left with the impression that you have such a firm grasp of the case that you can conduct most of it from memory. This tactic reinforces the notion placed with them during voir dire that counsel is possessed with a prodigious memory and complete control of the case.

EXPLOITING THE PAUSE BETWEEN DIRECT AND CROSS

In almost every trial I see the action between the direct examination and the cross-examination is the same. The lawyer conducting the direct examination announces he is finished with the witness. He then collects all the papers at the podium he has had with him during the examination and returns to his seat. Counsel who will conduct cross-examination assembles his papers (usually more than he should ever need) and carries them to the podium. During this time there is an awkward silence and the action of the case is interrupted. I have always thought this have a negative effect in the conduct of the case and quite often a missed opportunity for counsel beginning the cross. The attorney finishing the direct is at this moment quite vulnerable. He believes that he will have a brief moment to return to the counsel table and arrange his papers while you are taking that time to arrange your materials on the podium. This can prove fatal if you have the right situation.

Some years ago I was defending a union leader charged with conspiring to hire a convicted felon for the purpose of destroying an expensive motion picture screen in a theater with whom the union was having a labor dispute.

The government had made a deal with a convicted felon to infiltrate the union and inform on the activities. This witness was one of the most unsavory characters I had ever encountered. The government was in the unfortunate position however of having him as their only witness and did their best to minimize his shortcomings.

There was evidence to corroborate what he testified to and the fact he was unsavory did not necessarily mean the jury could not separate their dislike for the person and the truth of his testimony.

He was on the stand for a considerable amount of time and the district attorney had decided that it would be less damaging to his case if he brought out the negative factors about the witness before I did.

My seat at counsel table had been the closest one to the witness box and my disgust for the witness was such that I had gotten up during the direct testimony and taken one of the chairs just in from of the railing that separates the spectators from the participants in the case. I monitored the jury and could tell that they were as disgusted with the witness as I was, but that given time to reflect they might overlook the personal revulsion and credit the actual testimony. I felt that the witness had to be attacked and his credibility with the jury destroyed in a dramatic manner.

I was also sure the D.A. was prepared to try and deflect and dilute such an attack through objections. I sat somewhat pensively away from the counsel table and waited for the signal of the end of the direct examination. Just as the D.A. said "your witness" and began to turn from the podium I virtually leapt to my feet and without hesitation began my attack.

Q. *Mr. Ford, (this in a rather loud and aggressive voice) you have testified here today that you are a liar, a cheat, and a perjurer. That you have participated in assaults and armed robberies. And that the oath to tell the truth is without meaning isn't that true?*

The District Attorney was taken completely by surprise. His mind was on other things. Perhaps he was congratulating himself on traversing the minefield of this witness with relative success. Perhaps he was just giving himself a mental break in anticipation of the battle he anticipated in trying to prevent jut the thing I had said to the witness. Whatever the reason it threw him off stride. He appeared not to have heard all the question and his objection was hesitant and poorly worded. During the objection I continued to ask these kinds of questions until the judge stopped me and suggested we hear the D.A.'s objections. The damage had been done however. The witness was off stride and the D.A. had lost control of the situation and was never able to regain it. I continued to hammer home the aspects of the witness that would be repugnant to any decent human being and I am convinced that beginning the cross-examination in the way I did, and the timing involved, had a great deal with the fact the judge refused to accept the witness as credible and dismissed the case at the end of the government's evidence.

Delibrate Silence Distinguished

Sometimes it is useful to wait a moment before launching the cross-examination. The point of this tactic is to unnerve the witness, or in some cases, to gain the attention of the jury that may have lapsed. This carefully planned silence is not to be confused with hesitation. Hesitation is a demonstration of uncertainty, the confusion of not knowing what you are about or exactly where you want to go. Even if you decide not to ask a question for a few minutes in an attempt to cause the witness some discomfort you should do so in a commanding way. You should not sit at the counsel table and flip through notes or confer with the client. You should take command of the situation and approach the matter with confidence and not permit the jury to wonder if you really know what you want to do.

Principle Four

Lengthy Cross-Examination Exaggerates The Value Of The Direct Examination

Lengthy cross-examination is inherently dangerous. It risks boring the jury and losing their attention. It risks opening some new subject harmful to the side doing the cross-examination. It risks giving the impression that the testimony is so important that it must be impeached at all costs and therefore failure to do so gives it that much more credibility. It risks refreshing the witnesses mind about a subject he had failed to recall on the direct testimony. It risks having the case fly off into an area that is irrelevant to your case and which causes the jury to be put on a false trail.

Undoubtedly lengthy cross-examination is sometimes required. When the witness is so crucial that failure to discredit their testimony will result in failure of the case the advocate must make the painful choice between risking the lengthy cross or risk conceding the case with this one witness. The experienced examiner knows that even in the worst situation the most effective cross will not be unduly lengthy.

Cases are rare in which it is possible to conduct a lengthy cross-examination without losing the attention of the jury or worse to focus their attention to a greater degree on the validity of the direct testimony of the witness. Lengthy cross-examination usually results in the restatement of the witness' direct testimony without any telling points for your side.

What To Avoid

It is all too common to see a purported cross-examination degenerate into a reiteration of the direct examination with the attorney supplying the answers and the witness agreeing or disagreeing.

In this example the witness testifies on direct that he saw a collision at an intersection between the plaintiff and defendant. He further testified that the defendant was traveling over forty miles an hour and entered the intersection against a red light. The cross-examination follows these lines.

Q. *(By defense counsel) You testified that the defendant was traveling over 40 miles per hour. Are you sure of that?*
A. Yes.
Q. *Isn't it possible the defendant was traveling under the speed limit of thirty miles per hour?*
A. No.
Q. *You further testified that the traffic light was red when the defendant entered the intersection. Isn't it possible the light could have been yellow?*
A. No.
Q. *You seem quite certain about these two matters. Why is that?*
A. *Before I retired I was a bus driver for twenty five years and never had an accident. I have developed a good sense of judging the speed of city traffic and I know how important it is to observe the color of a traffic light.*

The attorney believing that he has set the witness up for the kill plays the ace.
Q. *Mr. Witness isn't it true that you observed these events looking west at four in the afternoon and the sun was directly in you eyes?*
A. *No sir it was cloudy that day.*

The only good thing about this example is that is mercifully short. Often such banality will be stretched out *ad infinitum*.

Avoiding the lengthy cross can be achieved by a full examination of the alternatives open to you, but it begins by a strict adherence to the rules I have discussed. In the example it seemed the advocate had decided on three points in his cross-examination; the ability of the witness to judge the speed of the cars; whether the traffic light was red, yellow, or green; and the ability of the witness to see the light. His analysis may have been correct but the execution was atrocious. He violated the rule against letting the witness repeat on cross everything he had said on direct, and he failed to ask himself if he could discredit or contradict the testimony of this witness through another witness or evidence. In this particular case, he would have been wiser to wait for another witness and raise the issue of the time of day and the direction of his vision. In that way the issue of clear or cloudy conditions may not have arisen in the case in chief and the advocate could have argued it in his closing argument.

Of course, there are cases in which the testimony of a witness is so crucial that one has no option but to examine the witness until every possibility of shaking the witness is exhausted or until some breakthrough is accomplished. Failure to discredit the testimony will enhance it in the eyes of the jury but in reality nothing will have been lost because not cross-examining at all would have been tantamount to conceding the case. In this situation one must plunge ahead and hope for the best.

Principle Five

Respond To A Harmful Answer By Immediately Posing Another Question

During any cross-examination the witness will inevitably respond with a harmful answer. How harmful this answer may be will depend on a variety of factors. Damage can be avoided by careful adherence to the rules of cross-examination that are designed to limit a witness' ability to respond to a question in a harmful way. Damage can also be controlled by laying a careful foundation with the witness in such a way that when an unexpected response occurs the witness can be impeached using his answers to previous questions.

Kinds Of Witnesses Likely To Make A Harmful Response

When the cross-examiner is caught unawares by a devastating answer, his recovery may depend on the extent to which he knows in advance the kinds of witnesses and situations that may produce the problem. The witnesses most likely to make a harmful response are:

* The honest witness who has no motive but to be honest and who is intent upon reciting the facts. Often this witness is so ingenuous and frank that the advocate is lulled into a sense of security and unwittingly allows the witness to blurt out something that is unexpected and harmful. It is with

this witness that such an incident can be most damaging because of the sense of honesty and decency that the witness has conveyed to the jury.

* The essentially honest witness who is not willing to perjure himself but who sees the cross-examination as a game and has laid a trap for the advocate. In this case the witness usually is so pleased with springing the trap that he takes time to exult over his victory and is particularly vulnerable at that moment to a quick and penetrating follow up. A good recovery by the advocate in this situation can be especially effective if the subject is an important one.

* The witness who has assumed the role of adversary and will invent a situation for the damaging answer if not presented with the opportunity by the advocate. This witness will inject something damaging into his answers gratuitously. The cross-examiner must then move quickly to another question or topic because the gratuitous response is usually of significance. However, because the response is gratuitous it is usually somewhat out of context and will be lost on the jurors if they do not have time to assimilate and digest it.

SHIFTING GEARS

When a witness delivers an unexpected response the reaction of the advocate should be to deflect the effects of the answer by posing another question as quickly as possible. By so doing he will accomplish some damage control by not giving the jury time to think about the statement of the witness. There is always the chance that by moving quickly to another issue the answer may be overlooked altogether. The possibility of this happening is directly proportional to the speed and cleverness with which the advocate proceeds

The well prepared advocate knows that the situation will arise and will have prepared himself for such an eventuality by having in his mind a topic or question that he can pose when the situation arises. This topic or question should be of sufficient impact that it will require that focus of the jury and make it even more likely that they can be diverted from the harmful response.

The damaging and unexpected response usually comes when you are surprised or make a tactical error. For this reason, you must anticipate the possibility of such a situation ahead of time so that your response will be automatic. The act of deflection must seem automatic and will lose its effectiveness with each moment that passes.

MASTERING THE ART OF RIPOSTE

The skills required by the advocate in responding automatically and effectively to the unexpected harmful response are the same skills employed in social situations in which people good naturedly or maliciously engage in the "put down". It is a game (if it can be called that) in which quick responses that are more clever than the opening gambit are the object. It is a game that requires a thick skin and a quick wit. The advocate would be well advised to seek out the kinds of social companions who are adept at this game of wits and practice the skills as much as possible. The skills acquired will serve him well when required to make a quick retort in court.

One of my favorite examples of this repartee was between George Bernard Shaw and the actress Cornelia Otis Skinner when she opened in a revival of Shaw's *Candida*. This exchange of cables took place:

Shaw: "Excellent. Greatest!"
Skinner, overwhelmed: "Undeserving such praise."
Shaw: "I meant the play."
Skinner: "So did I."

A popular anecdote on this subject deals with an accident case involving a man riding in a buggy and an automobile. The man in the buggy is suing for physical injuries suffered in the incident. It is an example usually given to demonstrate the damage that can be done by the advocate that asks the wrong question. It is a good example for that but rarely does the commentator provide us with advice on how the embarrassed cross-examiner might have extricated himself from the situation. First the example.

The witness testifies on direct examination that he was driving his horse drawn buggy along a road and a car driven by the defendant forced him into the ditch where he was thrown from the buggy and his horse was injured. On cross-examination the following took place:

Q. *Isn't it true that immediately after the accident while you were lying in the ditch you told a stranger that you were not hurt?*
A. *Yes.*

This is a remarkably good place to stop this line of questioning. The intrepid advocate goes on.

Q. *If you were hurt why did you say you weren't?*
A. *Just after the accident I was lying in the ditch unable to move and the horse was lying not far away. This man stopped his car and came over and looked at the horse then he went back to his car and returned with a large pistol and shot the horse. Then he turned to me and asked if I was hurt and I said "I'm not hurt!"*

Obviously the advocate as the result of a stupid question got an answer that was devastating and the lesson is not to ask a "why" question. I include it here because it offers an opportunity to explore what the advocate might have said to salvage the situation if only in a small way. The advocate should have proceeded as follows.

Q. *Are you asking this jury to believe that the only reason you lied and said you weren't hurt is that having seen a veterinarian put a horse out of its misery as an act of kindness, you believed that if you didn't lie to him he would shoot you?*

By this response the advocate has suggested the witness is

capable of lying, that his behavior conflicted with the common sense of the jury, and that he knew the stranger was a veterinarian. It may serve to put the witness on the defensive and to raise the credibility issues with the jury. It certainly has a better chance of success than to stand speechless.

Principle Six

No Cross-Examination Doesn't Always Mean No Questions

Assume a witness has completed the direct examination and opposing counsel indicates you may cross-examination. You may decide after listening to a witness that there is no need to cross-examine. You may base this decision on the fact the witness did not say anything damaging to the case. Or you may conclude the best way to impeach him is through another witness. Or the witness may be so good that the dangers of trying to cast doubt on the testimony are greater than any potential benefits.

The decision not to cross-examine in the traditional sense of trying to cast doubt on the witness or their testimony is different than deciding not to ask the witness any questions at all. Often the advocate can decide not to cross-examine the witness and overlook the fact that there are many other goals that can be achieved with a witness under the guise of cross-examination. In other words, having made the decision not to cross-examine the witness, the advocate should go one step further and analyze whether or not there are any other goals that may be achieved while the witness is still on the stand.

An important aspect of any trial is the ability of the advocate to present to the jury as often as possible the key aspects of his case. Cross-examination should not be overlooked as one of these opportunities. The advocate should carefully consider whether or not this witness can be used to ratify the favorable aspects of the some other testimony. With careful handling this witness may be used to cast some doubt on another witness' testimony without realizing he is doing so. Or perhaps the advocate can use him to restate crucial points before the jury by cleverly worded questions.

Any decision to use an opposition witness for purposes other than cross-examination will depend on a great many variables that differ from case to case. Nevertheless there are constants in every case that must be taken into consideration.

A trial has one purpose. It is to persuade the jury that past events happened in the way your client says they did. It is a reconstruction of the past about which two sides differ dramatically. The work of the advocate is to convince the jury that his version of these past events is the correct one. No opportunity should be missed to reiterate points that should lead the jury to the conclusion most beneficial to the client.

Most lawyers think that their only opportunities to present their version of the past directly to the jury are voir dire, opening statement, and closing argument. They think of direct examination and cross-examination only as the time for presenting testimony and exhibits. this view has led many trial lawyers to squander valuable opportunities to address the jury. The examination of an opposition witness can be used to present many positive points to the jury which have little or nothing to do with an attack on the witness's credibility or his testimony.

When To Question But Not Cross-Examine

The decision approach an opposition witness in this fashion will depend on a variety of factors. The number and strength of your witnesses is an important consideration. Usually in criminal cases, the defense will have few or no witnesses. And will be unable or unwilling to call the defendant. In this situation it is vitally important to use opposition witness to make some beneficial points with the jury.

Generally the types of witnesses that present this opportunity are those that are neutral, those that are honest in their recollection of the facts, and those that are called to give background testimony or to establish some link in the chain of evidence. To some lesser degree, this consideration also applies to the witness that has damaged your case terribly. Instead of plunging into cross-examination as a sort of desperate attempt to make something good happen, or declining to cross-examine altogether and face the serious risk of losing the case, you might be able to mitigate the problem by scoring some collateral points.

The length of the opposition case may also have some bearing. If the case is quite long it may be wise to use some of their witness to keep your points of defense before the jury so they are not forgotten.

The advocate must carefully analyze what other opportunities exist for making certain points and what the effect may be of allowing a witness to be excused without any questions at all.

What Questions To Put Forth—Some examples

If the advocate feels that the jury sees the witness as being honest, he can seek to have the witness ratify something another witness has said by asking the witness if he has any quarrel with the previous statement. His answer that he does not have any quarrel is fundamentally meaningless but serves to reinforce the statement by suggesting that he too adopts it. Proceeding along these lines, you can obtain apparent acceptance by this witness of something you intend to present through one of your witnesses who is less credible.

In a case of identity the witness may simply be taken through a series of questions such as "You don't know of your own knowledge whether the defendant is the person who robbed the store do you?" "The fact that what you have testified to is correct is not to say that the defendant is the person who committed the robbery. Isn't that correct."

These techniques often have the effect of pointing out to the jury that an apparently honest and truthful witness is not impliedly testifying to the ultimate fact in the case and that their testimony while truthful has nothing to do with your ultimate defense. It also serves to remind the jury of the defense you are presenting and may suggest to the jury that if this witness had all the facts he would have concluded your client was not the culprit.

You can ask a police witness who may be a records custodian and is obviously testifying only in a custodial way without any knowledge of the facts whether or not he would agree with a statement made on cross-examination by a fellow officer that was beneficial to your case. Obviously the witness will agree to the extent that he will not risk contradicting a fellow police officer. Later on closing or at some other stage in the trial you can point to the statement of the first officer and buttress its validity by pointing out that another police officer agreed with it.

This technique is also a valuable tactic in enhancing a statement by a less credible witness through an apparently more credible one. It is also effective in calling the juries' attention to some previous testimony that is beneficial to your side.

You can extract from he witness the names of any service organizations or professional associations they may belong to and at some other time bring it to the attention of the jury that your witness or client belongs to same organization. This suggests to the jury that a witness called by the other side may in fact share the same integrity as those on your side.

Often a great deal can be accomplished with a witness by making a statement that takes the form of a question. This form of tactics can be accomplished by using such forms of question as 'Isn't' it true that . . . ' or 'Don't you agree that . . . ?" followed by the facts you wish to place before the jury.

Here's an example. The witness is a police property custodian and has been called to the stand to establish the chain of custody of a revolver used in a homicide. Your client's defense is that the shooting occurred in a crowded bar and that while he was present he did not shoot the weapon and because of the confusion and lighting at the time the witnesses are mistaken in their identity of him. The questioning might go something like this:

Q. *Officer you have no personal knowledge whether the person who shot the deceased is Mr. X, Mr. Y, Mr. Z. or the defendant do you?*
A. *No.*
Q. *You are aware are you not that the shooting occurred in a crowded bar?*
A. *No. (You may get lucky and have him say "I believe so" or "that is what I understand").*
Q. *You are also aware, are you not, that the lighting in the bar was very poor at the time?*
A. *No*

Depending upon the opposition's acumen, an objection will have been raised to each of these questions. It usually comes in the form of relevance or of the question being outside the scope of the cross-examination or something similar. The advocate parries the first by saying "your Honor I'm only inquiring if the witness knows." The court quite often turns to the witness and asks "do you know officer?" The answer is "no". The court says "go on to something else counsel" and you ask the next question and a similar colloquy takes place. This goes on until the court says "counsel either ask the witness something about which he has first hand knowledge or release the witness."

By this time you have reminded the jury of the crucial elements of your defense and perhaps even have caused them to focus their attention on the questions of identity and credibility of other witnesses at the expense of the direct testimony of the witness.

PRINCIPLE SEVEN

Avoid Exaggerating Trifling Discrepancies

Every witness will utter some minor contradiction in their testimony that is at odds with their own testimony or that of another witness. This may occur because of nervousness of the inherent intimidation of the courtroom. The advocate must always keep in mind that of all the participants in the trial it is the jurors and the witnesses who are the strangers and the result is usually an affinity between them. They are the one's injected into this foreign turf in which the judge and the lawyers are at home. The result more often than not is the sympathy of the jury will naturally be with the witness and remain there until the advocate convinces them the witness is unworthy of their sympathy.

This natural affinity for the witness will not be obviated because the witness has uttered some inconsistency or demonstrates a lack of knowledge on a minor point. The demonstration of a poor memory with respect to all the details of the testimony is not sufficient in and of itself to warrant an attack on the witness. Quite the opposite is usually the case. The jury will consider the witness whose testimony is without these errors as being too good to be true. It is the natural state of the human condition to not remember everything with exactitude. This is especially true when a witness is testifying to some event that was unusual and happened very quickly.

Every witness will mis-state some fact in the testimony. Most mis-statements fall in the category of the insignificant. Often they are obviously attributable to nervousness created by the strange and intimidating conditions of the courtroom. Almost always it is clear to all in the courtroom that the misstatement is not of a serious consequence and does not serve to raise questions about the legitimacy of the testimony.

Many advocates pounce on these tiny morsels of inconsistency as if they have won a major victory. The advocate rushes to the attack as if he has discovered some glaring error in the testimony. The result is usually that the witness corrects the error with some ingenuous explanation and exhibits even more distress at their embarrassment, which, in turn, generates more sympathy from the jury.

This often occurs with respect to matters the witness has not reviewed thoroughly or which are tangential to the matters at hand. When this takes place it is easy to spring little traps which put the witness in an apparent contradiction but the advocate must show a great deal of care in exploiting these deficiencies.

Juries believe that this tactic amounts to nitpicking and probably means the advocate is covering up the fact he doesn't have much of a case. Rather than exalting over some small victory it is quite often better to admit that there is nothing wrong in a witness being confused over trifles. If the advocate shows understanding about small inconsistencies it may serve to emphasize those he points out to the jury as being large ones.

Being empathic to a witness' minor errors may also serve to put the witness at ease in a difficult situation and dispose the witness to provide you with more neutral responses than might be the case if you increase the embarrassment by pointing out the inconsistencies.

The tactic of putting a witness at ease and making them feel disposed towards you and your case was a favorite tactic of Earl Rogers. He always began a case with the assumption that the witnesses wanted to tell the truth. To the extent they testified to something Rogers felt was wrong he attributed to the fact they had perceived the matter in that way. As soon as he had the chance to have a conversation with them and point out the correct perception he believed they would come around to his point of view. He was correct in this assumption more often than he was wrong.

SMALL INCONSISTENCY OR TIP OF THE ICEBERG?

While making much of trifling discrepancies often damages a case the advocate must be watchful for the situation in which the small inconsistency is merely the tip of an iceberg made up of large inconsistencies. The decision therefore to ignore apparent minor inconsistencies should not be automatic. The advocate must develop a sense of when the small error is symptomatic of the large one and he must also develop a sense of how far to probe the small one before abandoning it and moving on to something else.

One good indication of when to pursue what appears to be a minor inconsistency can be garnered from the jury. On the other hand the advocate may perceive an opening which is not apparent to the jury. What the jury may see as a trifling discrepancy may in fact be a part of a larger one waiting to be brought to the surface. In this case the advocate must pursue it even at the risk of offending the sensibilities of the jury at the outset. In this case the advocate must be careful to monitor the jurors reaction to this course of action and cease the line of attack in the event it is only serving to alienate the jury, or you should alter the tactics to deflect the resentment they may feel until you have convinced them of the correctness of your position.

The good advocate develops a sense of when he has the jury on his side of an issue and when the jury resents a witness. One technique is to probe the spot of inconsistency only slightly and see what reaction one gets from the jury and the judge. If it appears they expect you to pursue the matter then you should probably proceed.

Principle Eight

Cross-Examination Should Not Be Conducted From Written Questions

Seen all too often in the courtroom is the advocate who conducts the cross-examination from questions written down on a yellow legal pad on the podium in front of him. The pages usually extend over the rear of the podium in a somewhat sloppy way and counsel then conducts his examination with frequent reference to the pages, flipping them back and forth seeking a note or reference. Inevitably the points he wishes to make come about painfully and boringly. The jurors get so distracted by the seemingly interminable delays between questions, while the lawyer flips through the notes, that their attention strays and concentration lapses.

The trial is a drama in which the advocate hopes the jury will be swayed by the evidence and be predisposed to the point of view of one side because of the manner in which the evidence is presented. When the advocate conducts the cross-examination in a slow, hesitant and meandering way, searching through a note pad for the next question, the sense of drama is gone and even the most telling points risk being lost. Imagine an actor delivering one of Hamlet's soliloquies during which he must pause and seek out the next line by turning a variety of pages on a note pad in front of him. As an audience you would become restless and bored and the impact of the message would be lost completely. It is not dissimilar to the courtroom situation. The advocate who can conduct the cross-examination in a fluid way with minimal reference to notes will be much more compelling.

Seamless Verses Fragmentary Questioning

The advocate should conduct the cross-examination as if it were a conversation between him and the witness in which the advocate asks the questions and the witness answers "yes" or "no". If the advocate can style his cross-examination in such a way that the jurors feel they are eavesdropping on a conversation, the effect will be much greater.

Rufus Choate once defended a stock broker against a claim by a woman for the return of stocks that her husband had pledged. She claimed the stocks belonged to her and had been pledged without her knowledge or consent. The husband took the stand and swore under oath that this was indeed the case. Choate examined him using the technique of placing the witness in a position because of their answers of being confronted with having to chose one of two answers neither of which are beneficial to them.

Q. *When you ventured into the realm of speculations in Wall Street I presume you contemplated the possibility of the market going against you, did you not?*
A. *Well, no, Mr. Choate, I went into Wall Street to make money, not to lose it."*
Q. *Quite so, sir; but you will admit, will you not, that sometimes the stock market goes contrary to expectations?*
A. *Oh, yes, I suppose it does.*
Q. *You say the bonds were not your own property, but your wife's?*
A. *Yes, sir.*
Q. *And you say that she did not lend them to you for purposes of speculation, or even know you had possession of them?*
A. *Yes, sir.*
Q. *You even admit that when you deposited the bonds with your broker as collateral against your stock speculations, you did not acquaint him with the fact that they were not your own property?*
A. *I did not mention whose property they were, sir.*
Q. *Well, sir, in the event of the market going against you and your*

collateral being sold to meet your losses, whom did you intend to cheat, your broker or your wife?

This examination gives a sense of drama and purpose. Reading it compels the reader and the jury to be interested and to concentrate. The result is great dramatic impact. Now here is the same exchange with interlineations of how it would appear as conducted by the advocate using notes.

The witness is given over for the purpose of cross-examination. The advocate goes to the podium. Arranges his note pad on the podium and turns several pages.

Q. *When you ventured into the realm of speculations in Wall Street I presume you contemplated the possibility of the market going against you, did you not?*
A. *Well, no, Mr. Choate, I went into Wall Street to make money, not to lose it."*

There is a pause and counsel consults his note pad and appears to make a mark beside something on the page.

Q. *Quite so, sir; but you will admit, will you not, that sometimes the stock market goes contrary to expectations?*
A. *Oh, yes, I suppose it does.*

Again counsel consults his notes, and again goes back and forth between several pages.

Q. *You say the bonds were not your own property, but your wife's?*
A. *Yes, sir.*
Q. *And you say that she did not lend them to you for purposes of speculation, or even know you had possession of them?*
A. *Yes, sir.*

Another pause of many seconds, more flipping of pages.

Q. You even admit that when you deposited the bonds with your broker as collateral against your stock speculations, you did not acquaint him with the fact that they were not your own property?
A. I did not mention whose property they were, sir.

The advocate sensing that the next question will be his last and desiring not to have forgotten anything before releasing the witness takes an extra amount of time consulting his note pad and may even consult with an associate to reassure himself that nothing has been overlooked.

Q. Well, sir, in the event of the market going against you and your collateral being sold to meet your losses, whom did you intend to cheat, your broker or your wife?

Clearly the first example is by far the preferable one. Indeed when reading the second one the reader finds themselves getting lost and having to reread parts of it to get the full impact of the exchange. This is precisely what occurs in the courtroom. The jury finds itself with nothing to do while counsel refers to the notes and quite easily becomes distracted. The jurors begin fidgeting, they take a drink of water, examine their fingernails, look about the courtroom, and generally do everything but that which the advocate should be striving for which is to hang on every word of the exam.

SOME WAYS TO AVOID EXCESSIVE USE OF NOTES

There are several ways the advocate can minimize or avoid this problem. A good memory will help and developing one should be the goal of every advocate. Formulating a shorthand system is also a good technique. In this case the advocate develops a system of words or brief phrases that in turn trigger his memory. At the very least the advocate should train himself to be able to formulate one question while the witness is answering another.

In the example given above Choate may of had a note in front of him with one or two words that reminded him of the points he wished to make. One possibility was to have written the words "who did you intend to cheat?" in large letters. This would have been sufficient for the exchange involved.

By extension these devices must be formulated to deal with the witness that may take several days to testify and for whom the cross will also extend over a several day period

The advocate must train himself to maintain a steady flow of questions during the cross-examination. He must develop his memory aids to cover a large number of subjects but these should serve only to remind him of the major points to be covered and the many questions required to cover those points should be asked in a flowing and spontaneous way. Another technique is a checklist that contains one or two words for each topic or point to be covered. Counsel can refer to this list without it being apparent to the jury and in a way that does not break the flow of the examination.

Above all being able to conduct the cross-examination without unnecessary pauses and references to pages of note paper requires a clear understanding of the case and the points the advocate intends to rely on. The advocate should not appear to be on a fishing expedition, even if he is.

Principle Nine

Exposing The Lie Does Not Complete The Cross-Examination

There is more to cross-examination than exposing the lie or error. The jury must be made aware of it and of its significance. If the point isn't hammered home then it may just as well have not been extracted or exposed at all. It is a fallacy to believe that the mere utterance of the error or lie will automatically make an impact on the jury. The import of the error and its significance in the entire case must be brought home to the jury. The matter must be so firmly entrenched that no amount of effort on the part of opposing counsel will undo it.

The object of cross-examination is to test the truth of the testimony by exposing any or all of it as being a lie or significant error. To fail to take advantage of the hard won victory by not pursuing it sufficiently to impress it on the conscience of the jury is to not have examined at all.

The advocate must not only be aware of the lie and have the skills to expose it he must pay attention to the circumstances in which he chooses to expose it. It is not enough to engage in a dialogue with the witness and extract some admission that a fact he has testified to is wrong. The admission and its significance may be clear to you but may be completely lost on the jury.

There are many reasons this occurs. It may be a result of the sequence in which the examination is conducted. The information is brought out before the jury is aware of how it fits into the entire picture. It may result from something as simple as the time of day. If it is late in the day the jurors attention may not be as keen. This may be true just before the lunch recess when jurors are thinking of food or mentally making a list of the things they must catch up on during the brief free time they will have during the day to conduct some business or check in with their employer.

When the advocate becomes aware that he has a opportunity to gain an admission of error from a witness he must then carefully consider the time and circumstances of presenting it to the jury. If the tactic is to not confront this witness with the error but to point out through another witness then take the offending witness through a series of questions stressing the error and firmly implanting in the mind of the jury. In this way, the jury will remember the matter when the other witness testifies. And the present witness will have so committed themselves to the point that to attempt to change the position will only appear ludicrous.

This situation may arise in a case where the witness has recited correct and harmful facts but has attributed them to a person you can prove was out of the country on the date in question.

If the advocate confronts the witness with this fact the witness may simply say he was wrong and thank you for pointing it out to him. He will go on to say it was Mr. Smith, give some plausible reason for the confusion and then restate the facts. The better approach is to take him through the story again with the emphasis on the fact is was Mr. Jones he spoke with but do so as if you agree with the witness that is was Mr. Jones. This can be done by repeating Mr. Jones's name frequently in the questions so that it will be remembered by the jury.

Q. *When you purchased the automobile Mr. Jones assured you it would never be in an accident is that correct?*
A. *That is right.*
Q. *Your are sure Mr. Jones told you this and didn't say if you drove carefully it would not be in an accident?*
A. *No.*

Q. *Mr. Jones was a supervisor?*
A. *You remember the statement because Mr. Jones joined you and the other salesman during the negotiations?*
Q. *Yes.*

The cross should continue in this vein. Its purpose is to try and cast doubt on the direct testimony of the witness but in so doing have the witness combine the memory of the events with the presence of Mr. Jones. When it is shown later that Mr. Jones could not possibly have been involved you can point out to the jury that every question about the matter involved the name of Mr. Jones and not once did the witness contradict the fact. If the witness could be so mistaken about the person he was speaking with how could he be sure of the words spoken?

If the opposition recalls the witness to correct the mistake it will seriously dilute the testimony and call into question the memory of the witness and the accuracy of the facts testified too.

Hammer The Nail Until It Sticks

"Some men," said a London barrister who often saw Sir Charles Russell in action, "get a bit of the nail, and there they leave it hanging loosely about until the judge or some one else pulls it out. But when Russell got in a bit of the nail, he never stopped until he drove it home. No man ever pulled that nail out again."

The use of a nail as a metaphor for exposing the lie or error in the cross-examination is an apt one, and illustrates the problem many advocates face when they believe they have exposed an error or lie. Often it is done in such a way that the significance of the matter is lost on the jury. This may occur because the advocate has not laid the necessary foundation.

Before confronting the witness with the lie or error, a great deal more foundation must be laid. This can be accomplished by first ignoring the lie and moving to another subject which can be used to return to the subject of the lie from a variety of angles. Each approach should require the witness to reaffirm his position in a variety of ways before allowing him to understand the nature of your attack.

Once you have made the witness restate the lie or error in a variety of ways then the confrontation should occur and if the witness tries to recant you can take him through each of the incidents in which he restated the point and emphasize through repetition both the error and the fact the witness had many opportunities to correct it.

In the example of Mr. Jones above the witness from time to time should have been asked if he remembered such and such a statement because Mr. Jones said it. He might further have been asked it the fact Mr. Jones was a supervisor had a bearing on his remembering. In all of the examination Mr. Jones should be made to be an integral part of the incident. The testimony should be cast in such a light that the memory of the witness may stand or fall on the presence of Mr. Jones.

In this case when the witness is confronted with the fact that Mr. Jones could not have been present and then attempts to say the witness was incorrect about that fact but that everything else, he will sound hollow at best.

Don't Rush The Climax

The lie or error could not be pounced on immediately. To do so is to give the witness an opportunity to recant immediately and diminish the significance of the matter.

If you are sure a lie has been committed and that you can prove it, then it is best to do so with independent evidence. If you do not have great impeaching evidence it becomes all the more important to drive the point home during cross-examination. This should be done only after the witness is well committed to the position and should be done with as much drama as possible, insuring that the jury is aware that a significant point has been reached and that their attention is focused on the matter.

One time Abraham Lincoln defended a murder case with this cross-examination of an eyewitness.

Q. *And you were with Lockwood just before the shooting?*
A. *Yes.*
Q. *And you stood very near to them?*
A. *No, about twenty feet away.*
Q. *May it not have been ten feet?*
A. *No, it was twenty feet or more.*
Q. *In the open field?*
A. *No, in the timber.*
Q. *What kind of timber?*
A. *Beech timber.*
Q. *Leaves on it are rather thick in August?*
A. *Rather.*
Q. *And you think this pistol was the one used?*
A. *It looks like it.*
Q. *You could see defendant shoot-see how the barrel hung, and all about it?*
A. *Yes.*
Q. *How near was this to the meeting place?*
A. *Three-quarters of a mile away.*
Q. *Where were the lights?*
A. *Up by the minister's stand.*
Q. *Three-quarters of a mile away?*
A. *Yes—I have answered you twiste.*
Q. *Did you not see a candle there with Lockwood or Grayson?*
A. *No! What would we want a candle for?*
Q. *How then did you see the shooting?*
A. *By moonlight (defiantly).*
Q. *You saw the shooting at ten at night-in beech timber, three quarters of a mile from the light-saw the pistol barrel-saw the man fire-saw twenty feet away-saw it all by moonlight? Saw it nearly a mile from the camp lights?*
A. *Yes, I told you so before.*

Lincoln at this point removed an almanac from his pocket introduced it into evidence and confronted the witness with the fact that the entry for that night was that the moon had risen at one AM and was not seen. The result was an acquittal and a confession by the witness that he had killed the victim.

Part Four

Achieving The Objective

Principle One

The Object Of The Examination Must Be Clearly Defined Before Confronting The Witness

The objectives of cross-examination must be clearly defined. These objectives can range in importance from obtaining a concession with respect to point to be relied on in summation to a complete destruction of the witness or the testimony. If only one or two simple concessions need be extracted from the witness, the advocate should be careful to make the points and end the cross-examination. In other cases, the case will stand or fall on the success of totally discrediting the testimony.

Regardless of the magnitude of the objective, the advocate should be careful not to pursue some unfocused or tangential, matter no matter how tempting it may be. Countless cases have turned on minutia that the jury hears because the advocate simply could not resist cross-examining on some subject that had nothing to do with the ultimate issue in the case. On the other hand, the advocate must pursue the important objective without regard for time and must maintain his focus on the issues until the objective is achieved or proves to be unobtainable.

Earl Rogers, before beginning his cross-examination of a key witness in a murder case, walked to his daughter who was seated just behind the bar in the front row of the courtroom. He handed her a list of eight questions that he had for the witness and the answers that he felt were it necessary to obtain if he had any chance of success in the case. His cross-examination took three days, but he never lost sight of his goal. As soon as he had the answers to those questions he sat down.

Focusing on the objective is necessary to aid the advocate in recognizing the difference in the effect the witness has on the jury and what the advocate expected the effect to be. The advocate must have the flexibility to react to the real situation and not the one for which he prepared. Often, an important witness will make statements outside the courtroom that seem to have devastating consequences for the case. The advocate prepares as best he can for the inevitable confrontation that will come. The point in the case arrives for the witness to testify and the testimony falls flat; the witness may change ground; or the timing is bad; or the witness adds something helpful to your side; or the direct examination has such an impact on the jury. Here, the advocate must be able to put aside all the preparation for this witness and discipline himself to forego the examination or change it in such a way as to meet the specific exigencies of the situation presented.

This same discipline extends to deciding whether to follow a new path opened by the witness. Some of the most brilliant examples of cross-examination have resulted from the advocate seeing and pursuing some totally unexpected opening. Before attempting to traverse new terrain, the advocate must have a firm grasp of his case sufficient to allow him to make a split second decision about exploring new material and he must possess the skills to do so. The advocate must have the skills to decide where a new subject is leading and abandon it if it appears to be harmful. Important to this tactic is the ability to see where the path leads before the jury and opposition does.

Pursuing a new subject on cross-examination will create curiosity in a juror that causes him to want to see the outcome. If you suddenly change courses because it appears that the ultimate result will be harmful without some explanation, the juror may draw an adverse inference. In this case, it often serves a useful purpose to abandon the subject while leaving the jury with the impression that you will return to it at a later time. Often, language such as "Mr. Witness, let's leave this subject for the time being and turn our attention to something else. We'll come back to it in a minute," is helpful. Of course, you never do and hope the jury will be diverted to something else and forget about the matter all together.

Often, judges are inclined to grant wide latitude in the cross-examination. Cross-examination will begin with the advocate thinking that he has the basis and technique to punch some holes in the testimony of the witness only to discover, as the examination progresses, that he is unable to. Rather than simply accept defeat, the advocate should have the techniques to use the situation in a positive way.

This may be done in one of several ways:

- Recite some favorable testimony from another witness under the guise of asking the witness if he is aware of the information, which may take the form of asking the witness if he is aware that a different witness has testified to something favorable. This has the effect of repeating the testimony of the prior witness to the jury and may suggest to them that this witness while not agreeing or disagreeing with the statement doesn't disapprove of it.
- By asking the witness a series of questions to which you are reasonably confident the witness will say he doesn't know.

Q. *Isn't it true that Detective Jones didn't see blood on the hands of the defendant when he arrived at the scene?*
A. *I don't know.*
Q. *Isn't it true the Mr. Smith told officer Jones the defendant was several miles away from the scene when the crime occurred?*
A. *I don't know.*

With these questions the advocate has restated to the jury two points he wishes to make without them being contradicted.

After several questions along this line the witness can be excused.

IMPORTANCE OF CONTROL

The advocate must take care to know whether the jury has accompanied him in achieving his objectives. Often, the advocate will conduct the cross-examination thinking that he has made the necessary points only to later discover that the importance of them was lost on the jury. The advocate must be careful to hammer home each point in such a way that the jury is aware of the importance and the opposition cannot remedy the damage.

The specific objects of cross-examination must be pursued in the most direct line possible. This means controlling the witness and the pace of the examination; otherwise, the cross-examination is ineffective. Control can best be accomplished by asking questions that require a 'yes' or 'no' answer. The ideal cross-examination is the advocate testifying and the witness agreeing or disagreeing with what the advocate says. Avoid questions which invite the witness to answer with an essay, or those which contain the word 'why'. Open-ended questions are generally dangerous to the advocate's case and will usually lead the advocate to a cliff from which he will then be pushed.

Questions must always be clear and unambiguous. The less clear the question the greater the possibility of the witness using the ambiguity to inject something into the answer that will hurt your case. If the question is unclear, the jury may not understand it and the opposition may call attention to it in summation and turn it to his own advantage.

PRINCIPLE TWO

The Objectives Of Cross-Examination Often Exceed Impeaching The Witness

The important threshold question before beginning cross-examination is whether the witness has damaged your case. If he has not then he should not be impeached. If he has done damage then the next question before undertaking cross-examination is whether or not there is a better way to impeach the witness than through cross-examination. For instance, with another witness or in closing argument.

If the witness has done no damage or there are better ways to impeach him the advocate should consider whether the witness should be questioned for other reasons. Some of these reasons are:

- To gain some concession outside the witness's direct testimony that will aid your case.
- To adopt the witness as your own in some way.
- To anticipate positive points you expect to come into the trial later.
- To contradict something a previous witness has said.
- To repeat favorable testimony from another witness.

Once the decision to question the witness has been made the advocate must be careful how he deals with new material that may arise during the questioning. This is a delicate matter because it is always tempting to leap on an apparent contradiction or omission by the witness only to receive an answer that damages your case even more.

Not Every Witness Does Damage

A witness who has hurt or made an impression against your case must be cross-examined. The advocate should not confuse the fact that a witness has been well received by the jury with the fact that no matter how well the witness is received the testimony has not hurt the case. There is a temptation to believe the witness has hurt your case when all that has really happened is that the witness has appeared truthful and sympathetic in the eyes of the jury and has not contributed anything to negating your strategy.

When this occurs, it is better to courteously dismiss the witness and rely upon your rhetorical skills to make the jury understand that, while the witness was kind, honest, or sympathetic, he contributed nothing to the case against your client.

Assessing The Witness

Before deciding to cross-examine, it is a good idea to assess each witness and his testimony by asking yourself some of the following:

* Who is the witness in the sense of his relationship to the parties in the case?
* What are his motives?
* What information does he have that has not been adduced in the direct examination?
* What light, if any can he shed on your own theory of the case?

The advocate must always ask himself whether he has a realistic expectation of scoring some beneficial points through cross-examination and weigh that against the issue of whether he has other ways and opportunities to make the same points that may be more efficacious than through cross-examination.

Opening The Door

An ever lurking danger in cross-examination is to open a door through inadvertence or neglect that will send the jury, or the opposition, down a path you did not intend. It is a better choice not to examine at all and risk the jury wondering why you didn't cross than to cross on issues that are not precisely germane to your overall case and, thereby confuse the jury over basic issues.

Nothing can be so disheartening in a case than to have it veer off onto another path. The jury inevitably becomes confused and you must spend time (assuming *you* recognize the confusion) getting them back to the real issues. Another possibility is that the other side, concerned that an issue of some significance has inadvertently risen, decides that they must pursue it. The result, at best, is a waste of time and, at worst, results in a loss of the case because the jury was influenced by an issue that you never intended.

On the other hand, the cross-examiner cannot be inflexible. The very essence of the great cross-examiner is his ability to recognize openings during his examination and, indeed, to create these openings solely for the purpose of exploiting them. However, the advocate must be very careful in analyzing which of these openings are worth pursuing and which are not. Exploring each and every opening simply because it exists or to demonstrate how clever you are at recognizing the opportunities, risks losing control of the jury and the case.

The wise advocate takes advantage of the opening only if it serves his purpose in developing the themes he has set out for the jury. The advocate who launches an assault on the witness by throwing as many possibilities into the discussion in the hope that something will develop will, more often than not, find that after all the fishing, he has caught nothing and has alienated the jury.

Principle Three

Timing Is Everything

When and how you ask a question is as important as the subject of the question. Each cross-examination must be thought through with a sharp awareness for creating the correct ambiance and sense of drama.

Often the advocate will have several good points he can make during his cross-examination. Unfortunately they are often brought out in such a way that their impact and importance are lost on the jury.

Points that the advocate hopes to make in his cross-examination must be carefully timed so that the jury in aware of the full impact, the witness is put in a position from which he cannot escape and the opposition is placed in a situation from which they will have difficulty extricating themselves.

The greater the fall you have in store for the witness then the greater the height to which he should be led to before being pushed. It is not enough to simply extract some damaging concession from the witness it must be done after you have created an atmosphere in which the concession is made that will have maximum impact on the jury.

Timing is important in other respects. It comes into play as a device for creating tension. Often it is good to begin your examination by merely looking at the witness for a longer period of time that seems appropriate. As if to give the witness time to reconsider his perfidy before being confronted and allow him time for penitence. This devices often makes the witness uncomfortable and they begin to fidget. It serves in some small measure to begin to break down their confidence. After all, they have by then gone through the relatively easy part of direct examination and must be feeling rather smug. As is to say "this wasn't so difficult after all.". They have probably been coached on how to respond to what you ask on cross but have not been coached on how to deal with silence. Every advocate knows that moments of silence in the courtroom tend to magnify and what may only be thirty seconds seems like eternity.

LATITUDE AND HOW TO EXPLOIT IT

In cultivating a strategic sense of timing, the advocate should consider the wide latitude judges generally permit for cross-examination. This permissiveness is based on the belief that the advocate is responsible for exploring every possibility in impeaching a witness and should be allowed to do so with minimum interference.

The advocate should take advantage of this and use it to craft his cross-examination in the most imaginative way possible. On the other hand, courts grow impatient very quickly if the cross-examination wanders, is unfocused, is unartfully stated, boring, or tedious. So long as you avoid these problems and keep every one's interest by voice modulation, clear and unambiguous questions, variety and clarity of purpose most judges will permit a broad ranging cross-examination.

When the court cannot see what the strategy is or whether it is coherent, the court will inevitably cut the examination short. This is damaging because the jury will see this as a negative assessment of the judge.

Maintaining a balanced and focused approach will allow you to exploit a witness for some purposes that may technically be considered outside the scope of cross-examination. These include the use of a witness to validate the testimony of another witness by demonstrating that they share a profession or that one respects the other, or that one knows the other by reputation, or that one may be believable because the two share an interest. Wide latitude on cross-examination can also exploited by the tactic of making statements to the jury in the form of questions that will serve to reiterate points you may have little opportunity to make otherwise. This usually takes the form of asking a witness "is it not true that (here you make the statement you wish to reiterate to the jury)?" The witness may say he does not know or it may draw an objection but if you have gained the respect of the court for not wasting time or for being focused the response from the judge will usually be "I'll allow it. This is cross-examination."

WELLMAN IN ACTION: SETTING UP THE DECISIVE BLOW

Francis Wellman describes a cross-examination which demonstrates the quintessential use of timing. The case involved a civil suit brought by a man named Reader against one named Haggin for an alleged commission Reader said he had been promised.

> I had some very damaging letters written by Reader to his friend Garland in Peru which I hoped he had forgotten all about—or at least never suspected they could be any possibility be in my possession. (I learned after the trial was over that he had assured Mr. Stanchfield that there were no writings that could in any way contradict his testimony.)
> My absorbing problem was, therefore, how to get these letters admitted in evidence so I could use them to the best advantage. If I let Reader have the slightest suspicion that I had them, all he had to do, if he was quick-witted enough—and he surely was unscrupulous enough—was to disclaim his handwriting. I had no way of proving the authenticity of the letters unless from his own lips.

He was turned over to me for cross-examination at two o'clock in the afternoon. The court adjourned at four. I must gain his confidence during those two hours; puff him up with pride in his own importance; let him—in pugilistic parlance—punch me all around the ring; let him feel his superiority when it came to a matching of wits between us, and then, just when he felt the money already in his pocket, just at the stroke of four o'clock—and as the judge was rising from the bench to adjourn the court—I might—might, mind you—be able to put a bunch of papers under his nose and ask him, in the most nonchalant way I knew how, please to identify his handwriting on a few papers which might be of no importance but which I could look over before the next session of the court—and trust to my congenital luck to do the rest.

Mr. Wellman: (In a modulated and most respectful tone.) Mr. Reader you say that the only witness to your arrangement with Mr. Haggin was Mr. Van Slooten?

Mr. Reader: He was the only witness present in person at our conversation, yes.

Counsel: And he is dead?

Witness: He committed suicide.

Counsel: Well he is dead isn't he? And you have already testified that you had an arrangement with Mr. Van Slooten for ten per cent, haven't you?

Witness: Mr. Van Slooten offered me ten per cent commission for Mr. Haggin.

Counsel: You called Mr. Haggin's attention to that?

Witness: I did.

Counsel: Did you have that ratification in writing?

Witness: No. I have given it in my evidence that I asked Mr. Van Slooten whether I should get it in writing.

Counsel: So that as to whether or not Mr. Haggin really ratified *what Mr. Van Slooten had said to you on a prior occasion, practically depends upon you and Mr. Haggin. It is a question of veracity between you and Mr. Haggin or at least a question of memory? In view of Mr. Van Slooten's suicide it becomes a question whether or not we in this courtroom, hearing the two stories, the statement and the denial, believe your's or Mr. Haggin's statement.*

Witness: There are other things as well.
Counsel: Yes. To some of those I propose to call your attention. But let us first settle the question about the capacity in which you went to Mr. Haggin.

(The plaintiff, as well as his friend Van Slooten, were both undoubtedly promoters—the most precarious occupation any man can possibly adopt. He hears of some new invention or enterprise, seeks out the impecunious owner and by exaggerating and misstating his influence with many well-known rich men, with whom he claims to be acquainted, obtains a short option and authority to try to interest them or someone else in the venture. My cross-examination of this witness was an effort to point out to the jury that both these men were only acting as promoters, and employing their well-known methods in their contacts with Mr. Haggin. Throughout his testimony Reader made every effort to represent himself as a broker, to the point of even not knowing what was meant by the word promoter.)

Counsel: Were you a promoter?
Witness: I was not a promoter.
Counsel: Were you a broker?
Witness: I was in that matter.
Counsel: In all other matters were you a promoter?
Witness: No, sir.
Counsel: What was your business? What do you call it?
Witness: I was an owner of properties in Peru and elsewhere.
Counsel: And you tried to get capitalists to invest in them?
Witness: With respect to some of them, yes. I tried to sell them.

Counsel: To sell them?
Witness: To raise working capital for some of them.
Counsel: (good-naturedly) Then you were a man of large property?
Witness: I had a considerable property, yes.
Counsel: You mean you were a man of considerable wealth?
Witness: Yes, I was.

(One of the witness's letters—which I hoped to introduce in evidence later on—was written to a friend in Peru telling him that he had arrived in New York just before seeing Mr. Haggin, with only fifty dollars in his pocket, and begging his friend to send him a few hundred dollars to tide him along.)

Counsel: And these different properties that you bought were all over the world, were they?
Witness: No, the majority of them were in Peru. I also had property in London, and I had some property in New Zealand.
Counsel: If you don't mind, won't you tell us some of them—some of the different properties that you own?
Witness: I owned 10,000 hectars that would be 25,000 acres of rubber in Peru.
Counsel: And you were trying to sell those to capitalists in London and America?
Witness: I had an offer to buy them.
Counsel: And you would not accept it. Do you still own them?
Witness: I still own them.
Counsel: Those are rubber properties. Now take up something else. What else?
Witness: I had some copper mines in Peru.
Counsel: In this Cerro de Pasco region?
Witness: No, outside of that.
Counsel: Which you own?
Witness: Yes, I owned them. I owned, myself, the mines entirely at first, afterwards I took in a partner.
Counsel: But you originally owned the mines?
Witness: Yes.

Counsel: So much for the mines in Peru. Now what else?
Witness: I was a part owner of about 100 acres of coffee plantation. Then I also had properties in New Zealand.
Counsel: Of what nature were these properties?
Witness: They were real estate.
Counsel: All these you were trying to sell, or perhaps trying to keep some of them?
Witness: Yes, sir.
Counsel: Were you interested in any sulphur properties or in any borax property?
Witness: No.
Counsel: Then, have you given all the properties that you can think of as being interested in about this time?
Witness: I was also interested in and steel patent.
Counsel: In a steel process you mean?
Witness: Yes.
Counsel: What was that just in a word?
Witness: It was a steel process for the improvement of steel, for the hardening of steel.
Counsel: Did you at one time own the Lima Tramway?
Witness: I had an interest in it.
Counsel: Were you trying to sell that?
Witness: I was trying to electrify it at one time.
Counsel: Did you have an interest in any quicksilver property?
Witness: I had an option once in a quicksilver property.
Counsel: What was the Morocuche property? Is that a mine?
Witness: That was a group of mines.
Counsel: Were you trying to sell them?
Witness: Yes.
Counsel: Did you have anything to do with a railway tunnel?
Witness: No, not that I know of.
Counsel: A tunnel or a railway? You see (good-naturedly), I know very little about these things and I have to look to you for information.
Witness: The drainage tunnel of the Cerro de Pasco I had considerable to do with. I opened an option on it. I was going to buy it for Mr. Haggin.

Counsel:	I see. And the Acari—what was that?
Witness:	The Acari copper mines.
Counsel:	Did you own them?
Witness:	I did own them, yes.
Counsel:	Were you trying to sell those?
Witness:	No.
Counsel:	And so, in all these things you apparently had large sums of money invested.
Witness:	Yes.
Counsel:	And you considered yourself a wealthy man. (By these preliminary questions I had three objects in view: first, to get the witness in a good humor and rid him of any fear of me, personally; second, to lead him to admit that he was in fact only a promoter and not a broker working on a commission, and third, to so exaggerate his wealth, that, later on, when I could produce his letters, the discrepancy between his testimony and his own writings would discredit him completely.)
Counsel:	You have spoken about Mr. Van Slooten and of seeing Mr. Haggin with him in March 1901. How long had you yourself known Mr. Van Slooten?
Witness:	I had known him two or three years.
Counsel:	Was he a promoter?
Witness:	I don't know what he was.
Counsel:	You know what I mean by promoter, don't you?
Witness:	I don't know, really.
Counsel:	You don't know what I mean?
Witness:	It is a very large term.
Counsel:	Have you never happened to hear of the term promoter?
Witness:	Very often.
Counsel:	(with surprise) And you don't know what it means?
Witness:	I would find it hard to define what you mean by promoter.
Counsel:	I use it in the ordinary sense that we all use it. Was Mr. Van Slooten a promoter in that sense?
Witness:	I only know Mr. Van Slooten as the agent of Mr. Haggin.

(I was prepared to show that he and Van Slooten has been working together to sell properties in many parts of the world for several years.)

Counsel: So that your first talk with VanSlooten about Cerro was somewhere around the end of 1900.
Witness: Yes, Christmas day.

(I had letters to show this was a complete mis-statement.)

Counsel: Then the years you had known him you had gotten to trust him I suppose, hadn't you?
Witness: I had the highest recommendations from a very old friend of mine about him.
Counsel: And your experience with him accorded with that?
Witness: My experience with Mr. VanSlooten was perfectly satisfactory.
Counsel: I am asking you if your own experience with him accorded with the very high recommendation you had received about him when you finally entered into business relations with him. That, perhaps, will account for your not making any written contract with him when he arranged to give you ten per cent. Before you saw Mr. Haggin was there any arrangement between you and him that you two would be in it together?
Witness: None whatsoever.

(In one of his letters, which I had in my pocket, he calls Van Slooten a "wily bird," "untrustworthy," etc.)

Counsel: Then so far as you recognized him in the matter you looked on him as a man who was trying to secure the mines for Mr. Haggin, is that right?
Witness: That is right.
Counsel: When you went to see Mr. Haggin you said something about some London People. Were you under obligation to any London syndicate?

Witness:	No, sir.
Counsel:	You had to get rid of them before you could take the subject up with Haggin. Didn't you say you went to London? Wasn't that for the purpose of getting rid of them?
Witness:	No sir, it was to see whether they wished to take up the property or not.
Counsel:	Oh, then you would have thrown down Van Slooten if the English people had concluded to take the property.
Witness:	No, sir, Van Slooten begged me to stay in New York and throw them down for Mr. Haggin.
Counsel:	You would not do that of course:
Witness:	No, sir.
Counsel:	You went to see them, and you found they were not particular about the property. Did you tell them that you had a better chance here?
Witness:	No, sir.
Counsel:	Then sometime in March you went to see Mr. Haggin with Mr. Van Slooten:
Witness:	Yes.
Counsel:	I will ask you to give me again the conversation you had with Mr. Haggin. He asked you if you had options on the Cerro de Pasco. Is that right:? And if they were still in your possession.
Witness:	Yes.
Counsel:	Now go on from that.
Witness:	Do you want me to repeat the conversation?
Counsel:	Yes.
Witness:	Mr. Haggin asked me if I had options on Cerro de Pasco. I told him I had them until March 8 but that from a cable I had received from Witness: Garland in the last few days I knew that I could hold them for a month or six weeks if Mr. Haggin would send his engineers immediately without loss of time, to Peru.
Counsel:	Then what did he say?
Witness:	Mr. Haggin asked me if I had power to transfer the options and I showed him my power from Garland.

Counsel:	Did he ask you if you were quite free from an English syndicate?
Witness:	He asked me if I had any obligations to the English syndicate and I told him no.
Counsel:	Then what? Now comes the contract.
Witness:	Then I said to Mr. Haggin, "I understand Mr. Haggin that you have authorized Mr. Van Slooten to pay me ten per cent commission on the cost price of the Cerro mines subject to your examination." Mr. Haggin said, "That is satisfactory to me. Mr. Van Slooten is my representative in this matter and you arrange details with Van Slooten."
Counsel:	Then you went out?
Witness:	Then I explained that Garland was to receive five per cent from the mine owners for his services, as his pay.
Counsel:	Garland is the man whom you have spoken of as getting the options?
Witness:	Yes, sir.
Counsel:	Now you say that your conversation with Mr. Haggin ended practically with his remark, "Mr. Van Slooten is my representative." Those are the words he used?
Witness:	"My representative. He represents me."
Counsel:	And you were to arrange all details with him?
Witness:	Mr. Haggin told me to do so.
Counsel:	Were you looking upon this ten per cent as a detail?
Witness:	I certainly was.
Counsel:	Did it occur to you to arrange this little detail of ten per cent with Mr. Van Slooten by putting it in writing in the form of a contract?
Witness:	It did occur to me, yes.
Counsel:	So that detail occurred to you? You went outside and said something about a writing, you told us.
Witness:	I did.
Counsel:	What was it?
Witness:	I said hadn't I better get Mr. Haggin to put his offer of a commission to me in writing. That was in the passage outside Mr. Van Slooten's Office.

Counsel: Van Slooten said, "He is an honest man"?
Witness: Van Slooten said, "He is an honest man. It is not necessary. I have worked for Mr. Haggin for over four years. He is a man of great wealth and I have found him to keep his word and to prove it I will show you a letter I have just written out with his signature showing how much he trusted me.
Counsel: (looking straight at the witness) I thought you said just now that Haggin told you he was his representative. Why did you need any proof of it from Van Slooten? How could you have it better from Van Slooten than from Mr. Haggin himself? You told us that Haggin said, "Mr. Van Slooten is my representative. Arrange details with him." What better proof could Mr. Van Slooten give you that would be more convincing than Mr. Haggin's own words?
Witness: (doggedly) It is hard to think of any better proof.
Counsel: (sarcastically) You said you regarded this ten per cent commission a detail—a mere detail of $250,000. At that time didn't that seem to be a large sum of money?
Witness: Oh, yes, it was quite a sum of money.
Counsel: Then it was an important detail?
Witness: It was a very important business.
Counsel: (very impressively) Did it occur to you at the time as strange that a man whom you had just met for the first time should tell you orally—having only seen a sample option of some properties you claimed to have in Peru-(a place anyone could reach by streamer in twenty-five days)—that he would give you ten per cent of $250,000 to get those mines?
Witness: He was not a perfect stranger.
Counsel: I am speaking of it as between you and Mr. Haggin. You never had seen him before. You said you had just arrived in New York from Europe. You go into this office; tell him that you have an agent who is in your employ down in Peru who has gotten some mines, or some options on some mines; you show him a sample; you tell him the options are nearly run out but that you think that you can hold them together long enough for him to send someone down to look at them, and

	then Mr. Haggin tells you that if you will hold them he will give you $250,000. Didn't that seem strange to you?
Witness:	Not a bit.
Counsel:	Did it not seem strange to you? Just think a moment, when, if you had told him that your options had nearly run out that he should agree to pay you $250,000 instead of sending down there and getting them himself?
Witness:	Yes, sir.
Counsel:	(with marked emphasis) Does it appeal to your business sense that if a man wants to sell at his own price there is only one man in the world who could make him do it?
Witness:	That is what occurred.
Counsel:	Did Mr. Haggin ask you to go down and look over these things?
Witness:	Yes, he did.
Counsel:	Did he pay your expenses?
Witness:	He did not.
Counsel:	Did you ask him to, or did he offer to? Was anything said about expenses?
Witness:	No, sir.
Counsel:	(sarcastically) Did you explain to him how rich a man you were and that expenses, even for so long a journey as that to Peru, was a matter of no importance whatsoever?
Witness:	The question of expenses did not crop up between us.
Counsel:	Did you explain to him how many properties you were interested in and what a man of affairs you had become, or did you omit that part of it altogether?
Witness:	Mr. Van Slooten had already told him.
Counsel:	I didn't ask you what Mr. Van Slooten said before you went there because perhaps you would not know, but when you were there was anything said about it?
Witness:	No, sir.
Counsel:	Now, as a matter of fact, how were you earning your living at this time?
Witness:	I was living as I tell you.
Counsel:	No, I mean how were you earning your living. You have

	told us that you were going around London, Peru and America. Didn't you have any salary?
Witness:	No, sir. I raised money on my properties.
Counsel:	You mean you borrowed money on the chances of selling your properties?
Witness:	I sold participation in some of them.
Counsel:	Why are you so constantly fighting shy of the term promoter?
Witness:	Not at all. I understand it is a very honorable business.
Counsel:	As distinguished from capitalist? Please tell us was anybody paying your expenses?
Witness:	I was paying my own expenses on the trip to Peru. (He had really written to friends trying to borrow the money.)
Counsel:	And you started with Van Slooten and McFarlane, the expert, to go to Peru?
Witness:	That is right.
Counsel:	I ask you if you did not know, as a matter of fact, that a man by the name of McCune later had Mr. Haggin's power of attorney to buy these mines and that eventually they were all bought through Mr. McCune.
Witness:	That is right.
Counsel:	There were about four or five hundred?
Witness:	Over four hundred.
Counsel:	Apparently, it all comes down to this. That all during these transactions Mr. McCune was the only man who was signing the contracts or handling the money to buy all these mines. I wish you would tell the jury just what conversations you have ever had with Mr. McCune on this subject.
Witness:	With whom?
Counsel:	McCune. He is alive, isn't he?
Witness:	I understand he is.
Counsel:	What, if any conversations did you ever have with him on this subject—on the subject of Cerro mines or your ten per cent commission in them.
Witness:	I had none!
Counsel:	(excitedly) Although you were in Peru, and in New York for nine months after you alleged contract with Mr. Haggin for

	ten per cent commissions, you never had any conversation with Mr. McCune on this subject?
Witness:	No, sir.
Counsel:	Had you at any time come to distrust Mr. Van Slooten?
Witness:	No, I can't say I distrusted him. I distrusted his discretion.
Counsel:	Perhaps that is one reason why you did not talk with McCune?
Witness:	There was no necessity to talk with McCune.
Counsel:	Well was that one of the reasons? Because you had this complete understanding with Van Slooten?
Witness:	Not at all. I had my conversation with Mr. Haggin.
Counsel:	But you told us just a little while ago that Mr. Haggin directed you to go to McCune when you came to see him about the contract.
Witness:	Mr. Haggin refused to pay my commission.
Counsel:	I understand that, but didn't he tell you to go and see McCune?
Witness:	He said, "I can't recognize you. Go and see McCune."
Counsel:	Did you "go and see McCune?"
Witness:	I had no reason to!
Counsel:	(shouting) No, that is not it. Did you go?
Witness:	I did not go and see him. There was no sense in going.
Counsel:	But you admit that you never even mentioned the subject to him. How can you now say there was no use in going to see him after Mr. Haggin had told you to do so.
Witness:	I had not bought the mines for McCune; I had bought them for Haggin.
Counsel:	But Mr. Haggin told you to see McCune. Why was there no use in going to see him?
Witness:	It was not likely that McCune was going to pay me.
Counsel:	Wasn't the commission large enough to see whether or not McCune was going to pay you? You said McCune had only been buying a trifle of two and a half million dollars worth of mines down there and handling all the money. Was it not worth while to go and see him on a little detail of $250,000?
Witness:	In my opinion it was not.

Counsel: (throwing down his papers) *As a matter of fact, did you not dine with him at the Waldorf and spend a large part of the evening with him—and never even mention the subject at all?*

Witness: That is right.

Counsel: *Then why didn't you tell us about that? I ask you again did you discuss the Cerro de Pasco mines at dinner without ever once suggesting that there was any question of your commission, or that Mr. Haggin had recommended you to go to him, or that Mr. Haggin had turned you down saying that he had nothing for you in the matter?*

Witness: (sheepishly) We never mentioned anything about Cerro de Pasco!

Counsel: *Were you not introduced to him at the Waldorf on this occasion?*

Witness: That is so, yes.

Counsel: *Introduced in November to the very man who had been buying mines, whom you yourself admitted was the only broker with power to purchase, and when you are introduced to him after the thing is all over, you don't even mention it during the entire Waldorf dinner.*

Witness: That is so.

Counsel: *I suppose, in as much as you were to get this ten per cent from Mr. Haggin, you appreciated that you were employed as his broker,*

Witness: Well, I don't know. My special business was to hold those options in line for him to buy.

Counsel: *But you said that you had no interest yourself. You were not an owner of the options because Garland had the options. In any event, were you acting in Mr. Haggin's interests?*

Witness: Absolutely.

Counsel: *You appreciated, when you were taking commissions from him that it was your duty to act entirely in his interests?*

Witness: Absolutely.

Counsel: *And to make Mr. Garland, for instance—acting as your employee—act entirely in Mr. Haggin interest.*

Witness: I certainly did.
Counsel: That is, your instructions to him were to get them as cheap as he could.
Witness: Absolutely.
Counsel: You and Garland were both acting in Mr. Haggin's interest then, as best you could, just as loyally as you knew how?
Witness: Most decidedly.
Counsel: And taking commissions from both sides?
Witness: I did not take commission from the other side.
Counsel: But he did.
Witness: That was agreed to by Mr. Haggin.
Counsel: It was agreed to by Mr. Haggin that you should act entirely for him; both you and Garland, and yet get paid by the other side also? Didn't you find that your duties conflicted in any way when trying to get the interests as cheap as you could for Mr. Haggin and at the same time get as good a price as you could for the mine owners who were giving you an extra five per cent? Wasn't this all something of a strain on your conscience in any way? Your effort to be honest to both sides when getting commissions from both sides?
Witness: No answer.
Counsel: If he should get ten thousand pounds for the miners, his commission would be double what it would be if he only got five thousand pounds from Mr. Haggin for the same mine. Did you tell him to get the mine for five thousand pounds and let the commission go?
Witness: I certainly did insist upon it.
Counsel: You appreciated that you could not take commissions from both sides? That has been explained to you by the lawyers, I suppose?
Witness: I never would have dreamed of doing it.
Counsel: You appreciate that the courts would never let you dream of doing so either. You knew that would be an illegal contract.
Witness: There was never any question about it.
Counsel: I am asking about what you know. You had been told, had you not, that if you were taking commissions from both

Counsel:
Witness:
Counsel:

Witness:
Counsel:

sides, *without the knowledge of the principals, that you would have no case in law or anywhere else. You knew that?*
Quite so.
Yes, of course. *And you have been informed that an agent could not act in a transaction where he had an adverse interest, had you not? You could not act as the broker for Mr. Haggin if at the same time you had an adverse interest from the mine owners.*
I don't understand that question at all.
Well, *what I am asking you is, did you not know that it was incumbent upon you to use your utmost good faith in your dealings in regard to this matter out of which you hoped to receive $250,000?*

(It was to appear later that he had a secret written agreement with Garland that he was to receive one-half of the five per cent paid by the mine owners.)

Counsel: After Mr. Haggin refused to carry out the agreement with you, did you see Mr. Van Slooten?
Witness: I saw him every day.
Counsel: Did you take Mr. Van Slooten around to Mr. Haggin and say, "Here, Mr. Haggin. You agreed to give me ten per cent commission in Mr. Van Slooten's presence. Why not carry it out?" Did you do that?
Witness: I took Mr. Van Slooten's advice.
Counsel: Did you do that?
Witness: I did not do it.
Counsel: You said that Mr. Haggin referred you to McCune. Did you, then, take Mr. Van Slooten, who was alive, to Mr. McCune and say, "Mr. McCune, Mr. Haggin referred me to you. Here is Mr. Van Slooten. He is a witness to what Mr. Haggin said to me. He heard Mr. Haggin say he would give me ten per cent. Mr. Haggin says you are the man to see. Now let me have my ten per cent"?
Witness: I did not go to Mr. McCune at all.

Counsel: But that was before Van Slooten died. At that time you claim you had a witness to the conversation with Mr. Haggin?

Witness: I certainly had a witness.

Counsel: Well, did you let Mr. Garland know anything about Haggin's repudiation?

Witness: I did. I wrote him. I was in constant correspondence with Garland, writing frequently and getting letters from him. (I had these very letters in my pocket.)

Counsel: Did you let Van Slooten know you were going to sue Haggin?

Witness: Van Slooten died—committed suicide.

Counsel: I asked you when it was that you made up your mind to sue him. You answered in January. But Van Slooten died in December. Could it be that you waited until your witness was dead before you made up your mind to sue?

Witness: (almost in a whisper) I was very much upset in the matter and my affairs prevented it.

Counsel: (preparing for the final coup about the letters) Did you let Garland know that Van Slooten was dead?

Witness: Yes, I let him know.

Counsel: Write him?

Witness: I wrote him.

Counsel: Did you keep him posted?

Witness: Why, of course.

Counsel: Well, I don't know, of course. I am asking for information, that is all. I have got a few things. I don't know that they throw any light on the subject but I would like to see whether they do or not. Do you recognize this as one of your letters to Mr. Garland?

Witness: That looks like my writing, yes.

Counsel: Here is another one of November 3. I don't know as there is anything in it of importance, but I would like to mark it for identification.

Witness: That looks like my writing.

Counsel: Here is one of November 27.

Witness: Yes, that is mine.

Counsel: October 5?
Witness: Yes.
Counsel: January 4?
Witness: Yes.
Counsel: November 19?
Witness: Yes.
Counsel: February 1?
Witness: Yes.
Counsel: July 7?
Witness: Yes.

And the letters were all in, just as the clerk announced that court was adjourned until the next morning.

Principle Four

Decide Whether The Object Of Your Cross-Examination Is To Discredit The Witness Or Discredit The Testimony

The sympathies of the jury are most often with the witness. They perceive that the attorney is on his home turf; and the witness, like them, is a stranger to the courtroom. How you handle the witness in the early stages will go a long way in winning the jury over to your point of view.

Confusing the witness is not good cross-examination nor is browbeating or shouting at the witness. Such tactics more often provoke the jury into sympathizing with the witness.

Discrediting testimony is always permissible; it is the style and manner of the cross-examiner that may make it fail. Rarely should a decision be made to attack the witness rather than the testimony. Discrediting the witness is a tactic that must be employed judiciously since it is a risk.

Witnesses that may be discredited are the perjurer, especially if you have convincing independent evidence of the perjury; the expert with suspicious qualifications; someone with a clear interest in the outcome of the case; the criminal informant who has a despicable history and is receiving a reward for his testimony.

There is a significant difference between discrediting a witness and destroying a witness. Discrediting the witness involves an attack on him with respect to the motives and other personal reasons for testifying. Destroying the witness attacks him at every possible level of his life and seeks to place him in such a repugnant light that, not only does the jury disbelieve him, but they may bend over backwards to find a solution in the case that serves to deliver an insult to the witness. It is a nice result, but the opportunities to achieve it are rare and the chance that the tactic will backfire is great.

Move From Courteous Opening To Final Attack

As a general rule, any approach to a witness should begin with the courteous and kind and then progress along the spectrum, as need dictates, towards the final extreme of destroying a witness. Before undertaking such a drastic step, the advocate should be convinced that no other approach will achieve the necessary result.

Louis Nizer faced this choice in the executive clemency hearing of convicted murderer Paul Crump. The job was even more difficult than usual because the witness was an experienced judge and was a surprise witness. The issue was whether Paul Crump was sufficiently rehabilitated to have his death sentence reduced to a term of imprisonment. This is how he described it.

The lawyer's ordeal is even more forbidding, because he has only moments to decide on a campaign. We had not expected Richard Austin to appear. Indeed, District Attorney Thompson, whether guilefully or not, had announced that the State "has, as such, no witnesses to call." Our strategy had to be improvised on the moment. The risks could not be assessed by reflection.

MR. NIZER: Judge, were you requested to come here by the State Prosecutor to testify?
A. I was.
Q. As a witness for the State?
A. I was asked by them, and I stated to the press that I was available for either side to come here and relate any knowledge of Crump's

background that extended for nearly 9 1/2 years. I have been available for either side.

Q. *I did not ask you whether you were available, Your Honor.*
A. *They did ask me to come.*
Q. *When was that, sir?*
A. *Well, let's see, they sounded me out about a week ago. And I then indicated that I would come.*
Q. *Who was it that requested you on behalf of the State to testify, sir?*
A. *No one asked me. They asked me if I might be available, and I gave them an answer.*
Q. *Did anyone, specifically on behalf of the prosecutor, ask you to come here as a witness, sir, or did you—*
A. *Perhaps Mr. Thompson asked me to come here as a witness.*
Q. *When was that?*
A. *The latter part of last week.*
Q. *Did he state to you that he asked you to be a witness in this proceeding, or did he merely ask you whether you would be available if necessary?*
A. *Well, I don't know how he specifically told it. I know that I told him that I would be available if he wanted me. And, I think, perhaps, I got definite word over the weekend that they wanted me.*
Q. *And who gave you that definite word?*
A. *Mr. Thompson.*
Q. *Do you know that Mr. Thompson announced that he had not called you as a witness to this proceeding?*
A. *He hadn't called me originally. And I don't know what he announced. I wasn't here this morning.*

We had already fared better than I had hoped. From "No one asked me. They asked me if I might be available" to "Perhaps Mr. Thompson asked me" to "Mr. Thompson gave me definite word to come" to "He hadn't called me originally. And I don't know what he announced," there was none of the certainty of his original testimony, which had sounded more like a lecture by an expert to the uninformed.

It is a curious phenomenon in cross-examination that the effect upon the witness and judges of uncertainty dragged from him, may be out of all proportion to the importance of the subject matter. A witness who flounders about whether he was subpoenaed or appeared voluntarily, may cast a shadow on his most impressive recital of important facts. Reliability is a continuous string. It depends on complete consistency. To be partly reliable is to be unreliable.

I stepped up the attack:

MR. NIZER: *You have given a recital of some of the events at the time that you were a prosecutor in this very case.*
A. *That's right.*
Q. *And a very able and conscientious prosecutor. Have you read the transcript of that trial, which lies in front of the prosecutor?*
A. *I have not read the transcript. I have not.*

I faced him with the records which revealed that "immediately" after the confession Crump had been examined by his own doctor, as Judge Austin had just said, but by Dr. Brams, who was Judge Austin's doctor and friend. I could not pin him down on this error, because he had recalled that other doctors had examined Crump. Of course one of them was Dr. Rosen, whom Crump had visited long before the confession night. Thompson and Moore later skirmished over this point. However, Judge Austin had been further shaken by our quick resort to specific passages from the trial testimony.

I attacked from another direction:

MR. NIZER: *You also, in referring to the original circumstances of this terrible crime, said that Mr. Crump knew that Ted, the victim of the crime, who was killed, was his friend?*
A. *I can't point to it in the testimony, but I can refer you to the widow, who said that Crump used to call her deceased husband, 'Ted.'*

I was sharp with him for avoiding the question and trying to prejudice the Board with a statement of supposed knowledge outside of the record.

MR. NIZER: *Is there anything in the testimony that indicated that he was his friend; is there to your knowledge, or it there not to your knowledge?*

A. *Nothing in the record. Nothing in the record.*

He had yielded under pressure. I took a deliberate pause. The time had come for the main attack.

Q. *Now, Judge, you have recited in rather vivid terms some of your descriptions of this terrible crime. Have you read the 220 pages of affidavits submitted by fifty-seven witnesses for Paul Crump in this clemency proceeding?*

A. *I have not.*

Q. *You have never seen them?*

A. *Never seen them.*

Q. *You knew that they were in the hands of the prosecuting attorney before you came here?*

A. *That's right.*

Q. *Do you know who those fifty-seven affiants were?*

A. *I understand a great number of them were guards at the Cook County Jail.*

Q. *Do you know who the others were?*

A. *No I don't.*

Q. *You referred to the kind of testimony that has been given here. Were you present this morning when any of the testimony was given?*

A. *I was not here. I had it summarized for me during the noon hour.*

Q. *You had the testimony this morning summarized for you, by whom?*

A. *By Mr. Thompson.*

Q. *So you are going on a summary of the prosecuting attorney within a half hour, or an hour, during your lunch hour . . . is that what you referred to as the testimony that was presented here, in characterizing it?*

A. *That's right.*

Q. *And telling this Honorable Board that testimony is inadequate on that basis, is that correct?*

A. *That is correct.*

Q. Do you recognize, or do you not, sir, that if there is a case of genuine rehabilitation—a man who has changed his outlook on life to be a social instead of an anti-social creature—that is a proper element in the exercise of the conscience of the Governor for commuting a death sentence to 199 years in prison, is that a factor, is my question?
A. This is something that only the Governor and this Honorable Board can determine. I'm not going to determine it for them.
Q. I'm not asking you to determine it, Judge. I'm asking you whether there is any reliable evidence of rehabilitation.
A. I say the point involved in this case is whether there is any reliable evidence of rehabilitation.
Q. I am asking you, sir, not to pass on whether it is reliable. I say, if there is, assume, sir, that there is genuine rehabilitation . . . is this a proper vital consideration of this Board in making its recommendation to the Governor to commute sentence?
A. I have no opinion on that.
Q. You do not wish to express an opinion on that. Do you agree with the following sentence here:

"*Rehabilitation, whether real or honestly imagined should not govern a recommendation of this Board. It is not a basis for clemency.*"

A. I believe . . . in this case, that that is my feeling on the matter. I believe that there are unrehabilitatable people. And this defendant has heretofore deceived and misled this Parole Board when he convinced—not this Parole Board—
Q. Judge, you have told us that. I do not want you to make any repetitious remarks, so as to prejudice the court. My question is, and would you be good enough to answer it: Do you agree with the philosophy that rehabilitation is not a basis for clemency?
A. And I believe that.
Q. You do believe that?
A. Yes. In regard to this particular case, as I have heretofore said.
Q. No, I didn't ask you with regard to this particular case. I distinctly asked for a direct answer. I thought you gave one, but I will give

you a further opportunity to elaborate. Do you believe in the principle as state—

CHAIRMAN KINNEY: *Just a moment.*

As I drew close to eliciting an answer which would contradict the entire theory of the prosecutor "that rehabilitation is not a basis for clemency," Thompson arose and signaled that he wanted to interrupt.

MR. THOMPSON: *Mr. Chairman, Mr. Nizer is asking Judge Austin if he agrees with a quoted statement he is reading.*

Judge Austin has stated that he agrees with that statement as it relates to this case.

Now in fairness to the Judge, I think it should be made clear the statement Mr. Nizer is reading, is a statement from the answer [brief] of the State's Attorney in this case.

So that the answer of Judge Austin is responsive to his question. And that Mr. Nizer not be allowed to go beyond that.

MR. NIZER: *I do not think that it is well taken, Your Honor. The statement obviously is a general statement of philosophy. And I didn't say in this case.*

MR. THOMPSON: *It's a statement in response to the petitioner in this case, which is a capital case.*

MR. NIZER: *I do not think it is necessary for me to argue with counsel.*

I turned to another attack.

Q. *Judge, do you recognize that there are objective tests of whether a man is rehabilitated; objective in the sense of his conduct over a period of years . . . confirmed by third persons, such as inmates, guards . . . would you recognize that objective evidence as a proper weight of consideration on the subject of rehabilitation?*

THE WITNESS: *I would like to answer it in my own way, if I might.*

Q. *If you will answer the question first, and then elaborate on it, I do not care. But give me an answer. Do you consider that a proper subject for rehabilitation?*

A. *I would think that there would be some evidence of rehabilitation.*
Q. *Thank you, sir.*
A. *But I would say that it's to the advantage of a certain person, under certain circumstances to appear to be rehabilitated. And I'm aware of perfectly sane men malingering to the extent that two of the outstanding psychiatrists in this city rendered an opinion that he was insane, and only after intercepting a letter written by this defendant, awaiting trial in a capital case, in which he instructed the witnesses how to testify. And stated that he fooled the psychiatrists into writing an opinion that he was insane.*

   I'd say you can feign rehabilitation, just as you can feign insanity. And it's much less difficult.
Q. *Judge, there is no doubt that it is possible to feign some posture in any circumstances in human experience. It is just as possible for there to be genuine rehabilitation, isn't there?*
A. *It's possible.*
Q. *And you have not read the 220 pages of affidavits, which in this case indicate a genuine rehabilitation . . . you have not read those, have you?*
A. *I have not read them.*
Q. *How many times since March 28, 1953 [a period of nine years] have you had a personal conversation with Paul Crump?*
A. *Never.*
Q. *How many times since 1953 have you visited Cook County Jail where Paul Crump was confined?*
A. *Well, on many occasions, but on none of which did I see Paul Crump.*
Q. *So that what you are giving us, as you characterization of his non-rehabilitation, is based, as I think you have stated, upon your observations of him during the time that you were the prosecutor . . . when he was concededly a savage and desperate criminal. That is the basis upon which you have given your testimony here?*
A. *Mr. Nizer, you don't put words into my mouth.*
Q. *I'm not attempting to, sir. Let me ask it another way.*
A. *Let me answer the question that you have asked.*

Q. *All right, fine.*

A. *My opinion is based upon the feigning at rehabilitation that he used to get out on parole from the—by the predecessors of these gentlemen. The eloquence and the persuasion with which he talked himself out of the Stock Yards Police Station, that he had nothing to do with this killing.*

And in addition to my observations of him during the time he was in the custody of the State's Attorney. And during the time he was on trial in the Criminal Court Building.

Q. *And that was all before 1953, right?*

A. *That's right, sir.*

Q. *And most of it in 1953 and 1954?*

A. *That's right. The second trial, I think, was in 1955.*

Q. *Would you consider the opinion and testimony under oath of the guards, many inmates, the chaplain, the head of the medical department, the head of the linen department, the chief nurse, and many others who have dealt in daily contact with Mr. Crump over a period of nine years, as having some significance on that subject of rehabilitation?*

A. *Not as to genuine rehabilitation. I would consider it in regard to whether he was acting purportedly rehabilitated.*

Q. *You are assuming in that answer, Judge, as a basis for your answer that he is feigning, and therefore all this testimony is the victimization opinions of those against whom he has feigned, is that right?*

A. *His background indicates that to me.*

Q. *On the basis of his background.*

Now sir, with respect to capital punishment, do you recognize any case at all . . . in which clemency by the Governor . . . may be exercised without necessarily being in derogation of capital punishment; do you recognize that?

A. *Let me say that the last commutation of the death penalty that I'm aware of in the State of Illinois, I thoroughly approved of. It was granted by Governor Henry Horner to a man by the name of Henry Budrick, who was a seventeen-year-old lad. And I thoroughly approved of that.*

Q. You still feel good about that, don't you?
A. That's right.
MR. NIZER: *No further questions.*

There is an infallible sign as to how effective a witness has been. If the judge examines him, one can tell whether the questions are designed to aid the witness in establishing a point more clearly, or to finish the cross-examiner's task of drawing admissions from him. Unless the judge remains inscrutably silent, he will psychologically reveal himself, no matter how carefully he phrases his questions to appear unbiased. Not only the direction of the inquiry, but the tone and manner of the judge can be read by the discerning observed as if the judge unfurled a plaque saying "I agree" or "I disagree with this witness." We soon had such an acid test of Judge Austin's final impact on the members of the Board. One of them put a series of questions to him, and I could almost see the strings of cross-examination being picked up and drawn in tighter.

Member Craven wanted to know whether the Governor's power to commute "was part of the judicial process, or do you consider that when he exercises his executive power to grant clemency, that this is an interference with judicial power?"

Judge Austin conceded that "it's perfectly legal for the Governor to commute for any reason that may come to his mind."

Member Craven pressed on. "Under what circumstances do you believe a Governor in good conscience could commute a death sentence?"

Judge Austin specified two circumstances, "when there is reasonable doubt as to guilt, or where the penalty appeared too severe."

Craven pursued him. Would subsequent insanity be another circumstance for commuting? Judge Austin agreed. Then he put the ultimate questions:

"Now where there is a death penalty, no reasonable doubt as to guilt, and no question as to the penalty being too severe for the crime, would a Governor, in your opinion, in good conscience, be properly exercising his executive power to pardon, in the event that the defendant is in fact rehabilitated?"

A. Well, in my opinion, no.

Craven had used the word pardon. I wanted to make sure the Board understood the difference between the words pardon and commute.

MR. NIZER: "Or to commute."
MEMBER CRAVEN: I'm using the word "pardon" as to reducing something from a death sentence to a lesser sentence.

Judge Austin did not answer again, he was excused.

Principle Five

Cross-Examination Should Not Open A Subject Otherwise Closed To The Other Side

In every case, there are some subjects that one side may not inquire into unless the opposing side inquires into them first. For the most part, these are subjects that are irrelevant or so potentially damaging to someone that the law forbids their presentation by the opposition. However, if the side that is the presumed beneficiary of this exclusion introduces forbidden evidence, then the court may rule that, the subject having been raised, the other side cannot be precluded from pursuing it.

This is a real mine field for the inattentive cross-examiner. Often, a seemingly harmless question put to a witness on cross-examination may be so broad as to permit the witness to utter matters that would otherwise be excluded. This innocuous question will be construed as permitting the other side to introduce evidence on the issue because you have opened the door. An example of this is a defendant's criminal record, or prior acts of similar misconduct.

To avoid opening a door closed to the other side the advocate must conduct the cross-examination in a way that leaves the witness no opportunity to elaborate. The advocate should be in control at all times and the questions should be clear and unambiguous.

Avoid "Why" And "How" Questions

Questions that are open ended or suggest the words "why" or "how" should be avoided because they invite a witness to elaborate and thereby say something that puts a fact in issue that may otherwise be excluded. Often lawyers will file a motion *in limine* before a trial to have the court order that certain matters are irrelevant and may not be inquired into during the trial by opposing counsel. Such an order must be adhered to by the proponent as well as the opponent. If the proponent allows one of their witnesses to address the matter inadvertently then the opponent may make full inquiry. The clever examiner is ever watchful for such an opening and the one doing the questioning must craft his questions very carefully and in a constricted way so as not to permit something to happen by accident that has been excluded by the court.

The problem of opening the door to a subject that has potential for harm often arises when an advocate successfully invokes a rule of law during direct examination which prevents the opponent from extracting damaging testimony from a witness only to ignore the rule during his own examination and thereby allowing the opposition to bring out the forbidden subject during the re-direct.

Often the advocate allows this to happen through carelessness or inadvertence. Oftentimes it is a failure to recognize that a clever opponent may be able to successfully argue that a question that appears on its face to be removed from that which he attempted to elicit from the witness during direct examination is in fact the same situation as your question on cross-examination and that your having done it should permit him the same latitude.

For example, a prosecutor may try to elicit a statement from a police officer that was made to him by another officer and is damaging to your client. You object because it is hearsay and the judge sustains the objection. During the cross-examination you seek to elicit form the witness a statement made by a third party that is favorable. There is no objection and the statement comes in. The clever prosecutor will now seek on re-direct examination to re-open the original subject that you had successfully objected to.

Unfortunately for you, the judge now may rule that since you elicited hearsay testimony during cross-examination you have waived any objection to the prosecutor doing so.

It is not enough to keep the opposition from inquiring into a subject and then as a result of inattention or inept questioning during your cross-examination to open the to a damaging subject that is otherwise closed.

Principle Six

The Jury Must Be Made Aware Of Any Mistakes

When a witness is testifying, he may contradict prior testimony or utter some mistake, the significance of which is lost on the jury. When this occurs on direct examination, the other side, will quickly pass on to another subject before the jury focuses on the situation. For this reason, the cross-examiner must be attuned to the witness's slip-ups and make sure that the jury is made aware of them. There are several techniques for accomplishing this goal.

If something occurs during direct examination that you feel may not have been fully appreciated by the jury, you can appear not to have heard or understood the response, and interrupt by saying something to the effect of, " . . . your honor I was distracted just then. Did I understand the witness to say . . ." then repeat the statement. This has the effect of repeating the statement you wish the jury to be aware of; and (assuming the judge says yes) may have the additional benefit of suggesting by the judge's response that he is somehow giving approval to what was said.

If the error arises during cross-examination, the advocate should take time to repeat material directly to the jury by engaging them; that is, turn to the jury, make sure you have their attention, establish eye contact, and while looking at them, repeat the material to the witness as if to affirm it was said.

You can also reiterate the witness's direct examination in this respect by saying " . . . is it not true that on direct examination you testified as follows . . . ?"

You can also repeat the favorable material through another witness, especially one that has made a favorable impression on the jury, by saying "there has been previous testimony that (repeat the testimony), were you aware of that fact?"

Great ingenuity is required by the advocate when he is attempting to place before the jury mistakes and contradictions by a witness that occurred outside the courtroom, This is particularly difficult when the judge is bent upon restricting the use of such materials. And, of course, the opposition will be using every objection at their disposal to restrict the matter.

Principle Seven

Never Ask A Question That Contains The Word "Why" Either Express Or Implied

Because control of the witness is crucial to any successful cross-examination, the advocate must develop the skill of phrasing questions in such a way as to limit the ability of the witness to elaborate on his answer.

Any open-ended question will provide the witness the opportunity to respond with gratuitous remarks that may harm your case. Open-ended questions are those that do not call for a precise answer or do not set forth a clear set of alternatives from which the witness must choose.

The open-ended question can usually be spotted because of the existence of an interrogative in the question. Which, what, how, who, when, why are common examples. While the existence of one of these words in the question does not necessarily mean the question is open ended, one can be reasonably certain that all open ended questions contain one or more of these words.

All of these words can be used effectively in cross-examination by a skilled questioner with the exception of "why?". "Why?" should never be used. The use of the other interrogatives can be successful if the question is phrased properly. But the better practice is to learn to ask the question without resorting to them. When they are used the question must be phrased so as to limit the possibilities of response.

Assume that the case involves a defendant commandeering a witness' car, forcing the witness to drive him at gun point to someone's place of employment where the defendant shoots the deceased. Assume it is important to inquire into the color of the vehicle, the route taken and the speed of travel. A question such as 'what was the color of the car' seems safe enough because it calls for an objective response. But, what if the witness says something like "its was the same color as the blood on my face where the defendant hit me". The question was broad enough to invite that response. If it is important to your theory of the case that the car was red and you want that before the jury, then the question should be "The car was red wasn't it?"

The witness should not be asked "How did your travel the deceased's place of employment?" The answer may be "With a gun to my head." The question should be "Did you travel by car?" "What speed did you travel?" should be "Was the car traveling fast or slow?". Any question that uses a common interrogative should be couched in precise language in order to limit the response.

While it is true that some interrogatives can be used in a way that limits the response it is because they usually call for an objective response. Where did the accident take place? (Geography) When did the accident take place? (Time). How did you travel? (Mode of conveyance). This is not true of the interrogative "why?". "Why?" always calls for or permits a subjective response from the witness. It asks for the state of mind of the witness; and, if the advocate is foolish enough to ask it, he must live with the answer which, in the hands of an expert can go on forever.

The advocate must also keep in mind the fact that, in certain circumstances, the word "how?" is merely a substitute for "why?" and must never be used in that context.

In a murder case where the key evidence was that of ballistics, the prosecution had called an FBI laboratory technician to testify with respect to the matching of the slugs taken from the victim and those fired from the gun found in possession of the defendant. The lawyer asked the FBI technician how he knew the slug fired from the defendant's gun was the same as that recovered from the victim. The technician answered the question for about thirty minutes before the judge interceded more out of mercy than from a point of law.

I learned the lesson regarding the use of why quite early in my career. Three men, of whom I represented one in a separate trial, had been charged with assault and battery on one Sanford, who was short, slight, wore hearing aids in both ears and glasses with very thick lenses. On his way home from work, Sanford met three men who were drunk and pushing and shoving pedestrians, one of whom called the police.

Sanford testified in his direct testimony that, just after he passed them, he felt a hard blow to his back and fell to the ground. After he was on the ground he was hit and kicked repeatedly by all three men. A policeman arrived before Sanford suffered anything more serious than bruises. The policeman had to control the three Navajos until help arrived, and any witnesses to the events disappeared.

The object of my cross-examination was to cast doubt on Sanford's ability to say with certainty that my defendant had hit or kicked him. I freely conceded that the two other defendants had assaulted him. My defense was that they had done so but that my client had not and that Sanford could not possibly say he had with certainty. The policeman said he had not seen any blows struck and there were no other witnesses.

Mr. Sanford testified in a straightforward manner putting a hand to one of his hearing aids from time to time and asking that the question be repeated and bringing the attention of the jury to one aspect of his frailty. He testified that, after being knocked to the ground, all three men began to hit him and to kick him with most of the blows being directed to his head.

The cross-examination began.

A. Yes.
Q. You didn't see who hit you?
A. One of the Indians did it.

Q. But, assuming that is true, you don't know which one hit you, do you?
A. How could I; my back was turned.
Q. Thank you. You were stunned by this blow?
A. It knocked me down.
Q. But coming as a surprise as it did and with enough force to knock you down, it must have stunned and confused you somewhat.
A. Well you can see it doesn't take much to knock me down. I only weigh . . .
Q. All right, Mr. Sanford, let's go on. You were struck by somebody from behind, fell to the ground and then felt some more kicks and blows?
A. Yes.
Q. So you can't say with certainty that this man (indicating the defendant) either hit or kicked you?
A. Oh, he hit and kicked me all right.
Q. But up to this point you hadn't seen him do it, had you?
A. No. But I did later.
Q. But, Mr. Sanford, isn't it natural in such a situation to cover one's head with arms for protection?
A. It may be natural but when I rolled over I could see all three of them.
Q. You didn't try and protect your head?
A. Oh, you bet. But I didn't cover my eyes.
Q. You didn't try and protect your glasses?
A. No.
Q. Were they hit or kicked?
A. Yes.
Q. Did they come off?
A. No. My arms were holding them on (he demonstrates).
Q. Are these the same glasses you had on when you were attacked?
A. Yes.
Q. Did you repair them after the incident?
A. Didn't have to.
Q. Mr. Sanford, you were struck from behind by someone you can't identify; you fell forward to the pavement and were struck again by

one or more of the three men but you can't be sure that the defendant did it; you rolled over, covered your head but not your eyes and were kicked and punched repeatedly around the head but your glasses were never knocked off nor broken. Is that your testimony?

A. Yes.

Q. (Now the fatal blunder resulting from exasperation and inexperience) If you were kicked or hit in the head, why weren't your glasses damaged or broken?

A. I can tell you why. (Sanford removes his glasses) I make glasses. I made these glasses. (Sanford now has the glasses in front of him and is holding them by the ear piece.) You cant hurt these glasses. (He now begins to strike them against the oak rail in front of him and he holds them up for the jury to see.) See, no damage. (He begins again to strike the glasses on the rail harder than before. Now the sound doesn't sound like Bang! Now it says GUILTY, GUILTY, GUILTY.

Principle Eight

Questions Should Be Simple And Unambiguous

Questions on cross-examination which are not simple and unambiguous will confuse the jury and cause it to lose confidence in the cross-examiner and his case. These types of questions cause the cross-examiner to lose control of the witness and, hence, the case.

The advocate should not ask a question that is so convoluted as to confuse the witness or, worse, to give the clever witness to launching into a damaging narrative.

Some rules for questions on cross-examination are:

- Train yourself to compose questions that are ten syllables long. They can be slightly more or less but ten is a good benchmark. It is a good number to aim for because it will force the short and simple question, it is the meter that the English language is best spoken in, and is most pleasing to the ear.
- Questions should require a 'yes' or 'no' answer.
- Questions that occur to you in a longer form must be divided into several questions of shorter and simpler form.
- If a question requires some preface before getting to the important part, the prefatory questions should be divided into separate questions. All too often during cross-examination one hears something along the following lines:

"Mr. Witness, is it true that on the day in question you entered the bank, walked to the rear of the bank, filled out some forms, then returned to the teller's window and when you stepped up to the window you heard the teller scream."

This question kind of question can only lead you to trouble. The process should be:

Q. Mr. Witness, on the day in question you entered the bank?
A. Yes.
Q. You went to the rear of the bank?
A. Yes.
Q. You then filled out some forms?
A. Yes.
Q. You then returned to the teller's window?
A. Yes.
Q. Then you heard the teller scream.

The first form of the question risks having the jury be confused about what is important in the question. It also gives the witness to the opportunity to equivocate. And it gives the opposition the chance to argue that the answer of the witness was may have been directed to one part of the question and not another.

An amusing result coming from a simple question but, as it turned out, not unambiguous occurred in a motion picture. The comedian, Peter Sellers, was checking into a hotel in France. He was standing at the registration desk and a dog lying on the floor next to the desk was growling. Sellers looked at the concierge and inquired: "Does your dog bite?" The concierge answers "No". Sellers resumed his filling in the registration form; and, suddenly, the dog attacks him. There is the usual comedic scene in which Sellers destroys much of the reception area while extricating himself from the dog. Having done so, he returns to the concierge who has remained seated. Sellers straightens his clothes and asks, "I thought you said your dog does not bite?" The concierge replied; "It is not my dog."

The advocate should avoid using language that may not be understood by the witness or the jurors. Often the witness will understand a question that a juror may not understand. The jury should always be monitored during the cross-examination for signs that they may not understand certain questions, phrases or words.

The advocate should develop a sense of when certain words or language may be lost on a particular jury. It is important to be aware of the limitations of a particular jury, and to avoid condescending language. If there is a doubt it is better to repeat a question in alternative language.

The problems associated with failing to ask clear and unambiguous questions can often assume the following form:

Q. *(By Defense counsel) Prior to the alleged incident at the intersection of 10th and Broadway what was your location?*

The witness appears confused.
(Be the court) Counsel wants to know where you were before the shooting.

A. In the Barber shop.
Q. *Subsequently did you remove yourself from the barber shop and travel to the intersection.*

Another confused look.
(By the Court) Counsel wants to know if you went to the intersection.

A. Yes.
Q. *Were you present at the intersection when the defendant is alleged to have perpetrated an assault on the complainant?*

(By the court) Counsel wants to know if you were there when the defendant shot the woman.

Not only has the cross-examiner accomplished nothing by using legal jargon he has caused to judge to intervene and in effect announce to the jury that from his point of view the defendant is guilty by assuming the fact in his last attempt to clarify a question.

Part Five

Developing A Style

Principle One

The Advocate Must Control The Subject Matter And Pace Of Cross-Examination

Controlling the subject matter of the cross-examination is important if the advocate has any hope of presenting the jury a coherent and well structured case that will lead them to the inexorable conclusion that what happened in the past is the way he has portrayed it. This kind of control is accomplished by the nature and form of his questions. It requires having a clear idea of the goals he's set for the trial and cross-examination.

The pace of the direct examination and the cross-examination is important because it allows the attorney to build his examination to a dramatic climax for the jury. This means the advocate must be able to deflect any attempts by the opposition to disrupt the pace, and, conversely, to be able to disrupt the pace of the direct examination and cross-examination of the opposition.

Disrupting And Fending Off Disruption

This is a subject that every advocate must approach with caution. There is a thin line between the legitimate use of trial tactics to gain advantage and unethical behavior. The advocate must be keenly aware of this and tailor his behavior in a way that conforms to the ethical.

The best way of dealing with the opposition disruption of

your cross-examination is a direct approach. By objecting to the court, the cross-examiner can show the jury that the opposition is interjecting an objection for the purpose of trying to distract the juries' attention from some crucial information. In other words make the opposition pay such a high price for the tactic that they will stop. A second method is to use humor to deal with the opposition's disruption.

You can disrupt the pace of the opposition by interposing objections or inquiries that have more as their object the disruption of the pace than to achieve the exclusion of an answer of the witness. This may be made in a speech to the jury pointing out that what the witness is saying has been asked of another witness and a different answer was forthcoming, or that there is no evidence this witness is competent to testify regarding this matter. These interjections will usually be rejected by the court as being premature or that they should be saved for cross-examination. Nevertheless they may serve to put the opposition off stride at a crucial moment. Any of these tactics should be used sparingly and saved for those moments in a direct examination that might be particularly harmful to your case.

What Some Leading Trial Lawyers Have Done

How far some lawyers have gone to distract the jury are shown by the anecdotes that follow. I will leave it to the reader to draw any ethical inferences. The first involves Earl Rogers and his behavior during the summing up of the prosecution in a criminal case.

This is the most difficult and uncomfortable time of any trial for the criminal defense lawyer. It is the final word to the jury and you are helpless to say or do anything to counter the telling points the good DA will make. Rogers for some of his practice was in courts that allowed the participants to smoke. When this was the case Rogers would take a very long cigar to court with him. When he had finished his summation he would sit down and light his cigar. As the DA began his speech Rogers would puff contentedly on the cigar. As the speech reached the most telling parts the ash of the cigar was growing longer and longer. Soon the jury began to wonder when the ash would fall. As it grew the jury became more fascinated with how a cigar ash could possibly remain on the cigar. By the time the DA was getting to the most dramatic part of the argument the ash was of such a length as to defy all laws of gravity and the jury had lost all of their ability to concentrate on what the DA was saying. Beforehand Rogers had inserted a piece of wire the length of the cigar. The effect of the wire was that as he smoked the cigar the ashes would remain on the cigar, held there by the wire.

The second incident involved the best trial lawyer I have ever seen. No advocate I have ever seen was quicker on his feet, more eloquent, possessed a better sense of timing, and could develop a greater rapport with the jury than Irving Andrews. He was defending a murder case once along with an associate in which the DA was seeking the death penalty. It was a case where the death penalty was a good likelihood and Irving's primary goal was to avoid it.

The DA made his customary short opening summation saving the real oratory for his last speech. Irving gave his usual moving argument and finished by saying that the case didn't come close to a death penalty case and that if the DA had the audacity to even speak the words he would leave the courtroom. Of course the DA reached the question of the death penalty rather soon in his speech and the moment he said the words Irving rose, gathered his papers, and strode indignantly from the courtroom. The jury was amused and the DA never dreaming Irving would follow through on his threat was so disrupted that the remainder of his argument was ineffectual. The jury convicted but did not impose the death penalty.

The adroit advocate can turn an attempt by the opposition to disrupt him to his own advantage. Jerry Geisler told a story of an incident early in his career when he worked for Earl Rogers. Rogers was defending Patrick Calhoun, the president of the San Francisco street railway system, who had been indicted for various kinds of crookedness. Francis J. Heney was prosecuting the case and between him and Rogers every tactic for breaking the other lawyers stride was known, and used. What follows is an example of what happens when the parties get too cute in attempting to upset the other side's pace.

Rogers was cross-examining the head of the Board of Supervisors. The cross-examination had the witness on the ropes and Rogers was pummeling him. Heney realized he had to upset Rogers or his star witness would never be effective. He decided to cause a diversion:

Heney: *'Your honor, I'd like to call attention to the young man sitting behind Mr. Calhoun. [this was Jerry Geisler] When anything favorable to the prosecution is brought out, he frowns at the jury. When anything favorable to the defense occurs, he smiles at the jury. It is the opinion of the prosecution that his behavior is improper, reprehensible and is designed to influence the jurors.'*

A defense lawyer: *'Mr. Heney's remarks are a barefaced attempt to prejudice the jury, since the young man in question was innocent of anything except pulling for his side to win, and that was certainly normal.'*

The defendant Patrick Calhoun stood up.

Calhoun: *'Your honor, in reality it is my life which is at stake here, because these proceedings involve my reputation, which is more valuable to me than my life, and for Mr. Heney to interrupt the proceedings upon which a man's precious reputation hangs with such foolishness is unseemly. This young man has been sitting near me throughout this trial and I have never seen him do anything which would be described as reprehensible. But apparently Mr. Heney is willing to try any trick, no matter how cheap or tawdry, to create a momentary interruption.'*

What had started out as an attempt by Heney as a simple attempt to divert the jury and court from the cross-examination of his witness in the hopes the witness could reassemble himself turned into a an opportunity for the defendant himself to address the jury.

Principle Two

Begin The Cross-Examination Courteously

With rare exception the advocate should begin the cross-examination courteously never losing sight of the fact that the resolution of disputes by trial is an example of civilization at its highest. The entire case should be conducted with decorum, and the advocate should remember that jurors expect erudition, civility and good manners, and will tolerate the angry, indignant, aggressive approach only when they feel the advocate has been provoked into it by an evasive, lying, or manipulative witness.

The advocate can always advance from the courteous to being aggressive or indignant. However, it is very difficult to begin with the aggressive or indignant style and retreat to a courteous one. Even where you know in advance that eventually you will employ an aggressive and indignant approach toward a witness the examination should begin courteously and the witness should be given the opportunity to redeem himself in a civilized atmosphere before you launch a more vigorous attack. This civilized approach will serve to disarm the witness and draw the jury into indignant censure should his recalcitrance require you to become more aggressive.

A Soul Stripped Bare

One of the more interesting capital cases in England in the early part of the twentieth century was the charge against Mr. and

Mrs. Seddon for the poisoning of a tenant for her money. Mr. Seddon was a well respected member of the community and highly polished in his speech and was able to think quickly. A formidable foe for any advocate. He took the stand in his own behalf and made a convincing case for his innocence. The Crown was represented by Sir Rufus Isaacs and his cross-examination of Seddon is a classic of its kind.

Issacs begins the cross-examination in a dispassionate and courteous voice designed to disarm the witness.

Isaacs: *'Miss Barrow lived with you from the 26th of July, 1910, till the morning of the 14th of September, 1911?'*
Seddon: *'Yes.'*
Q. *'Did you like her?'*
A. *'Did I like her?'*
Q. *'Yes, that is the question.'* [*Seddon had so mistreated the deceased that a 'yes' answer would ring false. A 'no' answer paint him as uncaring. Issacs had put the witness in a box with only one question.*]
A. *'She was not a woman that you could be in love with, but I deeply sympathised with her.'*
Q. *'During the time she was living with you at your house did you advise her on her financial affairs?'*
A. *'Certainly I advised her.'*

There was a serious of questions in which the witness admitted the facts of the deceased's small fortune.

Q. *'She came to you, then, with India Three and a half per cent. Stock bringing in one pound a week, the leasehold property bringing in one hundred and twenty pounds a year, and over two hundred pounds in the Finsbury Saving Bank; that is right?'*
A. *'Yes.'*
Q. *'On the 14th of September, 1911, when she died, was all the property that was found of hers a sum of ten pounds in gold, and furniture, jewelry, and other belongings to the value of sixteen pounds, fourteen shillings, and sixpence?'*

A. *'According to the inventory taken by Mr. Gregory, a reputed auctioneer and appraiser, it was sixteen pounds odd.'*

Isaacs continued for some time increasing the intensity of the questions, but by all accounts never wavering in his courteous tone of voice and gentlemanly treatment of the witness always calling him 'Mr 'Seddon'. Finally Seddon showed his first sign of anger when he was asked as to the counting of the gold on the day of the victim's death,

A. *'The prosecution are suggesting that I am dealing with the deceased woman's gold. That I should bring it down from the top of the house to the bottom, into the office in the presence of my assistants, and count it up—is it feasible? . . . I am not a degenerate. That would make it out that I was a greedy, inhuman monster . . . . The suggestion is scandalous. I would have all day to count the money.'*

This is where Isaacs' patience, and quite courteous approach paid its dividends. Seddon's falsity had been stripped away in such a fashion that the witness was the only one of the participants that was unaware of losing the confrontation. What he believed were clever answers were ever increasingly taken with disgust by the jury, and one he showed this side of himself Isaacs was ever increasingly able to show his true personality.

Principle Three

Don't Confuse Cross-Examination With Examining Crossly

The popular idea of the cross-examiner engaged in a blustering, rapid fire of questions in a harsh tone that is bullying and browbeating at a witness who hardly has time to answer bears little relation to reality.

Indeed, jurors understand that the confrontation between witness and lawyer is essentially stacked in favor of the lawyer. The lawyer selects the subject matter, controls the kind of answer that may be given, can shut the witness off, and if he wishes can make the witness appear to be confused, uncertain, or even to have a diminished mental capacity. The advocate who overplays his advantage will inevitably alienate the jury to such an extent that any legitimate points he has to make will be lost or offset.

Advantage Gained By A Courteous Approach

The object of cross-examination is not to bully a witness but to persuade the jury that events happened in a certain way and that what the witness has to say on the subject is wrong or so unreliable as to be impossible.

In his defense of one McComas for the murder of his mistress it was Earl Roger's defense that the mistress, Charlotte Noyes, had thrown acid in the face of McComas believing him to be an intruder and that McComas fired in defense of his life. The DA took the position that McComas had deliberately killed the woman and then thrown the vitriol on his own face. To substantiate his story McComas then had put some of the acid on the victims face. The pathologist called by the state testified to the cause of death and the DA carefully avoided asking anything about the acid hoping to limit the cross-examination by Earl Rogers. Rogers always believed the gentle courteous approach to the witness was the ideal one and how he handled the acid and the pathologist is a fine example of the art.

"Dr. Campbell," said Earl Rogers quietly, "you used the term 'return spray.'"

Instant activity in the prosecution's bull pen. Paul Fleming was on his feet. "Dr. Campbell did not use such expression during my examination." he said warmly. "I object on the grounds the question is not proper cross-examination, Your Honor."

He had no idea what return spray was, nor why Rogers was asking about it. He and his first assistant, a young man named Horton, and a battery of seven other assistant D.A.'s were there to watch. They were not going to give Earl Rogers an inch. If you let him take an inch—

"Dr. Campbell did use that term," Earl Rogers said as he lifted one finger. Quietly, Jerry Giesler put a blue document in his hand.

After an intense if hurried conference with Captain Fredericks, Fleming said again, "It is not on evidence in this trial, Your Honor."

With the blue document in hand, Rogers walked to the Bench. "Here it is, Your Honor," he said still quietly. "Page Forty-five—Dr. Campbell used this term—return spray—in his original examination at the coroner's request."

Fleming, with a mind as quick as Alexander Hamilton's had seen that return spray must have something to do with the acid-throwing business of this case. His strategy—and always the strategy was Fleming's—had been mapped not to bring this up until he had laid his foundation. The long interval between the shot, heard by several people, and the call McComas made to the police. The call from a nearby phone in another hotel to Earl Rogers' home during that same time lapse. Then cross-examination of McComas himself.

This was too early. Nor did he wish Earl Rogers to be the one to bring it up at all, though what return spray had to do with it he hadn't yet figured out.

He was to know very soon.

Both Fleming and Fredericks made a long and sound attempt to exclude the question.

Unless, Fredericks said, throwing all his persuasion into the objection, the question had been asked on direct examination in this court during this trial, the defense counsel could not cross-examine on it.

If at any time any place in any official hearing, said Earl Rogers, the witness has used that term in connection with this case, he may use it now and I may inquire into it.

The court now said, after some time, to the witness, "If you at any time have used that term as a description of what you saw in connection with this case, you may explain to the jury as to the conditions to which you applied it."

Mr. Rogers said, "Thank you, Your Honor." now that the court had so ruled, he began to use the two words as a fulcrum. His tone was entirely professional as he began. One physician consulting another. A general practitioner, uninformed at a high level of this special matter, ready willing to learn from a consultant of note.

"Dr. Campbell," he said, "what did you mean exactly, when you used the term return spray?"

Dr. Campbell said, "I applied it to the form and line the drops of acid took on the face of the dead woman."

Q. *(by Mr. Rogers) the face of the dead woman, Mrs. Noyes?*
A. *Yes, on the face of Mrs. Noyes at the time I studied the case.*
Q. *Yes doctor, I see. You studied the case carefully, of course. Now would you be kind enough to describe for us the condition left on her face?*
A. *Well, I found that from above downward, on the right side of the face was a line of acid drops. Or rather the marks, let us say, left by their passage. The lighter ones being above, these marks gradually became heavier as they passed downward. showing me that the line*

of fluid, of acid, had formed itself by gravity and struck the face in that perpendicular manner along the right side of the face.
Q. *Therefore you think she was standing up?*
A. *Yes.*

The doctor's manner had succumbed to that of Earl Rogers. They had forgotten they were in a courtroom, it appeared. They were two medical men. Doctors just plain never would discuss anything with you, or tell a layman anything about all these fascination details, even when it was your own family. Now, by the simplicity of manner and style and language, the jury felt they were being allowed to listen in on a real consultation. They were eavesdropping.

Q. *This meant that in other words the acid was running down?*
A. *Remember, the burns became deeper downward, the lower part of the face contained considerable eschar.*
Q. *By that, doctor, you mean dead tissue?*
A. *Yes, yes, I mean dead tissue or the crust or scab occasioned on the skin by burns or caustics.*
Q. *Then Mrs. Noyes was alive when the acid struck her?*
A. *Oh yes otherwise no eschar could form.*

—

Q. *Now doctor, if you will, may we go a little further into your reason for saying Mrs. Noyes was standing up?*
A. *The acid burns had been caused by a return spray. The heavy drops took the lower course, showing that the force of gravity had lined it. She must have been in an erect position to receive it that way.*
Q. *Receive it? Mrs. Noyes had thrown the vitriol, she had flung the acid. Now you are talking about her standing to receive it.*
A. *she received the return spray.*
Q. *Dr. Campbell, speaking of your use of the term return spray, will you please now tell us very explicitly what you mean buy it?*

A. *Well, I mean a comeback, from the acid striking something else, anything, and spraying back.*
Q. *You mean by that, then, what we might also call a splash back?*
A. *Yes, Mr. Rogers, as the ocean would strike a rock and spray back.*
Q. *In your best medical judgment, is that the way those burns were inflicted on this woman Mrs. Noyes?*
A. *Oh yes, most definitely. I'm quite sure about that. No other possible explanation from the nature of the burns on her dead face.*
Q. *When she was alive and erect she was struck by the return spray of the acid she had thrown?*
A. *Oh yes yes, had to be so.*
Q. *Did you so testify at the autopsy and the preliminary hearing?*
A. *I must have. That's the medical fact, I couldn't very well have testified otherwise, could I?*
Q. *I'm sure you couldn't doctor. Thank you, we all thank you, you have been of great help to us all.*

Then for the first time, Earl Rogers turned and looked at the district attorney's bench. Quietly, he said, "I haven't any more questions, Dr. Campbell. Perhaps the district attorney has."

But it seemed that the district attorney hadn't.

Principle Four

Never Open With The Last Subject Covered In Direct Examination

It may be useful with this principle to resolve the exceptions at the outset. Witnesses that are inconsequential or that are called for only one piece of information are obvious exceptions. With respect to the former, it is of no consequence what the order of questioning is; and, with respect to the latter one doesn't have a choice. This principle may not apply in situations where you are in possession on such damaging in incontrovertible impeaching material that one should move directly to the attack. The chances of this happening, however, are so rare as not to be very valuable.

That leaves the witness who has testified at some length on a variety of topics and must be damaged if your case is to prevail. With this type of witness it is best not to begin the cross-examination with the subject last covered on direct examination. The reason why is that the last item covered is usually the most dramatic of the witness's testimony and the one that needs most to be impeached. To launch into the subject denies the cross-examiner the opportunity to develop points on which the witness can be impeached, and thereby weakens the examination.

The opposition, having saved the best for last in the direct examination has probably impressed the jury with the strong points of the subject. Moreover, since the witness has just gone over the matter in direct, he will have it firmly in mind and be at his best in answering the cross-examination. The wiser course of action is to leave the subject alone and take the witness through a series of questions that will ultimately place him in a position of having to change his direct testimony or appear foolish.

This tactic can only be accomplished through patient effort and skilled maneuvering with the witness. It can never be successful if the advocate launches into the strong suit of the witness immediately.

An interesting and amusing example of this is found in the transcript of the proceedings relating to the trial of Errol Flynn. In 1942 a young girl named Peggy Satterlee (age fifteen) accepted an invitation to join Errol Flynn on his yacht for a cruise to Catalina Island. During the early morning hours Miss Satterlee was visited in her room by Mr. Flynn and was forced to have intercourse. The following evening while they were on deck Mr. Flynn suggested that Miss Satterlee, who was admiring the moon, join him in his stateroom because the view of the moon was much better through the porthole. She went along with him and much to her surprise and chagrin he forced her to have intercourse with him again. She complained to the District Attorney and Mr. Flynn was charged with statutory rape.

Jerry Giesler represented him and one of the more amusing and effective cross-examinations in the case was that of a Canadian flyer named Cathcart-Jones who had spent a great deal of time with Miss Satterlee. The cross-examination is preceded by a portion of the cross-examination of Miss Satterlee in which Giesler attempted to establish the relationship of Satterlee to Cathcart-Jones.

Q. *'Now, pardon me, Miss Satterlee, for asking you, but did Mr. Jones have any particular pet name that he knew you by—that he applied to you?'*
A. *'Oh, he had quite a few of them.'*
Q. *'Quite a few?'*
A. *'Yes, sir.'*

At this point the prosecutor, Mr. Cochran, indicated he had not heard the question and answer and asked that it be read back.

Q. BY MR. COCHRAN: 'That was Mr. Jones, you say?'
MR. GIESLER: 'Mr. Jones.'
MR. COCHRAN: 'That is objected to as immaterial—what nicknames Mr. Jones may have used.'
THE COURT: 'Objection will be overruled.'
Q. BY MR. GIESLER: 'What was the particular one? Do you remember, Miss Satterlee?'
A. 'Rather silly names, but Scrumpet, Bitchy Pie, and so forth.'
MR. GIESLER: 'May that be read, your honor? The jurors did not hear.' A wonderful device for emphasizing the answer, and making the jury think you are looking out for their interests.
THE COURT: 'All right. Will you read the answer?'

[Answer read.]

Q. BY MR. GIESLER: 'Scrumpet, Bitchy Pie, and so forth?'
A. 'Scrumpet.'
Q. 'Did you say Scrumpet or Strumpet?' [A wonderful play on words].
A. 'Scrumpet or something. It is an English name for crumpet or . . .'
Q. 'Well?'
A. 'I know it was something.'
Q. 'You know it sounded something like Scrumpet?'
A. 'Yes, sir.'
THE COURT: 'I understood her to say Strumpet.'
MR. COCHRAN: 'No, it is a little cake, I think.'

Giesler through this humorous side trip had set the bait the DA couldn't resist. Giesler wanted him to call the Canadian flyer. Under the rules then existing if Giesler called him he would be bound by his answers and could not cross-examine his own witness except under strict circumstances.

Q. BY MR. COCHRAN: 'Did you ever call Miss Peggy Satterlee any pet names, as we might say it?'
A. BY CATHCART-JONES: 'Well, I called her a kind of an English idea of what a ragamuffin is, which is Scruppet.'

Q. 'How do you spell it? You know we have had some considerable controversy over this thing.'
A. [spelling] 'S-c-r-u-p-p-e-t.'

Cross-examination by Giesler:

Q. 'And shortly after you got back Peggy visited you, didn't she?'
A. 'After I got back from Canada?'
Q. 'Yes.'
A. 'No, I went up to Santa Barbara to visit her.'
Q. 'But after you had been back—when you came back to Los Angeles—she came down to visit you, isn't that correct?'
A. 'Well, she came to Los Angeles.'
Q. 'She visited you here, didn't she, down here?'
A. 'Yes, she visited me here. Yes.'
Q. 'And that was in the month of August?'
A. 'Yes.'
Q. 'And you were still living at the Alto Nido Apartments?'
A. 'Yes.'
Q. 'And she visited you at the Alto Nido apartments?'
A. 'Yes.'
Q. 'And she visited you at the Alto Nido Apartments before you went to Canada, had she not?'
A. 'Oh, yes.'
Q. 'She had visited you up there alone at times, hadn't she?'
A. 'Yes.'
Q. 'And she visited you while—just after you came back from Canada, didn't she?
A. Oh, yes.
Q. And she visited you quite frequently up there alone, didn't she?
A. Oh, yes.
Q. Both before and after you went to Canada?
A. Oh, yes.
Q. And she visited you up there alone in the evening sometimes, did she not?

- A. *Oh, yes.*
- Q. *Didn't you call Peggy Bitchy Pie?*
- A. *No.*
- Q. *You never did?*
- A. *No.*
- Q. *Did you ever call her bitch?*
- A. *No.*
- Q. *You are sure of that?*
- A. *No. Absolutely.*
- Q. *You are sure that you never called her Bitchy Pie?*
- A. *Absolutely.*
- Q. *As a matter of fact, you used to call her Grummet?*
- A. *No.*
- Q. *Do you know what that means?*
- A. *It is a rope that you throw on a quoit.*
- Q. *It is a rope that you throw on a what? Well, maybe we better—*
- THE COURT: *Well, have him explain it, have him explain so that we can understand what he means.*
- MR. GIESLER: *Yes.*
- A. *The English, I think, of 'grummet' is a piece of vertical rope which you throw along the deck of a ship.*
- Q. *BY MR. GIESLER: And doesn't it have any other English expression?*
- A. *Not that I know of.*
- Q. *Now, you have gone other places with Peggy other than the Coleman ranch and to Arrowhead, have you not?*
- A. *Oh, yes, I have been all over places with her.*
- Q. *Never alone?*
- A. *No.*
- Q. *Who was with you there?*
- A. *Her sister June.*
- Q. *Well, you also were with her down to a mortuary down here in Los Angeles, were you not?*
- A. *Yes.*
- Q. *And she was kind of playing hide-and-seek around the corpses, wasn't she? Do you remember that night?*

A. Yes.

Q. Do you remember she showed you—opened it up and showed you—the body of an elderly lady?

A. Yes.

Q. And pulled the sheet down in the mortuary on a Filipino who had been crippled across his center?

A. Yes, I remember that.

Q. And then went back to where they inject the veins of corpses and there opened and looked down at an elderly man lying there, and her head was pushed down against the man's face. Do you remember that?

A. Yes, I remember that.

Principle Five

Never Falsely Represent What A Witness Has Said

The well crafted and presented case should resemble a drama and produce the necessary ingredients of tension and rising action. Therefore, the advocate should also keep in mind Coleridge's axiom that all good drama requires the voluntary suspension of disbelief by the reader or observer. The jury, of course, is the observer in the drama of the trial.

Juries would prefer to come to most conclusions on their own and the good advocate will attempt to play the role of facilitator in this respect. When a small victory is achieved on cross-examination, there should be a dramatic pause to allow the matter to be fully appreciated by the jury; and the advocate must be sure the jury is aware of the fact.

Moreover, the advocate should never falsely represent what a witness has said. Doing so usually means that the advocate has underestimated the intelligence of the jury.

Jurors try to do a conscientious job in an atmosphere that to them is intimidating and confusing. Rarely do they abandon their innate sense of right and wrong, and of fair play. Often an advocate, having established a good rapport with the jury, will misstate to the jury what a witness has said. He may be attempting to cast a witness's testimony in the most favorable light or to explain damaging testimony. In either case, the tactic of misstatement is a deadly mistake. Jurors will abandon an otherwise just cause very quickly if they feel the advocate is attempting to mislead them.

The better to handle damaging testimony is to ignore it, treat is as inconsequential, or approach it in a direct way by stating the testimony honestly and offering an explanation that is consistent with your theory of the case and that conforms to the common sense of the jury.

How Mis-stating A Witness's Testimony can Backfire

A famous case in English jurisprudence is referred to as the Tichborne case. In 1854, the young heir to the baronetcy and the Tichborne estates was lost at sea. Hoping against hope and believing him to be alive his mother put an add in papers throughout the world seeking information. The result of this effort was that a man named Thomas Castro from Australia appeared and claimed to be the lost heir. After a lengthy trial his claim was rejected and he was then tried for perjury.

He was represented by a Barrister named Keneally who insisted throughout the trial in misrepresenting the evidence. It was an item addressed by the Lord Chief Justice in the summing up and shows dramatically what damage the advocate can do by exerting to imaginative an approach in recounting the testimony of a witness or other participant in the case:

"Our position was rendered painful from this, that we had, again and again and over again, to interfere with the defence of the learned Counsel in order to correct mis-statements and mis-representations which we would not allow to pass unnoticed. When witnesses are misrepresented and their statements are distorted, when facts are perverted and dates set at naught—and all this not for the purpose of argument in the case, but in order to lay the foundation for foul accusations and unjust imputations against parties and witnesses. When one unceasing torrent of invective, of dirty foul slime, is sent forth wherewith to blacken the characters of men whose reputations have hitherto been beyond reproach, it is impossible for Judges to remain silent. It is not enough to say that the counsel

should be allowed to go on with his address to the end and that the Judge should wait till it comes to his turn to speak to set matters straight—seeing that, especially in such a case as this, when weeks or months might elapse before the Judge could have an opportunity of expressing his opinion upon matters of that kind, and meanwhile a temporary impression—perhaps that is all that is hoped to be gained—may go forth fatal to the honour, to the character of persons thus assailed. We therefore felt it our duty to interpose and to check the torrent of unbridled and indiscriminate abuse which the learned Counsel for the defence thought proper to indulge in. And in what way were our remonstrances met? In ordinary cases, if in the heat of argument or the fervour of oratory or the zeal which a Counsel sometimes exhibits in examining or cross-examining a witness, the strict bounds of propriety are, as will occasionally be the case, overstepped (I am bound to say for the honour of the Bar of England it happens very rarely indeed), a word from the Judge is sufficient to restrain overflowing zeal within its proper and legitimate limits. But how were we met? By constant disrespect, by insult, by covert allusions to Scroggs and Jeffreys and judges of infamous repute—as though, by the way, if the spirit of Scroggs and Jeffreys still animated the Bench in the administration of justice, the learned Counsel would not have been pretty quickly laid by the heels and put to silence! But in that way we were met by suggestions that we were interfering with the liberty and the privilege of the Bar....

"Interfere with the liberties of the Bar! What! In checking the license of unscrupulous abuse, in restraining that which, instead of being fair and legitimate argument, amounts to misstatement and slander! ... And in this case, gentlemen, the living and the dead have been equally aspersed. There never was in the history of jurisprudence a case in which such an amount of imputation, accusation and invective was used before, and I trust that such an instance will never occur again. Though this prosecution is instituted by Her Majesty's Government and carried on on the part of the Crown, you have been asked to believe that everyone connected with it, from the highest to the lowest—Counsel, solicitors, clerks,

detectives, everybody—is in one foul conspiracy and has no hesitation in resorting to the most abominable means in order to purchase testimony and corrupt witnesses. Bribery you have been told had been unhesitatingly resort to; witnesses against whom I should have supposed that nothing could be said except that they might be mistaken in the evidence they gave, have been charged with having been bribed and having committed perjury. Imputations are cast out to the right and to the left. One man is called a felon, against whom there no more ground for charging felony than any one of us. The authorities of Stonyhurst are charged, upon no ground or foundation whatsoever, not only with not teaching morality to their students, but actually with designedly corrupting their minds. They are said to have adopted a system by which youths are sought to be brought up to be 'men with the minds of women' and a covert hint is thrown out of abominations half revealed at which one recoils and shudders, without any more ground for it than if the imputation had been brought against the Authorities of Eton or Westminster or any of our great public schools. The dead are assailed in the same way. Sir James Tichborne is called 'a degraded slave'. Lady Doughty is charged with base hypocrisy; it is alleged that having discovered that her nephew had attempted the honour of her own daughter, or even succeeded in the attempt, she shows him the door with bland smiles and honeyed words. Captain Bickett, who went down in the "Bella" when she foundered, is actually charged with having scuttled the ship in which he unfortunately perished . . . .

"I attempted to draw a distinction between that which is legitimate in advocacy and that which is forbidden; and I illustrated the difference between the fas and the nefas of advocacy by the analogous case of the Sword of the Warrior and the poisoned dagger of the assassin. The learned Counsel began by citing my language and then, applying it to his learned adversary, charged him with having been guilty of the use of the dagger of the assassin in the conduct of this case. A more unfounded charge, I am bound to say, in justice to the professional honour of Mr. Hawkins, has never been made . . . Gentlemen, it has been has been very painful indeed *for me to make these observations, but the case called for it. Liberty of the Bar! Till this time I should not have thought it capable of abuse, but we have unfortunately witnessed its abuse. Of that abuse, a fitting corrective is to be found in the censure of the Bench, which I know will meet, as it ought to meet, with the universal concurrence of the Bar of England."*

Principle Six

Never Use Violent Or Abusive Language To The Witness

With rare exception, a witness testifying on direct examination will be accepted at face value by the jury and his story usually believed. The advocate charged with cross-examining him must realize this, despite the fact that he, the advocate, is in possession of damaging and impeaching evidence.

The advocate must convince the jury first that its trust and confidence in the witness may be misplaced and that all the belief they developed during the direct examination may be unwarranted. After the jury has been brought to this position, (that is returned to neutrality), then the advocate can begin the task of winning them to his point of view.

To some degree, taking away the credibility of testimony or the witness involves suggesting to the jury it was wrong to believe the witness in the first place. This must be done gently; to attack the witness with violent or abusive language will generally serve to make the jury try and reinforce their earlier view of the testimony or witness, rather than to admit they were wrong.

Firmness, outrage, righteous indignation may be used as tools of cross-examination, especially when it appears that the jury expects it; but violent or abusive language towards the witness can only be counterproductive.

A Patient Approach Does In Parnell's Accuser

Charles Parnell was an Irish leader in the British parliament. Two English government officials were murdered in Ireland and some time after the occurrence, the letters surfaced allegedly written by Parnell which implicated him. The person claiming to have produced the letters was Richard Pigott; and, upon, his cross-examination by Sir Charles Russell, Q.C. Parnell's future depended. Also of importance was the fact that Pigott had written to the Archbishop of Dublin warning him that the letters were to be published.

Russell: Mr. Pigott, would you be good enough, with my Lords' permission, to write some words on that sheet of paper for me? Perhaps you will sit down in order to do so? . . .

Pigott sat down.

Q. *Will you write the word "livelihood"?*

Pigott wrote.

Q. *Just leave a space. Will your write your own name? Will you write the word "proslytism" and finally (think I will not trouble you at present with any more) "Patrick Egan" and "P. Egan"? There is one word I had forgotten. Lower down, please, leaving spaces, write the word "hesitancy"—with a small "h".*

Pigott wrote, and looked relieved.

Q. *Will you kindly give me the sheet? . . . The first publication of the Articles "Parnellism and Crime" was on the 7th March, 1887?*
A. *I do not know.*
Q. *Well, you may assume that is the date.*

A. *I suppose so.*
Q. *And you were aware of the intended publication of the correspondence (i.e. the incriminatory letters).*
A. *No, I was not at all aware of it.*
Q. *What*
A. *No certainly not . . . .*
Q. *Were you not aware that there were grave charges to be made against Mr. Parnell and the leading members of the Land League?*
A. *I was not aware of it until the publication actually commenced.*
Q. *What*
A. *I was not aware of it until the publication actually commenced.*
Q. *Do you swear that?*
A. *I do.*
Q. *Very good. There is no mistake about that.*

Russell then produced the letter to Archbishop Walsh.

Q. *Is that your letter? Do not trouble to read it; tell me if it is your letter.*
A. *Yes, I think it is.*
Q. *Have you any doubt of it?*
A. *No.*
Russell (addressing the judges): *My Lords, it is from Andertton's Hotel, and it is addressed by the witness to Archbishop Walsh. The date, my Lords, is the 4th of March—three days before the first appearance of the first of the articles, "Parnellism and Crime" (Russell then read): "Private and confidential. My Lord,—The importance of the matter about which I write will doubtless excuse this intrusion on your Grace's attention. Briefly, I wish to say that I have been made aware of the details of certain proceedings that are in preparation with the object of destroying the influence of the Parnellite party in Parliament."*
Q. *What were the certain proceedings that were in preparation?*
A. *I do not recollect.*
Q. *Turn to my Lords and repeat the answer.*
A. *I do not recollect.*

Q. *You swear that—writing on the 4th March less than two years ago?*
A. Yes.
Q. *You do not know what that referred to?*
A. I do not really.
Q. *May I suggest to you?*
A. Yes, you may.
Q. *Did it refer to the incriminatory letters, among other things?*
A. Oh! At that date. No, the letters had not been obtained, I think, at that date, had they, two years ago?
Q. *I do not want to confuse you at all, Mr. Pigott.*
A. Would you mind giving me the date of that letter?
Q. *(Answer by Russell) The 4th of March.—The 4th of March. Is it your impression that the letter had not been obtained at that date?*
A. Oh, yes, some of the letters had been obtained before that date.
Q. *Then, reminding you that some of the letters had been obtained before that date, did that passage that I have read to you in that letter refer to these letters, among other things*
A. No, I rather fancy they had reference to the forthcoming articles in the Times.
Q. *I thought you told us you did not know anything about the forthcoming articles?*
A. Yes, I did. I find now I am mistaken—that I must have heard something about them.
Q. *Then try not to make the same mistake again, Mr. Pigott. "Now" you go on (continuing to read from Pigott's letter to the Archbishop): "I cannot enter more fully into details than to state that the proceedings referred to consist in the publication of certain statements purporting to prove the complicity of Mr. Parnell himself, and some of his supporters with murders and outrages in Ireland, to be followed in all probability by the institution of criminal proceedings against these parties by the Government."*
Q. *Russell (to the witness): Who told you that?*
A. I have no idea.
Q. *But that refers among other things to the incriminatory letters?*
A. I do not recollect that it did.

Q. Do you swear that it did not
A. I will not swear that it did not.
Q. Do you think it did?
A. No, I do not think it did.
Q. Do you think that these letters, if genuine, would prove or would not prove Parnell's complicity in crime?
A. I thought they would be very likely to prove it.
Q. Now, reminding you of that opinion, I ask you whether you did not intend to refer—not solely, I suggest, but among other things—to the letters as being the matter which would prove complicity, or purport to prove complicity?
A. Yes, I may have had that in mind.
Q. You could have had hardly any doubt that you had?
A. I suppose so.
Q. You suppose you may have had?
A. Yes.
Q. There is the letter and the statement: "Your Grace may be assured that I speak with full knowledge, and am in a position to prove, beyond all doubt and question the truth of what I say." Was that true?
A. It could hardly be true.
Q. Then did you write that which was false?
A. I suppose it was in order to give strength to what I said. I do not think it was warranted by what I knew.
Q. You added the untrue statement to add strength to what you said?
A. Yes.
Q. You believe these letters to be genuine?
A. I do.
Q. And did at this time?
A. Yes.
Q. Russell (reading): "And I will further assure your Grace that I am also able to point out how these designs may be successfully combated and defeated." How, if these documents were genuine documents, and you believed them to be such, how were you able to assure his Grace that you were able to point out how the design might be successfully combated and finally defeated

A. —*Well, as I say, I had not the letters actually in mind at that time. So far as I can gather, I do not recollect the letter to Archbishop Walsh at all. My memory is really a blank on the circumstance.*
Q. *You told me a moment ago, after great deliberation and consideration, you had both (the incriminatory letters and the letter to Archbishop Walsh) in your mind?*
A. *I said it was probable I did; but I say the thing has completely faded out of my mind.*
Q. *I must press you. Assuming the letters to be genuine, what were the means by which you were able to assure his Grace that you could point out how the design* might be successfully combated and finally defeated?
A. *I cannot conceive really.*
Q. *Oh! try. You must really try.*
A. *I cannot.*
Q. *Try.*
A. *I cannot.*
Q. *Try.*
A. *It is of no use.*
Q. *May I take it, then, that your answer to my Lords is that you cannot give any explanation?*
A. *I really cannot absolutely.*
Q. *Russell (reading): "I assure your Grace that I have no other motive except to respectfully suggest that your Grace would communicate the substance to some one or other of the parties concerned, to whom I could furnish details, exhibit proofs and suggest how the coming blow may be effectually met." What do you say to that, Mr. Pigott?*
A. *I have nothing to say except that I do not recollect anything about it absolutely.*
Q. *What was the coming blow*
A. *I suppose the coming publication.*
Q. *How was it to be effectively met?*
A. *I have not the slightest idea.*
Q. *Assuming the letters to be genuine, does it not even now occur to your mind how it could be effectively met?*
A. *No.*

Q. *Whatever the charges were, did you believe them to be true or not?*
A. *How can I say that when I say I do not know what the charges were? I say I do not recollect that letter to the Archbishop at all, or any of the circumstances it refers to.*
Q. *First of all you knew this—that you procured and paid for a number of letters?*
A. *Yes.*
Q. *Which, if genuine, you have already told me, would gravely implicate the parties from whom these were supposed to come?*
A. *Yes, gravely implicate.*
Q. *You believe that charge to be true or false?*
A. *I believed that charge to be true.*
Q. *You believed that to be true?*
A. *I do.*
Q. *Now I will read this passage (from Pigott's letter to the Archbishop): "I need hardly add that, did I consider the parties really guilty of the things charged against them, I should not dream of suggesting that your Grace should take part in an effort to shield them; I only wish to impress on your Grace that the evidence is apparently convincing, and could probably be sufficient to secure conviction if submitted to an English jury." What do you say to that, Mr. Pigott?*
A. *I say nothing except that I am sure I could not have had the letters in mind when I said that, because I do not think the letters conveyed a sufficiently serious charge to cause me to write in that way.*
Q. *But you know that was the only part of the charge, so far as you have yet told us, that you had anything to do with in getting up?*
A. *Yes, that is what I say: I must have had something else in my mind which I cannot at present recollect—that I must have had other charges.*
Q. *What charges?*
A. *I do not know. That is I cannot tell you.*
Q. *Well, let me remind you that that particular part of the charges—the incriminatory letters—were letters that you yourself knew all about?*
A. *Yes, of course.*
Q. *Russell (reading from another letter of Pigott's to the Archbishop): ". . . I can assure your Grace that I have no other motive in writing save to avert, if possible, a great danger to people with whom your*

> *Grace is known to be in strong sympathy. At the same time, should your Grace not desire to interfere in the matter, or should you consider that they would refuse me a hearing I am well content, having acquitted myself of what I conceived to be my duty in the circumstances. I will not further trouble your Grace, save to again beg that you will not allow my name to transpire, seeing that to do so would interfere injuriously with my prospects, without any compensating advantage to anyone. I make the request all the more confidently because I have had no part in what is being done to the prejudice of the Parnellite party, though I was enabled to become acquainted with all the details."*—Yes. What do you say to that?
A. That it appears to me clearly that I had not the letters in my mind.
Q. Then if it appears to your clearly that you had not the letters in you mind, what had you in your mind?
A. It must have been something far more serious.
Q. What was it?
A. I cannot tell you. I have no idea.
Q. It must have been something far more serious than the letters?
A. Far more serious.
Q. Can you give my Lords any clue of the most indirect kind to what it was?—
A. I cannot.
Q. Or from whom you heard it?
A. No.
Q. Or when you heard it?
A. Or when I heard it.
Q. Or where you heard it?
A. Or where I heard it.
Q. Have you ever mentioned this fearful matter—whatever it is—to anybody?—
A. No.
Q. Still locked up, hermetically sealed in your own bosom?
A. No, because it has gone away out of my bosom, whatever it was.

Principle Seven

Hide Your Wounds

An advocate conducting cross-examination must maintain a serene appearance during the cross-examination and not display the fact that something said or done is a surprise or is particularly damaging. The jury will be watching him carefully and will instinctively draw some of there inferences about the case from the way the advocate reacts to setbacks, surprise revelations, and damaging evidence. The advocate's every move, his every display of emotion by word or gesture, will register with them and have an impact. If the advocate appears to be hurt by an answer or is hesitant when a damaging answer is given, the jury will pick up on it.

Reversals of fortune are inevitable—they happen in almost every case. There will always be unexpected testimony or evidence. A witness may divulge a damaging bit of testimony unknown before that very moment. It requires the greatest command of the emotions not to show that you have been damaged.

Often the problem arises when the advocate is at his most vulnerable: the rhythm and pace of the examination is just to your liking, you have scored some telling points, and you are being warmed by the comfort of your own cleverness. It is usually at this moment that the witness drops some bombshell. Maintaining self control now is a must. If you display weakness the jury will notice as will the witness and the opposition. On the other hand if you can retain you composure it may appear the material is of little or no significance and its impact will be significantly diminished.

The problem often occurs when you are confronted by something your client neglected to inform you about. The natural response to this is to express, by way of gesture or expression, your unhappiness with the client. But the urge must be suppresses lest you elicit a gesture or response from the client which only compounds the damage.

The greatest source for these unexpected disasters involves expert or "professional witnesses". (Policemen are good examples.) Most of these witness see the trial as a game, or a battle of wits with the advocate and often will spring the unexpected trap

Joseph Saint-Veltri, an attorney whose trial practice has brought him into countless encounters with undercover narcotics detectives, is excellent at "maintaining a serene appearance during cross-examination".

During his cross-examination of a detective, he is frequently faced with the most damaging revelation possible. Without missing a beat, he will throw out his hand in a act of dismissal and say in his calmest manner, "Detective we know all about that. (implying it was of no importance before and is of no importance now). I'm asking you now about something entirely different."

USING RIGHTEOUS INDIGNATION TO DEFLECT THE JURY'S ATTENTION

Another technique you can resort to, if necessary, to deflect the jury away from some damaging points being made against you case involves the display of righteous indignation. This can take the form of being outraged at something the witness says or at some oversight or tactic employed by the opposition. It is a useful technique in the correct situation because the opposition immediately gives credence to your indignation, for fear that they may have missed something that has also outraged the jury. They are, therefore, temporarily distracted while they review their case for possible oversights.

While righteous indignation can be a useful tool, it may also easily make the advocate seem foolish. One should be very sure of his ground and the timing before employing this device.

Principle Eight

Maintain A Serene Appearance

Even where the flow of testimony is in the cross-examiner's favor, a serene demeanor is indispensable. By retaining his composure, the cross-examiner keeps his unsuspecting prey off guard when launching his most devastating attacks, and, at the same time, keeps the jury tightly focused on the unfolding drama.

The libel case of Quentin Reynolds against Westbrook Pegler began when Pegler published one of his syndicated columns containing at least fifteen libels against Reynolds. Among other things, the column accused Reynolds of cowardice, debauchery, war profiteering and being pro-communist. Louis Nizer represented Quentin Reynolds.

Q. *[By Mr Nizer] Mr. Pegler, yesterday and the day before various clippings were shown to you and your were asked whether you had read them and relied on them prior to the time you wrote Exhibit 1 [the libel article], which is November 29, 1949. Do you recall that?*

A. Yes.

Q. *And before you were asked those questions you were on the stand when his Honor gave a learned instruction to the jury as to the purpose for which this kind of evidence might be accepted, namely, it went to punitive damages and not as to the truth. You heard that?*

A. Yes.

A. *And you also heard that if you testified under oath that you had relied on these clippings . . . prior to writing the November 29,*

1949, article, then his Honor instructed the jury they would be accepted for that limited purpose. You heard that?

A. *Yes.*

I then showed him one of the exhibits that he had so qualified and asked him if he had read it before November 29, 1949. he said he had.

Q. *You . . . told this court that you remembered reading that article about seven years before you wrote Exhibit 1 in 1949?*

A. *Yes.*

Q. *Isn't it a fact, Mr. Pegler, that you never saw that Hinsley article until after the publication of the November 29, 1949, column?*

A. *No.*

I proceeded to contradict him.

Q. *You signed an examination before trial in this action?*

A. *I recall testifying for 2400 pages, more than the entire record of this trial for the first four weeks.*

NIZER: *I move to strike it out.*

COURT: *Strike out the balance of the answer. Mr. Pegler, just answer the question. If there is anything on direct your counsel will ask you about it.*

Q. *Did you read your examination . . . before you signed it?*

A. *No.*

Q. *Didn't you read your examination . . . before you signed it?*

A. *No.*

Q. *Didn't you make specific changes of particular answers spread over the entire examination before you signed it?*

A. *The answer to the first part of your question is yes.*

Q. *Isn't it a fact that you made more than twenty-eight changes directly changing your answer from yes to no, and no to yes, after you read this examination and before you signed it.*

A. *I do not know how many.*

Q. *I show you this volume which ends with page 313 and ask you whether that is your signature?*

A. *Yes.*

I had, of course, approached the witness stand to show him his signature. The volume was on the table in front of him. I asked him whether he had read that volume before he signed it. Suddenly he shouted:

A. *Don't stand close to me; go down where you belong.*
COURT: *Please, Mr. Pegler. Please don't tell counsel where to go.*

I was surprised to have drawn blood so early. We all remained frozen for a moment. Then I said: "It will be a pleasure for me to comply with your request."

I walked back to the counsel table, but pressed the lie upon him.

Q. *Do you contradict or disavow your counsel's statement that the Cardinal Hinsley article was given to you after November 29, 1949, and not in 1942, seven years before?*
WITNESS: *Is that the statement of my counsel?*
NIZER: *Yes.*
COURT: *Show it to him.*
A. *I disavow nothing that my counsel stated.*
Q. *And you accept this as a statement of your counsel, that the Hinsley article was given to you after November 29, 1949, right?*
A. *Yes.*

So he had lied when he testified originally that he read and relied on that article before he wrote the libel column. I followed this and another illustration of his false "reliance" testimony.

Q. *Then . . . your counsel showed you a publication called the Tablet, which is now Exhibit U U . . . and you were asked whether you had read this publication and relied upon it—is dated January 9, 1943. Do you recall those questions, sir, about this exhibit?*
A. *Yes, I do.*
Q. *Do you recall that you said you read it at about the time it was published?*
A. *Yes.*

Q. *Of course, that wasn't true, was it?*
A. *Yes.*
Q. *You are now telling this court . . . that six years before you wrote Exhibit 1 of 1949 that you recalled reading this paragraph in the 1943 issue of the Tablet, and relying upon it six years later? Is that what you are telling this court?*
A. *Yes.*
Q. *Isn't it a fact that you never saw Exhibit UU, this Tablet, until after you wrote the article of November 29, 1949?*
A. *No.*
Q. *Didn't you testify under oath that you didn't see it until after November 1949.*
A. *I don't know.*
NIZER: *. . . I don't want any doubt about it. I am going to read from your examination before trial.*

I then read the passage from the transcript in which he stated that it first came to his attention in April 1950, long after this suit was instituted.

Q. *Did you make that answer?*
A. *I believe I did. If it is this text, I will say yes.*
Q. *Isn't it a fact, Mr. Pegler, that what you were doing [yesterday] was to accommodate yourself to the law as it had been instructed to the jury, to claim that you relied on Exhibit UU so that you could get that hearsay clipping into evidence? Isn't that the plain fact?*

When he answered "No" to the rhetorical question I pummeled him some more on this subject, drawing new admissions, such as the fact that he had sent this exhibit to his lawyer after the suit was instituted.

Q. *And that was the first time you saw it?*
A. *Yes, sir.*
His covering letter was dated April 1950. We adjourned for lunch. Upon return, I asked:

Q. Before recess you told us that . . . you mailed that to Mr. Henry in April 1950. do you recall that?
A. No, I don't recall it, but it is all right; I will accept it. I don't recall the date. I remember discussing it.
Q. You don't recall from an hour and a half ago that the date was April 1950 of this letter?
A. No, I certainly do not. I went out and had lunch and I didn't keep the date in my mind, but I am willing to admit if you say it is there on the record, that I said it before lunch, I will let it stand. I do not specifically remember that date even at this time after lunch. Why should I?
Q. Well, why should you remember that you read Exhibit UU six years before you wrote this November 29, 1949, article? Why should you remember that?
HENRY: I object to the form of the question.
    COURT: Objection sustained.

At another point, I asked:

Q. You couldn't remember that since Friday?
A. No. Something five minutes ago I couldn't remember.
Q. But you do remember reading Loomis's article in the Brooklyn Eagle in 1941?

We struggled through the tunnel of confusion concerning the Tablet exhibit, but we finally came out into daylight:

Q. And on June 1950 you had no recollection that you had read either that reprint or any other copy of that article, did you?
A. On that day I did not.
Q. But four years later in 1954 you discovered that you had read it?
A. No. I didn't discover it. I remember that I had read it.
Q. What was there that refreshed your memory, four years later, that you had read something that you didn't remember you read in 1959?
A. Nothing.

I then shifted to the fact that in the very clippings he claimed to have relied upon, there were some favorable comments about Reynolds. Did he also rely on those?

Q. When you red this article did you make a selective choice of the things you were going to rely upon and the things you were not going to rely upon?
A. Yes.

I showed him a clipping from the New Yorker which his counsel had introduced and read to him from it.

Q. "After an awkward silence during which we all admired the view of the East River, and some signed photographs of President Roosevelt and General Eisenhower..."—do you recall reading that in Exhibit GG?
A. I think I do, yes, I do.
Q. And did you also take into consideration the fact that there were personally autographed photographs from General Eisenhower and President Roosevelt to Mr. Reynolds?
A. Yes, I took it into consideration for what it was worth. It seems to me I also recall something about a mutt in there, a dog.
NIZER: I move to strike out that last statement.,
COURT: Strike it out.

I showed him a highly laudatory article about Reynolds written by Damon Runyon.

Q. Do you think Damon Runyon was a reliable reporter?
A. No.
Q. Do you think that he was an honorable man with integrity?
A. No.

I found that one of the easiest ways to reveal Pegler's extremism and irresponsibility was to question him about men who were generally admired and draw his denunciation of them.

Q. Did you rely on General MacArthur with respect to his judgment on this when you read it?
A. No, I don't think he knew head to finger side what he was talking about . . . .

President Eisenhower didn't fare any better in Pegler's lexicon.

Q. Have you ever referred to Eisenhower's Socialistic Republican Party?
Q. I think so . . . . I don't believe he knows what he is talking about.

In the examination before trial I read to him from his column: "All the crooks and Communists wanted to give us Ike."
I tested him on one of his own confreres on the Journal-American:

Q. Do you recall that this Exhibit 138—this is Louis Sobol's column. Do you consider him reliable?
A. No.
Q. Do you consider that fact that he writes for {HEARST'S} New York Journal gives him any reliability in his statements?
A. No.

He turned on another Hearst publication with similar unconcern.

Q. Do you think that the appearance of Damon Runyon's article in the Hearst publication, the Mirror, gave it any sense of reliability?
A. No.

Even the founder of his co-defendant publications had not escaped his wrath when he wrote for the World-Telegram. He referred to William Randolph Hearst as "that never to be adequately dammed demagogue and historic scoundrel."

As always his accusations had built-in boomerangs and returned to strike him, for he had also written that one who works for the Hearst organization sells his principles for some dimes. Thereafter, of course, he joined that organization.

He attempted to justify his support of the notorious Gerald L. K. Smith by stating in his examination before trial: "My version was that if you are going to have one lying scoundrel [Walter Winchell] poisoning the air on one side, it is no worse than a proper redress of balance to have a similar rascal propagating the opposite view in similar appropriate time." He testified that the New York Herald Tribune was a "heavily pro-communist" paper. Its support of Eisenhower was "evasive action" and its prior support of Thomas Dewey was "again a camouflage." The New York Times, according to him, was in part pro-Communist.

In a final effort to destroy the clippings and "reliance" testimony, I resorted to a daring device. I made photostats of the very clippings which he said he had read and relied on. The photostats had no court-exhibit markings on them so Pegler did not know that these were the same as those which had already been shown to him. I was gambling that he would not remember them:

Q. I show you these clippings and ask you whether you ever read these and then relied upon them.
A. No, I don't think I did.

The day before he had said of originals of these clippings: "Yes. I read them all."

I felt that the corroding prejudice of the hearsay testimony that had entered through the inviting door of Section 338 had been overcome. By various cross-examination techniques we had demonstrated that the claimed "reliance" was mostly fictional. I hoped that the clippings and the "he told me" or "I heard" testimony would be completely discounted by the jury. This neutralizing cross-examination had been chiefly improvised. It was designed as an opening effort to clear away the obstacles, as a football player takes out the interference, so that the runner himself may be tackled. I now addressed myself to the libels.

When Pegler originally testified on examination before trial, he did not mention Reynolds and a woman exposing themselves nude together while taking a shower in his house. Four years later, he added this claim. I asked him:

Q. And you further testified . . . that the only information you claimed to have on nudism was hearsay from Broun or Mrs. Broun?
A. I had forgotten this incident apparently.

I read this testimony that he had not personally seen any nudity. He replied:

A. It was a mistake.
Q. Another mistake under oath; is that right?
A. . . . Yes, another mistake under oath.
   Had he remembered this shower incident when he originally omitted it?
A. I had it in my mind, but I didn't recall it.

This was a neat psychiatric poser for the jury. He had fixed the date of this incident as 1933. Knowing that the lady whom Reynolds had escorted to Pegler's home (Reynolds emphatically denied the whole incident otherwise) had left the United States to go to England a year earlier (1932), it was obvious that Pegler had chosen an impossible date. The best way to induce him to stick to it, was to insist that the date he gave might be wrong and that the visit might have been earlier. Perversely enough, he then insisted it could not have happened before 1933.

Witnesses who gauge their answers not by recollection but by the tonal anxiety of the cross-examiner can be lead into such traps. A telling illustration of testimony adjusted to resist the cross-examiner's apparent objective, but which destroyed the witness, occurred in this very case. That error by Pegler became the most widely published incident of the trial. It involved Pegler's self-condemnation as a Communist. But its recital will have to take its place in the alter developments on cross-examination. So, wanting Pegler to adhere to the date of 1933, I had asked again in the examination before trial:

Q. Do you exclude a possibility that . . . it was 1931 or 1932, in other words earlier than 1933?

Q. *Well, do you say that the girl who later became his wife was present on that occasion"?*
A. *I did so, but I was mistaken.*
Q. *. . . That was wrong, you say, under oath?*
A. *The more I had pressed, the surer he was.*
A. *Yes.*
Q. *Then I ask you if it could have been earlier than 1933 and you say no. 1933 was the outside date . . . is that right?*
A. *Yes.*

Pegler maintained that there were a number of witnesses in his living room who conveniently could see from their orchestra seats the balcony where the male and female nudes were disporting themselves in full view of the audience. He identified these witnesses as his brother, Jack Pegler, and his wife Mable, his nephew, Bud Pegler, and his present wife, Nancy Hutchinson. But he forgot that this incident was supposed to have occurred twenty-two years before when Bud was only eight years old and his future wife Nancy was not even present:
   Yes, it was a mistake under oath, an error under oath.

Q. *Well . . . let's sum it up briefly. You had the year wrong.*
A. *Yes.*
Q. *You had the people wrong?*
A. *Yes, that was one out of four that was wrong.*
   And of course, he had "forgotten" to mention the matter when he first testified. I pushed him further in the direction that this story of the splashing nudes was really a recent invention.
Q. *Did you ever talk to Quentin Reynolds personally at any time about this alleged nudism?*
A. *I don't remember whether I ever did.*
   Would not a host, subjected to such embarrassment in the presence of his wife and family have protested to his guest about the extraordinary liberties he had taken?
Q. *After the shower incident did you invite Reynolds over to the house again?*
A. *I think so.*

Q. Did he come?
A. Yes, he came.
Q. I ask you now . . . did your wife join in the social invitation to Mr. Reynolds to come to your house?
A. I think so.

Would a fine woman like Mrs. Pegler, if she had been subjected to sexual exhibitionism in her own living room and in the presence of her eightyear-old nephew, have invited the offender to visit her home again?

During this cross-examination Pegler once more lost his composure. At one point while I was reading from his former testimony to contradict him, I punctuated my comment with an emphatic gesture of my hand, in which I held my glasses. He stood up and shook his glasses at me in a mocking manner, while imitating my voice. Such an incident could not be recorded in the stenographer's minutes and therefore could not be referred to on appeal to a higher court. I took the precaution of making a statement for the record.

COURT: He is standing on his feet now—
NIZER: Your Honor . . . I am referring to a mannerism of the witness in attempting to shake his finger at me in answering . . . and I ask your Honor to tell the witness not to indulge in that kind of gesture.
COURT: I can't control the gesture of anybody. The jury will make it's own observation . . . As a matter of fact the manner of giving the testimony is an item which jurors may take into account in passing upon the credibility of witnesses.

Yet the very next day, when Pegler was in another squeeze of "I was in error under oath" admission, he exploded again. I was questioning him about the libel column. he invited me to show it to him:

WITNESS: . . . Inasmuch as it is here, why can't I see it?
NIZER: It is right there [indicating].
PEGLER: Get away from me.
NIZER: Please, your Honor.
COURT: Please, Mr. Pegler, I ask you to refrain from these comments.

NIZER: . . . *I would like to make a brief statement on the record . . . with your Honor's permission. On several occasions the witness has asked me to hand him something or show him something. When I go up to show it to him, with great insolence he demands that I get away from him, as he said just a moment ago. I also call to your Honor's attention, respectfully, the fact that when I have put questions he has mimicked my manner, or if I have made a gesture with my glasses he has mimicked it, and I respectfully ask the Court to instruct the witness that he is insolent, that his behavior is improper; that it isn't enough merely for the jury to determine what his character or the credibility of his testimony is from his manner, but that I am entitled to the protection of the Court, as an officer of the court, against that kind of insult and insolence.*

COURT: *Please do not tell counsel where to go to. I thought I made it clear that this Court is the only one that issues instructions in this courtroom. With respect to the question of his conduct the jury may take into account his manner of testifying . . . .*

Politeness is the mark of a gentleman even in legal combat. I have rarely seen a successful trial lawyer who did not practice courteous amenities toward friend and foe alike. Similarly I have warned witnesses always to be respectful toward opposing counsel. They must never permit provocation to unsettle them. The jury evaluates the witness's character as well as his testimony. His credibility can be affected by offensiveness in demeanor. My feelings were ambivalent. On the one hand I felt insulted and was genuinely angered by Pegler's conduct; on the other, I was delighted that he could not stand a searching cross-examination. In his frustration and anger, he could not strike at Reynolds, who was sitting quietly on the side and enjoying the spectacle. So, as is often the case, the witness let out his venom toward his tormentor, the lawyer. I knew that if the questioning could maintain the pressure upon him, his malice might be fully exposed. I did not let up.

Pegler's charge that "Reynolds and his wench were nuding along in the raw" on Broun's property required an enveloping kind of cross-examination. I approached him from different sides in order to pierce his credibility.

Q. Have you ever taken a swim in the nude?
A. Yes.
Q. Do you know whether there were any people nearby at the time you did it?
A. Yes.
Q. Did you consider yourself immoral for having taken a dip in the nude?
A. No.

Then, another approach.

Q. According to you, your sole source for the statement in exhibit 1 [the libel article] that Reynolds and his wench were nuding along in the raw on a public road was pure hearsay, wasn't it?
A. I don't know the legal definition of hearsay.
Q. Haven't you testified that you have used the word hearsay in many columns when you were attacking certain propositions and claiming that it was simply based on hearsay?
A. Well we had a long discussion of that in pretrial examination. It left me with the impression that hearsay was something heard from a third party.

I moved back to the attack.

Q. Now, under your definition you never saw Mr. Reynolds in the nude any place on the Broun estate nuding along with a wench, did you?
A. No.
Q. The only source for that statement in Exhibit 1 according to you was hearsay of Heywood Broun?
A. It was the statement of Heywood Broun to me.
Q. And of course you knew when you wrote this column of November 29, 1949, that Broun was dead, didn't you?
A. Yes. I knew Charlie Duffy was dead, too.
NIZER: I move to strike it out.
COURT: Strike it out.

Now I approached on another flank.

Q. You say you relied on Broun for this alleged information, is that right?
A. Yes.
Q. According to you Broun was a notorious liar, wasn't he?
A. Yes.
Q. And you also called him a sneak?
A. That is right.
Q. Have you ever stated that Broun was in the habit of imagining and creating stories?
A. I may have said that.
Q. And according to you Broun upon whom you relied was also devoid of ordinary veracity, wasn't he?
A. Yes.
Q. . . . And also according to you, Broun, upon whom you relied in this instance, was not only accustomed to being called a liar, but proved a liar continuously?
A. Yes.
Q. And you thought Broun was such a liar that if he had recanted any position of his views you wouldn't believe him any more than you would believe Stalin or Hitler or Browder; that is what you said, too, isn't it"?
A. Yes.
Q. You said upon direct examination that he was an abusive liar?
A. Yes.
Q. Didn't you consider that statement abusive of Reynolds?
A. No.

Now, another approach.

Q. Incidentally, you had read, had you not, before you wrote this column . . . that Mr. Reynolds was allergic to the sun?
A. I think I had.
Q. Do you recall the sun poisoning which is described [in *Only the Stars are Neutral*] before you wrote this column?

A. yes.

> I came at him from a different side.

Q. You were in court when Mrs. Connie Broun testified, weren't you?
A. Yes.
Q. You heard her state under oath that Reynolds was never involved in any nude incidents?
A. I don't remember her words, but that is the effect of what she said.
Q. Did you testify as follows on your examination before trial: "Q. Do you believe Mrs. Connie Broun to be an honest person? A. Yes, sir. Q. And trustworthy and reliable? A. Yes, sir. Q. And certainly you would believe her under oath? A. Yes, sir."
A. I so testified, erroneously.
Q. During all these years that you knew her you found her trustworthy and reliable, up to the time that your counsel told you . . . she was going to testify against you, is that right?
A. That is when I changed my belief, yes.

> Then I made a surprise sortie which resulted in one of the most starling answers of the trial. First I asked Pegler whether Mrs. Broun's honesty was such that he would believe her even if she were not under oath. He replied:

A. I think everybody is subject to doubt not under oath.
> This opened a new door.

Q. When she is supposed to have told you these things about the rowboat incident [Reynolds climbing in stark naked?] she was not under oath, was she?
A. No.
Q. But you believed her?
A. Yes.
Q. And when she was here on the witness stand and she swore that there was no nudism . . . she was under oath, wasn't she?
A. Yes.

Q. *But you disbelieved her?*
A. *Yes, I disbelieved her.*

I returned to his cynical answer, "I think everybody is subject to doubt not under oath," and shot two words at him.

Q. *Including yourself?*
A. *Certain people make inexact statements that draw on their imaginations, to be amusing.*
Q. *And when you say that certain people draw on their imagination and made inexact statements, that has been true about you, has it not?*
A. *Yes.*
Q. *You have actually written, haven't you, sir, that it is perfectly all right to create fiction about a real person, because if you do it several years after it happens nobody will know the difference anyhow.*
A. *Yes, I wrote that.*

Incredible as it seemed, Pegler thus admitted that he "drew on his imagination to make inexact statements" and that it was perfectly all right to create fiction about a real person. Could there be a crasser credo? And what could be a more damning admission in a libel action?

I attacked from a different direction.

Q. *You never mentioned this alleged rowboat incident that you claim Mrs. Connie Broun told you about at any time during the entire examination before trial, did you?*
A. *No. I wasn't asked about it.*
Q. *At page 1129 was not the following question put to you and didn't you make the following answer:*
Q. *Except for this [shower incident] . . . is there any other incident of alleged nudism that you can recall or with to charge against Mr. Reynolds?*
A. *I never saw any.*
Q. *You did not . . . in the examination, mention a single word about*

the rowboat incident until you got into this Court and told us about it, did you?
A. No.

While I am endeavoring to give a full account of Pegler's tortuous testimony, its effect upon the courtroom cannot be fully reproduced in writing. The jury was watching him intently and I never ceased watching the jury. Were there signs of sympathy for him? Did any of the jurors think he was being badgered? I could detect no such reaction. I sensed that an atmosphere hostile to the defense was building up. It has been said that an old man has an almanac in his bones. I believe a trial lawyer can tell from the very air in the courtroom when his case is prospering. The "atmosphere" of a case may not appear for weeks. Then it is there and even the court attendants sense it. One side begins to predominate. It is not some particular evidence which creates the winning barometric pressure, but rather the total effect from all that has occurred in the courtroom.

It was important not to dissipate this atmosphere and to keep the defendant in a state of confusion and contradiction. I turned to the alleged marriage proposal in the funeral car.

A. I could have been mistaken under oath.
Q. Not only could you have been, you were again, weren't you?
A. I may have been; I don't know.
Q. And you didn't change that answer, did you?
A. I don't know. Did I?
Q. No.
A. No.
Q. You knew . . . that Monsignor Fulton Sheen was in the same automobile going to the funeral of Heywood Broun, didn't you?
A. No.

After a few moments of interrogation:

A. However I do believe that Bishop Sheen was there. Let us not quibble about that. I think he was there.

Q. Yes, let's not.... You knew before you wrote the [libel] article that Bishop Sheen was in the funeral car? ...
A. I think not. I think it was after.

After a considerable pummeling:

A. I think I knew that almost at the time of the funeral [ten years before he wrote the article].

He reversed his answers concerning Woody Broun, too.

Q. ... In the case of Woody you testified a few moments ago that you did know before November 29, 1949 [that he was in the funeral car], right?

In his examination before trial, Pegler had admitted that had he known Monsignor Sheen and Woody were in the funeral car "that would cast doubt" upon his statement in the libel article that Reynolds had "proposed marriage to Connie Broun while riding to the grave." This being so, the next question was, had he checked with Monsignor Sheen or Woody to "see whether you were accurate about this matter."

A. No, sir.
Q. Did you ask Connie Broun, to be sure you had that statement right?
A. No, sir.
Q. Did you do that before you filed your answer?
A. No, Sir.

By that time he knew a suit had been instituted charging the complete falsity of his statement. Yet, without any attempt to verity the facts, he and the Hearst defendants filed answers that repeated and enlarged these incredible accusations. Recklessness is proof of malice. We were making important strides.

Part Six
Understanding Witnesses

Principle One

Analysis Of The Witness Is A Prerequisite To Formulating Strategy

A successful strategy in cross-examination depends on the advocate understanding the type of witness he is dealing with. The honest witness will require a significantly different approach than the dissembling witness, and the cocky witness or the timid witness will require still different approaches. The advocate must recognize these differences and fashion his strategy accordingly. All too often one sees the advocate who has developed a style of cross-examination that he uses against every witness he confronts and the result is never very effective.

It is essential that the advocate be able to use all the styles and strategies that are available to the cross-examiner and be able to so so spontaneously. Each trial will have different kinds of witnesses. Whether the advocate decides on one of several tactics available to him will be dictated by an understanding of the nature of the person he is cross-examining. In cases where pretrial discovery is possible recognizing a witness type may be accomplished before the witness takes the stand in the trial. In other cases the advocate is faced with making the analysis during the direct examination. Often the analysis proves incorrect during the cross-examination and the advocate must have the flexibility to change his tactics based on the new knowledge. The advocate must be flexible enough to change his strategy to accommodate what is actually taking place rather than what he expected the witness to be like.

As in all things related to the skill of cross-examination, experience plays a major role in recognizing a witness type. Nevertheless, it is possible to define some general categories and provide suggestions for approaching them.

Witnesses fall into several types. A witness may be one of these or a combination of two or more. A witness may actually be one type who is posing as another type. When this is the case the advocate may have to change his strategy in the middle of his cross-examination.

General Types Of Witnesses

*** The Honest Witness

This witness should not be the subject of cross-examination in the sense of seeking to discredit the witness or the testimony. When a witness is honest it is usually apparent to the jury and any attempt to discredit the witness will only serve to strengthen the testimony, and give it added importance because the advocate tried and failed to discredit it. This witness can be made good use of on cross-examination however. Because the witness is honest any concession that can be gained from him that aids your case can have a substantial impact. If this witness can be made to admit that there is something plausible in your case, or that one of your witnesses is credible, the advocate can turn it to his advantage in the closing argument.

*** The Essentially Honest Witness.

This witness, while truthful, has the tendency to embellish a fact or emphasize one fact over another because they honestly feel one side should prevail over the other. This tendency can usually be recognized because the way the witnesses express themselves when embellishing or emphasizing a fact seems strangely incongruous to the rest of the testimony. The trained advocate in observing this witness will often think that something the witness says is out of balance with the remainder of the testimony. When this occurs the best approach is to try and point out to the witness the incongruity by allowing him to discover it himself. If the witness is honest he will more often than not retreat from the point because his inherent sense of honesty will overcome any indignation or outrage he may have felt that led him to the distortion in the first place.

*** THE SMART ALECK WITNESS

This witness tends to be facetious and believes he is a match for the lawyer. He tries to be witty and usually has some success doing so. His barbs are most often directed at the advocate and often strike home. The advocate must guard against losing his temper with this witness, and must discipline himself to take a few blows in exchange for scoring an important one. Hubris quite often drives this witness and irony is an effective tactic. Usually given enough rope this witness will hang himself.

*** THE TIMID AND HESITANT WITNESS

This witness is often the downfall of the advocate. The problem with this witness is that it is difficult for the advocate to determine the source of the hesitancy or timidness. Often the advocate will confuse the hesitancy or timidness with the witness being unsure of his testimony and therefore easily impeached. When this confusion occurs the advocate often launches an attack that results in the witness adding details to the direct testimony that are damaging and were omitted earlier in the testimony because of the witness's natural disposition.

It is important with this witness to make a preliminary determination of whether or not the witness is unsure of his testimony or is merely timid or hesitant in giving it. If the hesitancy stems from being unsure about the validity of the testimony then this witness can be an easy subject for cross-examination. If the hesitancy is by natural disposition the advocate can find himself in the middle of a mine field with no clear map to retreat by.

*** THE IGNORANT WITNESS

This witness may not possess the faculties for being a good witness. He may not be able to remember with accuracy the events that are the subject of the trial. He may not have the communication skills to recite what he saw. He may have been persuaded by the opposition through suggestion or flattery to give beneficial testimony to their side. Whatever the reason for the ignorance, this witness must be handled with some delicacy because the sympathies of the jury will be with him. The advocate must be careful to handle the witness in such a way as not to appear to be mistreating the witness or exploiting an apparent lack of intellect. The advocate must be careful to point out the errors in the testimony without ridiculing or demeaning the witness.

*** THE DISSEMBLING WITNESS.

This is a very difficult witness to cross-examine. Usually this witness attributes a literal meaning to the words of the cross-examination questions in a self-serving way. He then hides behind this literal interpretation in order to respond to the question in a way beneficial to his side. Usually his answers suggest that he has answered the question when, in fact, further probing with more exactitude will disclose something entirely different. The key to examining this witness is to listen very carefully to the answer and continually pin the witness down in order to eliminate the vagueness of the response. An example of this situation is where a question such as "Did your supervisor authorize your action?" the witness answers "I spoke to the supervisor and after the conversation with him took the action." This answer implies the supervisor approved the action but doesn't say so. The advocate must be alert to this and press the witness to answer the question. In this example the follow-up question would be "The question, Mr. Witness, was did your supervisor specifically authorize your action? Yes or no."

*** The Witness That Lies by Omission

This witness omits crucial information from his response and can be particularly devilish. He believes that a direct lie uttered by him is wrong but that merely leaving a detail out and thereby coloring the meaning of the testimony is all right.

*** The Evasive or Reluctant Witness

This witness can be turned to the cross-examiner's advantage quite easily. Usually the jury sees reluctance or evasiveness as concealment of facts or bias which seriously affects the credibility of the witness.

*** The Artful Witness

This witness often weaves a piece of perjured testimony into an otherwise truthful fabric and leaves it to the advocate to be clever enough to find the rotten thread. One of the most difficult of the witnesses.

*** The Professional Witness and Expert Witness

These witnesses often see the trial as a game and a test of intellect rather than a search for truth. Some try and manipulate the outcome of the case to serve what they perceive as a greater good. This often happens with a law enforcement officer whose frustration with knowing the reality of a defendant's existence and his inability to catch the criminal may allow him to rationalize perjury to bring about what he believes is a just result, namely putting the defendant in jail. Of the two the professional is the most difficult to cross-examine and requires the cross-examiner to make a careful analysis of the witness before applying the principles of cross-examination.

In the fictional account of the cross-examination of Galileo that follows we see a witness with mixed emotions about how he would like to see the case turn out. He dreads the punishment that may attend his wrong answers, he wishes not to abandon his science and what he intellectually knows to be true, and he has a deep and abiding belief in the church as the interpreter of God's will. Under a skillful cross-examiner his dilemma only grows.

Included in this example is fine use of several tactics. The inquisitor manages to shift the burden of proof from his side to Galileo; he uses the suggestion of lying to put Galileo on the defensive; he gives the witness room to roam and gains details for impeachment at a later time; his use of time and change of emotional direction keeps Galileo off stride; he makes clever use of assault on the witness as a tactic; he establishes bad memory as to some items and then attacks the witness on other matters using this show of bad memory as a rationale and shows impeccable timing in putting the witness on the defensive.

It was April 12th when they led him into the Council Room of the Holy Office. Two men supported him, the servant of the Embassy and a Dominican friar. They set him down in the anteroom. He was in great pain again, clenching his teeth and groaning; with all his strength he tried to control himself. From inside the Council Chamber came many voices, but their words were inaudible.

"Are those my judges?" he asked the Dominican.

"I can tell you nothing," the monk replied.

He waited, touching with his right hand his helpless left arm to move it slowly and carefully. Then he fingered the bandage of his rupture. He swallowed hard, his heart was pounding. The door opened and a monk called his name. They helped him up and into the room, which was large and well lighted. In the middle a long table with a crucifix. And on the other side of the table three priests: Firenzuola and two others. The accused was led to the center of the long table, face to face with his judges. The

President of the Court, who sat between the other two, glanced up.

"Is the accused ill?" he asked in Latin.

"I have sharp pains in my joints and ought really to be in bed."

"Then we permit you to be seated throughout the trial. But before you sit you must take an oath. I declare the proceedings opened."

The servant and the Dominican were still at his side, and he leaned on them. The clerk had soon taken his description: Galileo Galilei, Court mathematician, seventy years old, of Florence. Then Firenzuola rose with the other two judges. He announced the oath: "I swear to speak the whole truth..."

"So help me God, the Blessed Virgin, and all the Saints of God."

The judges sat down again; a chair was brought for the prisoner. He lowered himself slowly with many groans. Firenzuola signed to the Dominican and the servant, who bowed and withdrew. "Let the accused say whether he knows the reason why he is summoned here before the Holy Office."

"I have no official knowledge of it. But I think it is to answer for my recently published work."

Is this the book?" asked the President, holding up the copy.

"It is."

"Entitled *Dialogue*, etc. To save time we shall simply refer to it as *Dialogue*, throughout this trial, and shall not use its full title. Well, then. Do you acknowledge that you have written every word in this book yourself?"

"I do."

"Very well. Now let us turn to the preliminaries. Beginning with the year of Our Lord sixteen hundred and sixteen. Did the accused visit Rome in that year?"

"Yes, I did."

"What was the reason of your visit?"

"I had heard that the doctrine of the immobility of the sun and the movement of the earth, as stated by Copernicus, had various opponents in the Church. A certain Father Caccini preached against it in Florence and against its followers. I therefore came to Rome to assure myself as to the official viewpoint of the Church. This happened, not in 1616 but in December, 1615, though I stayed in Rome till the beginning of the following April."

"Never mind that. Let us say that you were here in 1616. Did you come by your own decision?"

"I did."

"Didn't you receive any call or summons?"

"No."

"Think again. Weren't you commanded by the Holy Office at that time to appear in Rome?"

"Not at all," he answered with surprise. "I had nothing to do with the Holy Office. I'd heard that there had been some denunciation; but the man Lorini didn't denounce me, only what he called my disciples."

"Are you quite sure that you hadn't been summoned? Have you any witness that you came of your own free will?"

"I discussed the journey with my Prince, His Highness Cosimo of blessed memory. The Prime Minister of Florence, Picchena, also knew of my decision. and Guicciardini, who was the Ambassador for Florence."

"I see. And all these are dead, of course."

Galileo did not answer. He began to see the trend of these questions. They wanted to prove that he had already been tried by the Inquisition. And in that case his offense would be judged with double severity. The instinct of the hunted animal sharpened his wits again.

"So you insist," the President said, "that you hadn't received any official summons and came to Rome of your own free will?"

"Yes, I remember it clearly; there cannot be any doubt of it. And if I had received any summons there would be a record of it in the archives. But that record cannot be found, because I myself decided to take the journey."

"Very well, let's leave all that for now. Tell me, what clerical persons did you meet at that time in Rome?"

Galileo first mentioned Bellarmin. Then he named Father Grienberger, Count Querengo, Cardinal Del Monte, Orsini, the Dominican General Maraffi, Cardinal Gaetani . . . .

"Now tell us what you discussed with these men."

"Yes, Father. I'll leave Cardinal Bellarmin to the last, because with him I talked most and discussed the most important things. With Father Grienberger we talked mostly about my beloved late master, Father Clavius, but also about Copernicus. Count Querengo I had met in Padua. I discussed with him the essential meaning of the Copernican system and the possibility of influencing the Prelates of the Church in its favor. The same questions I discussed with Cardinal del Monte and Cardinal Orsini, who enjoyed the special favor of Pope Paul. With Father Maraffi, I talked of the Dominicans who had attacked me. Cardinal Gaetani, and important official of the Holy Office, I asked to request Campanella, at that time still imprisoned at Naples, to give an expert opinion, which he did. But mostly I argued with Cardinal Bellarmin. He thought . . ."

He stopped suddenly. He had been going to say that Bellermin thought the doctrine of Copernicus would threaten the whole spiritual and temporal structure of the Church. But if he told these people that, he would give them arms to use against him.

"Well, why do you hesitate?"

"Forgive me, I was only collecting my thoughts. Cardinal Bellarmin thought that the doctrine of Copernicus contradicted the literal meaning of certain passages in the Bible. We talked often and at great length about this, but I was unable to convince him."

"What, generally speaking, was the source of these conversations.?"

"The interest shown by higher clergy. At that time proceedings had been started against the works of Foscarini, Zuniga, and Copernicus. The Prelates wished to be informed of the scientific essentials of the problem; therefore they consulted me, as an expert. But only in the capacity of an expert; I had no other status. I came freely to Rome; the proceedings of the Holy Office did not touch me personally. I was interested in them only as an astronomer. It was also important for me to know what the Holy Church said about this teaching in which I believed."

"Well, and what did the Church say?"

"The controversy on this teaching that the sun stands still and the earth moves was decided by the Holy Congregation of the Index as follows: To assert such an opinion directly is in contradiction to Holy Writ, and therefore forbidden; such an opinion must only be asserted in the way Corpernicus asserted it, as a mathematical possibility."

"Was the accused informed of this? And if so, by whom?"

"I was informed. By Cardinal Bellarmin."

"Very well. Tell us exactly what His Eminence told you, whether he informed you of anything else, and what it was."

"His Eminence told me that it was permitted to maintain the doctrine of Copernicus as a hypothesis, just as Copernicus himself had done. His Eminence knew that I conceived the doctrine only as a hypothesis. This is proved by the letter which His Eminence sent to the Carmelite Provincial Foscarini, and of which I possess a duplicate."

He selected the letter from among his documents and laid it on the table.

"Dated April 12, 1615, a year before the decree of the Inquisition. I have underlined one sentence here. 'Your Reverence and Messer Galilei would do wisely, I think, if you would be content to treat this matter hypothetically, and make no positive assertions.'"

The letter caused surprise. One judge handed it to the other. Galileo had treasured it for seventeen years. The Lynxes had given him the duplicate. The President said a little sharply:

"There is no need to talk about 1615. We want to know what happened in February 1616."

"Yes, Father. In February, Cardinal Bellarmin informed me that the doctrine of Copernicus taken as reality was in contradiction to Holy Writ; therefore it was forbidden either to maintain or to defend it, but permitted to conceive of it as a *theory and write about it in that sense. To prove this I have a document given to me by His Eminence Bellarmin on May 26, 1616, in which he says that the doctrine of Copernicus must not be directly asserted nor defended. Allow me to present a copy of it."*

He drew forth this paper. For a long time he had been uncertain whether he should use or withhold it. In the end he decided that it must be shown. The points against him he could not explain away. But the judges could see that Bellarmin did not force his scientific integrity.

"When you were informed of this, were you alone with Cardinal Bellarmin?"

"No. Some Dominican Fathers were also present. But I didn't know them and haven't seen them since."

"Were you told of any interdiction at that time? Think carefully."

"I want to tell you everything I know. His Eminence sent for me one morning. He reminded me of certain matters to which he felt I must first draw the attention of His Holiness before I talked to anyone else about them."

"What's that you're saying?"

All the judges stared in surprise at Galileo, who did not answer. The President shook his head. Firenzuola's face became still icier as he spoke:

"That must be put into the records. The accused can continue."

"Thereafter the Cardinal explained to me that I must neither uphold nor defend the Copernican doctrine. I must only treat it as a theory."

"Only as a hypothesis. I see. Did anybody hear him saying that?"

"Perhaps the Dominican Fathers..."

The President suddenly changed in tone. Up to now he had been asking his questions monotonously. Now he shouted at the accused.

"Perhaps. You say—perhaps! What talk is this? Were the Dominican Fathers present or not?"

The old man winced. Something told him that now it was beginning. now he must show absolute obedience and not a trace of argument.

"I don't remember. Seventeen years are a long time."

"So perhaps they weren't present at all?" Firenzuola continued his attack.

"Perhaps they weren't."

"So perhaps nobody heard the Cardinal say it?"

"Maybe. I don't remember."

"But if your memory is so bad, perhaps you can't even remember exactly what words the Cardinal said."

"He may have said something which I can't remember any more."

"Suppose that I refresh your memory? Suppose I read you the records of that hearing? Even then would you still be as forgetful?"

"I hardly think so, Monsignor."

"Well, listen to this. I have the record there in front of me."

Friday the twenty-sixth. In the Palace inhabited by His Grace the Cardinal and specifically in his private apartments, after the aforesaid Galilei was summoned and appeared, the Cardinal adjured Galilei in the presence of Fra Michelangelo Segnitius de Lauda, Chief Inquisitor of the Holy Office, to give up his erroneous convictions; immediately afterward the aforesaid Chief Inquisitor in my presence, in the presence of these witnesses, and likewise of His Grace Cardinal Bellarmin, commanded and prescribed Galilei in the name of His Holiness the Pope and the Holy Office to renounce completely the doctrine of the immobility of the Sun and the movement of the Earth, not to maintain it in any way, not to teach it, neither in writing nor orally, nor should he defend it, since otherwise the Holy Office would start proceedings against him. Galilei accepted this injunction and swore obedience. In witness whereof Nadino Nores etcetera, Augustino Mongard etcetera.

"*What do you say now, accused?*"

Galileo temple throbbed. He remembered clearly that it had not happened in this way. Only Bellarmin spoke; the Dominicans had hovered around in silence. This record had either been drawn up falsely at that time, or someone had fabricated now a pseudo-memorandum containing the fatal expression "*not to maintain it in any way, not to teach it . . . nor defend it.*" Not even in the form of a hypothesis! His first instinct was to cry out: "*This document is a forgery!*" But he could not. To accuse the Inquisition of forgery? His next step would be to the scaffold.

"*Well, why don't you answer? Do you remember that it was thus?*"

"*I can't remember.*"

"*You can't remember. But it might have been thus?*"

Galileo was silent. He felt giddy. Firenzuola roared:

"*Well? Might it have been thus? Or do you suggest that the records lie?*"

The words came slowly, hoarsely, almost like groans from the tortured old man.

"*It might have been thus.*"

"*At last! So you received an unmistakable injunction?*"

"*I can't remember what was said.*"

"*This protocol remembers better than you do, though, and you admit that it may have happened like this. Well, have you anything more to say?*"

"*I would humbly call the attention of Your Eminences to the fact that the document which His Eminence Bellarmin gave me does not contain the expressions 'neither to teach it orally nor in writing,' 'not to maintain it in any way.'*"

"*It doesn't contain them. But the records do. Well, who was it that issued the injunction?*"

"*His Eminence Cardinal Bellarmin.*"

"*Haven't you heard with your own ears from the record that* you were informed by the Chief Inquisitor of the Holy Office, the name of His Holiness the Pope and the Inquisition?"

"I'd forgotten that. Nor do I seem to remember the presence of His Reverence the chief Inquisitor."

"But he might have been present? Well? Speak! Speak!"

The Accused had great difficulty in answering. He answered in a voice that could scarcely be heard:

"Yes . . . he might have been present."

"Good! So now we can sum up the following facts: The Holy Office ruled that this doctrine was blasphemous; the Chief Inquisitor officially forbade the accused in the name of His Holiness the Pope and the Holy Office to maintain such a theory in any way, or in any form. Now answer my question: Did you, after receiving this injunction, ever ask to be released from it to write your Dialogue?"

"No."

"And why did you not request such permission?"

"I didn't suppose that I had infringed an injunction by my book."

"You didn't suppose that you infringed an injunction which you had received? And in spite of which you write our book! Tell me, how did you get the imprimatur from the Reverend Father Chamberlain at the Vatican?"

Galileo related in detail his dealing s with Riccardi.

"Did you tell the Father Chamberlain about the interdiction of 1616?

No? Then why not?"

"Because my book does not directly teach Copernicus. I enumerate all the counter-arguments."

"And are they stronger? Well? Did you hear my question? According to the accused, which arguments are stronger in his book? Those for, or against, Copernicus?"

"Those . . . against . . . him . . ."

"And the arguments for him? Are they weak?"

Suddenly the accused broke into sobs. He was being asked to pronounce judgment against the work of fifty years.

"Yes, they are weak."

Angelus bells rang through the window. At once the judges were on their feet. The prisoner had to rise unaided, groaning and gasping for breath. The Inquisitors finished their silent prayer, and the President said:

"Before I close the proceedings, the accused must take another oath."

He had to swear to say nothing about this examination to anyone in word or writing. Two priests came to support him. He took the oath.

"So help me God and the Blessed Virgin and all God's Saints!" and now the President gave his order.

Principle Two

Money Will Bribe A Few: Hate, Bias, Interest, Anger, Or Fear Will Bribe Many

Many people who would never consider allowing money to motivate their testimony are often motivated by some other emotion equally corrupting.

A witness may consider himself to be honest in the sense of not being for sale but will quite readily accept intellectual dishonesty as a course of conduct. This witness will permit themselves to be driven, whether consciously or unconsciously, by a wide range of emotions.

Pride, anger, and hate, either for a party or a cause leads many witnesses to color their testimony unconsciously. The testimony of a person with limited language skills, or reading skills, for example, will give testimony colored by the fact he is embarrassed by his shortcoming. Often jurors will fail to disclose a serious impediment to their serving because they couldn't suffer the embarrassment of disclosing the fact in open court.

The witness may have himself suffered a wrong similar to that of a plaintiff in a case and was not adequately compensated. He now perceives what ever he witnessed in a way that is colored by this long felt resentment. Witnesses in the hands of a clever attorney or investigator may be led to conclusions about events which coincide with their susceptibility to flattery, sympathy, bias, or fear and by the time they give testimony they themselves are not sure of the truth or the fantasy.

It is the task of the advocate to be sufficiently schooled in the forces, subtle or not so subtle, that may motivate the witness to embellish, shade or give nuance to the testimony. It is not a skill that can be readily achieved by reading a single work. It requires a keen interest in psychology and human nature.

BIRKETT ASSAILS THE SLANDER OF GLADSTONE

A journalist named Wright published a book of essays in which he attacked the character of Gladstone, the former prime minister of England. Even though Gladstone was dead, his two sons sought redress against Wright for what they considered a slander on their father. Norman Birkett represented the sons and his cross-examination of Wright stands as a good example, among other things, of probing the witness to find that motive which was the driving force.

Q. *Birkett began his cross-examination of the plaintiff in this customary quiet manner.* 'Captain Wright, do you regard yourself as a serious journalist?'
A. By Captain Wright. 'I try not to be dull.'
By the Court: 'Does that mean that all serious people are bores?'.
Q. By Birkett 'Do you regard yourself as a responsible journalist?'
A. 'I speak the truth.'
Q. 'Would you answer the question? Do you regard yourself as a responsible journalist?'
A. 'Certainly. The newspapers treat me as one, and I conclude that I am one.'
Q. 'Do you agree that the charge you make is about as horrible a charge as can be made against any man?'
A. 'No, because it has been made against innumerable great men.'
Q. 'It is not a charge which reflects on all the women who honoured Gladstone with their friendship?'

A. 'No, certainly not. He might behave very well at Carlton Gardens, but not elsewhere.'
Q. 'How many times did you see him?'
A. 'I saw Mr. Gladstone once when I was a boy.'

The witness went on to explain that when Gladstone played a part he played it so well that he became the real thing. When he was religious, therefore, it could not be said that he was completely insincere.

Q. 'Does it mean that he was the rankest kind of hypocrite?'
A. 'Yes, but, being a wonderful sort of man, he was a wonderful hypocrite.'
Q. 'Does it follow from that that his professed religion was a simple mockery?'
A. 'No.'
Q. 'Why not?'
A. 'Because he was such an actor and he threw himself so entirely into the part that he became it.'
Q. 'I take it that these assertions are based upon the evidence you have given us?'
A. 'You cannot say he disbelieved what he said. When he acted, he believed it. It was not merely in the matter of sex. Take anything else. He was always doing acts of jobbery and then condemning them.'

Birkett then read a passage from Morley's Life of Gladstone, recording the ideal married life of Mr. and Mrs. Gladstone, which he put to the witness.

Q. 'Take it on the footing for a moment that it was an ideal domestic life. Is this charge of yours that Gladstone was faithless to his wife for sixty years?'
A. 'Of course, it is, men who are very found of their wives are often faithless to them.'
Q. 'Are you ready to believe that there are millions of people in this country who believe that this charge is a horrible one?'

A. *'I should not have thought so.'*
Q. *'Do you regard immorality in a man as an ordinary thing?'*
A. *'No, I regard it as culpable.'*
Q. *'But not horrible?'*
A. *'No.'*
Q. *'If such a charge were made against a man falsely, would you not regard it as a foul charge?'*
A. *'Yes, most certainly.'*
Q. *'And the man who made it would be a foul man?'* Birkett pressed his attack.
A. *'Hardly, for a person who makes such a charge is not necessarily dissolute—that is the meaning of the word foul. That was Lord Gladstone's bad English, and I can't talk bad English to please you, you know.'*
Q. *'If a person made a foul charge against you or your dead father, what would you call him in your beautiful English?'*
A. *'I should call him intemperate.'*
Q. *'Is that the best you can do?'* Were you intemperate in that charge against Mr. Gladstone?'
A. *'I think that is the worst that can be said of it. It is a slightly intemperate phrase.'*
Q. *'If a man made charges which were false, and without evidence on which to make them, what would you call him?'*
A. *'I should call him a liar.'*
Q. *'When a writer makes a serious charge against a dead man, would you regard that as a responsible task?'*
A. *'A serious writer ought to regard all he writes as a responsible task.'*
Q. *'A responsible journalist would regard it as his duty to verity the facts before making a serious charge against anybody?'*
A. *'Not if he thought he knew them. Otherwise he could never write anything.'*
Q. *'He might proceed upon information given to him without verifying a single thing if he had formed a decided opinion?'*
A. *'In this case my charge against Gladstone is primarily one of hypocrisy. If a man has formed that opinion, and the reason is there, why should he go through some process of verification? It would paralyse him.'*

Q. *'Let me take what you said about Lord Milner and the use of the phrase that "Gladstone was governed by his seraglio". Was that the best evidence you had?'*

A. *'What I heard from Lord Milner, was the most reliable and best evidence I ever had.'*

Q. *'There is no question that it is the conversation with Lord Milner that you regard as the most reliable authority you have got?'*

A. *'It clinches the opinion I had formed long before.'*

Q. *'When you made the reference to the obituary notice, you knew full well that in that notice Mr. O'Connor was referring to Gladstone's devoted wife and daughter as "the seraglio"?'*

A. *'I was quite candid, and I referred to the notice to show that Mr. T. P. O'Connor used the same words. "Seraglio" could not mean wife and daughter . . . it was impossible.'*

Q. *'I put it to you plainly that when you write your letter to the executors' solicitors you wanted them to believe that you were corroborated by Mr. T. P. O'Connor?'*

A. *'That is childish; they could see the article for themselves. I have Murray's Dictionary here, and if you turn to "seraglio", you find that it does not mean wife and daughter.'*

The Judge: *'Don't shout please!'*

Q. *'Don't you think that the word could be used in jest without a serious meaning?'*

A. *'No! "Seraglio" in the mouth of a man like Lord Milner, who was a great literary artist, even when he was a young man, could not mean wife and daughter.'*

Lord Gladstone's counsel then passed to the question of Mr. Cecil Gladstone, whom the plaintiff had once seen at Eastbourne and who, so he had been given to understand, was the statesman's illegitimate son.

Q. *'Did you make any inquiries about Cecil Gladstone?'*

A. *'I did not deliberately make inquiries. I should never write anything if I did.'*

Q. *'You believed what you heard, and acted upon it?'*

A. *'I did.'*

At this point Birkett handed the witness two documents. The first was the birth certificate of Cecil Thomas Gladstone, which showed that he had been born in 1856 at Highgate, his father being described as 'William Gladstone, general merchant'. The second was a marriage certificate, from which it appeared that Cecil Thomas Gladstone had been married in 1902, his father being described as 'William Gladstone (deceased), merchant'.

Q. 'So those two documents would appear to show the birth of Cecil Thomas Gladstone?'
A. 'Yes, to William Gladstone.'
Q. 'You want to emphasize the "William" to the jury.?'
A. 'Yes. They both have the same Christian name and surname.'
Q. 'You mean that William Ewart Gladstone was also a William?'
A. 'Yes.'
Q. 'The certificates would appear to show that Cecil Gladstone was the son of William Gladstone, a merchant?'
A. 'A general merchant, yes, a very large category of people.'
Q. 'Do you think that a Prime Minister is covered by that description?'
A. 'I don't know that it does not. You are trying to show that Cecil Gladstone cannot be the son of the Statesman, but I am not certain whether your proof is quite conclusive.'
Q. 'Is the widow alive?'
A. 'I don't know.'
Q. 'Do you know whether she lives in Eastbourne now?'
A. 'I do not.'
Q. 'You have never made an inquiry about it?'
A. 'No. I was only showing the process of thought by which I arrived at my conclusion.'
Q. 'Do these documents influence your judgment at all?'
A. 'They don't seem to be quite so very conclusive on your side, because if Gladstone had an illegitimate son this is rather the way he would deal with it. It does not seem completely to refute my view.'
Q. 'In your view these documents are forgeries reeking with false information?'
A. 'They might be.'

Q. *'Given by the Prime Minister of this country?'*
A. *'If he had an illegitimate son. But he was not Prime Minister at the time. In 1856 Gladstone was apparently excluded from politics altogether.'*
Q. *'You think the certificates are full of false information?'*
A. *'Yes, by a Cabinet Minister who did not dare to speak the truth.'*
Q. *'Do you know a publication known as Lodge's Peerage?'*
A. *'Yes, but I have not studied it to such an extent as to be aware that it gave a genealogical tree of the Gladstone family and its branches.'*
Q. *'Do you know that William Ewart Gladstone had a first cousin named William, who is fully dealt with in this work?'*
A. *'No, I do not.'*
Q. *'Did you ever made any inquiry?'*
A. *'No, and when this case arose, what did it matter? What mattered were my processes of thought.'*

The copy of Lodge's Peerage was handed up to the witness box, where Captain Wright carefully scanned the entries to which Birkett directed his attention. He agreed, when they were put to him, that the entries bore out the certificates.

Q. *'Do you still say that Cecil gladstone was the illegitimate son of William Ewart Gladstone?'*
A. *'No, not now.'*
The Judge: *'Do you now withdraw what you said?'*
Q. *'Certainly, my Lord. That book convinced me at once.'*
The Judge: *'Don't you think you should be more careful before you make suggestions?' When you saw the birth certificate, did it not occur to you that it was not unusual for an illegitimate son to be registered in the name of his father?'*
A. *'It did not.'*
Q. *'You now agree that the information on which you acted was quite unreliable?'*
A. *'Yes. But I thought I was right at the time.'*

Next, Birkett questioned the plaintiff about the French actress named Brassin who was supposed to have known Gladstone.

Q. 'To what theatrical company did this actress belong?'
A. 'I don't know.'
Q. 'Let me see—'
Q. 'What play was she in?'
A. 'I cannot tell you that.'
Q. 'She is dead now?'
A. 'I should think so.'
Q. 'You never troubled to inquire?'
A. 'No.'
Q. 'Did you ever see her act?'
A. 'Yes, when I was quite young.'
Q. 'You are quite sure she existed?'
A. 'Oh, yes, I saw a reference to her in a book quite recently.'
The Judge: 'That is not conclusive.'
Q. By Birkett. 'In what year did she come to London?'
A. 'I cannot say.'
Q. 'Apart from the fact that a man, now dead, told you as a lad of twenty that an actress twenty years before had an intrigue in London with Gladstone when he was seventy-two, you made no further inquiries?'
A. 'No. Why should I?'

Captain Wright's self-confidence was astonishing. The trouble was that he always thought he was right, and unfortunately the majority of his informants were no longer available, as Birkett reminded him.

Q. 'Lord Milner is dead, Haslam is dead, Dr. Greatorex is dead, Morrison is dead, Novikoff is dead, Laura Bell is dead, Sir Francis Burnand is dead, Labouchere is dead, and Lord Morley is dead?'
A. 'Yes, and Gladstone was born six years before the Battle of Waterloo.'
Q. 'It is difficult when people are dead to get at the exact facts?'

A. *'Nearly every character in history is dead. I don't know whether you have observed that, Mr. Birkett!'*
Q. *'Where is Charlie Thompson? Is he alive?'*
A. *'I don't know.'*

[After some skirmishing over the fact that most of Wright's sources were then dead Birkett changes topics.]

Q. *'Mrs. Langtry is alive, is she not?'*
A. *'Yes. She lives on the Riviera.'*
Q. *'Do you think some of the answers you have given in the witness box might cause grievous pain to her?'*
A. *'I am afraid so. It very much annoys me that it should be so. I am very sorry about it—more than I can say. I would have done anything I could to avoid it."*
The Judge: *'You don't like reflecting on a living person?'*
A. *'Not a woman.'*

During the weekend recess Birkett received a telegram from Lillie Langtry saying she repudiated everything Wright had said. Wright's lawyer did not object because his defense was that Wright had believed what he had written. After this Birkett could not resist having one more go at Wright on the question of the word "seraglio"

Birkett had the witness read a passage from Boswell's Life of Johnson:
We surely cannot but admire the benevolent exertions of this great and good man . . . . He has sometimes suffered me to talk jocularly of his group of females and call them his 'seraglio'.

Q. By Birkett. *'Now it is quite clear that the use of the word by Boswell was a jocular use?'*
A. *'Yes.'*
Q. *'Do you agree that a man might use the word jocularly?'*
A. *'Boswell might jest, but Milner did not . . . He was not a jester.*
Q. *'Looking back upon all that has transpired in this litigation since the publication of the passage in your book, do you now regret the publication?'*

A. 'Yes, of course I do; and if Lord Gladstone would withdraw his charge, I would say, "I am extremely sorry that I hurt your feelings!"'

Principle Three

The Memory Of The Witness Is Made Up Of What He Sees And What He Thinks

Much of the advocates dilemma in approaching the witness is developing a cross-examination that will demonstrate to the fact finder that which is fact and accurate in the testimony and that which is fantasy. Psychological studies have demonstrated time and again that memory and perception of what events actually take place as someone is observing them can differ radically between observers with the same vantage point and same relative skills.

Associations judgments and suggestions enter into every one of our observations. People witness events and then overlay the events with a great many subjective factors which serve to alter the events in the memory bank. The cross-examiner is faced with the daunting task of illuminating these subjective factors for the fact finder in such a way as to allow the fact finder to reconstruct the past events in the way the advocate wishes.

This task for the advocate is made significantly more difficult because when it comes to the veracity of a witness most jurors will accept the fact that a witness may intentionally lie about something but are disinclined to believe that the witness may simply remember something that did not happen. There have been great strides in recent years with respect to how the memory functions. The advocate should be familiar with the evidence that is emerging in this fascination field. A review of this new and exciting material is not the subject of this book. How to cross-examine a witness with respect to separating fact from fantasy is, however, and the finest example of the art of cross-examining such a witness is found in the Archer-Shee case where a young navel cadet was accused of forging a money order and the key witness was the postmistress. Her name was Miss A.C. Tucker and she testified she remembered the young navel cadet coming into the post office and cashing the stolen money order. Edward Carson was required to cast doubt on the memory.

Q. Sir E. Carson: *I may take it that so far as those books are concerned they can give us no assistance at all as regards the order of issue, or the order of casing?*
A. *By Miss Tucker. Quite right; they do not give any assistance at all.*
Q. *Nor any assistance as to whether the same person cashed one and got one issued?*
A. *No.*
Q. *For that we must rely solely on your memory?*
A. *Yes.*

[Carson has quickly gotten the witness to commit to the fact that the only question is her memory. Something she will have difficulty denying when shown she has a faulty one.]

Q. *Do all these cadets look very much alike?*
A. *Very much.*
Q. *All about the same age? Do they all wear the same uniform?*
A. *I believe so.*
Q. *And they are all smart, good-looking little boys?*
A. *Nearly all of them, I think.*
Q. *I suppose you would agree with me that if one boy came to the counter and got something, and you had to step into the office, or go into the back office, and you found another boy there when you came back asking for something, you would not notice whether he was a different boy?*
A. *No, I certainly should not unless he was bigger or something.*

Q. *I think you would agree with me that we are driven entirely to your memory as to whether in fact you were called away when the person, whoever it was, cashed the five-shilling postal order?*
A. *I am perfectly sure at the time I was not called away.*
Q. *By Mr. Justice Phillimore: You have no book:*
A. *No, there is nothing to show.*
Q. *By Sir E. Carson: When did you first know anything was wrong?*
A. *The Petty Officer, Paul, came up that night and asked me if a cadet had cashed a five-shilling postal order.*
Q. *Did he suggest that a cadet did it?*
A. *I do not think there was a suggestion in it.*
Q. *By Mr. Justice Phillimore: Did he use the word "cadet"? Instead of saying "Did a man come in?" Did he say, "Did a cadet come in?" . . . Did he use the phrase "cadet"?*
A. *I believe so.*
Q. *By Sir E. Carson: Did Petty officer Paul say that a boy had signed an order which had been cashed, and that he was not the boy to whom it was payable?*
A. *No, I do not think so; I do not remember it. He may have done so, but I do not remember it at all.*
Q. *Will you deny that he said that?*
A. *I do not remember it; I will not deny it.*
Q. *Did he say he had only given leave to two cadets?*
A. *I am not sure.*
Q. *Did Paul say to you that a boy had signed an order which had been cashed, and that it was not the boy to whom it was payable?*
A. *I do not remember what he did say.*
Q. *Did he say that such people were not wanted in the Navy?*
A. *Yes.*
Q. *By Mr. Justice Phillimore: Did you ever tell Paul or anybody that it was the cadet who cashed the order until you saw Commander Cotton (i.e. on the following morning)?*
A. *I believe so. I believe I did, but I am not quite sure.*
Q. *Sir E. Carson: Whoever brought that five-shilling postal order there, did he sign it at the post office?*

A. No, it was handed to me signed.
Q. And you therefore know nothing about who signed it?
A. No, I do not.
Q. Nor did you ask any questions?
A. No.
Q. Now can you tell me anybody else who went in and had a transaction that day?
A. No, I do not remember.
Q. Come, cannot you recollect anyone else having a conversation?
A. No, I certainly cannot.
Q. How many went in that day?
A. A good many people would have come in, but there may not have been anything—
Q. There may, or may not, but was there? Can you recollect?
A. No.
Q. Can you recollect the appearance of anyone else?
A. No.
Q. Can you recollect whether any cadet servants were in there?
A. No, I cannot.
Q. Then you cannot call to mind any other person from that day except the cadets?
A. No, I could not.
Q. Nor what they did?
A. No.
Q. Nor what they said?
A. No.
Q. Nor any other day?
A. I did not see any cadet. I only saw two cadets, as far as I know.
Q. There is no doubt that cadet servants did go in that day?
A. They may or may not; I do not know.
Q. When the inquiry was going on at the College were you not asked any single word about anybody else going in there?
A. I do not remember that I was . . . .
Q. You paid no attention to any other transaction upon that day?
A. No, because there is nothing to mark it specially.

Q. *That is the very point I put to you, that nobody from the College requested you to recall anything else as regards that day?*
A. *No, I think not. I do not remember.*
Q. *Or anything with reference to the servants, or with reference to the other orders?*
A. *No.*
Q. *And nobody attempted to test your memory as to whether you could recollect at that date—that is, the day after the incident—anything that occurred with reference to other people who got orders?*
A. *No.*

With this examination Carson had first, gotten the witness to stake her entire testimony on her ability to remember, and then systematically shown the memory to be false. He won the case.

Principle Four

Witnesses Often Take A Position And Then Remember Facts To Support The Position

Police officers and detectives arrive at the scene of a murder. They make a preliminary examination of the scene and take the statements of witnesses and decide what happened and who the guilty part is. They then set about gathering the evidence to prove their conclusion. This is a scenario that takes place all too often with trained professionals that should know better. The inevitable result of this approach is that selective perception takes over and they only see that which is inculpatory and overlook that which is exculpatory.

Trained professionals fall into this trap, as do many lay persons. All too often the witness to an event makes a decision, either on the spot or over a period of time immediately after the event of what happened. He then creates a memory of events that support the conclusion.

With this type of witness, the cross-examiner has a reasonably easy task. The technique is to point out to the witness the factors that he obviously ignored, and either make the witness accept the illogic of his conclusion or make it clear to the jury how illogical the conclusion is.

When the witness has taken a moral position and then selected the facts to support the position, the problem is somewhat more difficult but the technique, as demonstrated here by Lloyd Paul

Stryker remains the same. Stryker was cross-examining a woman from whom his client had obtained a divorce on the grounds of adultery. The issue was whether the woman should have custody of their two young daughters. The witness could not deny the adultery and was placed in the position of having to invent answers to reconcile her position.

Q. *In other words, you a married woman, supported by your husband, and with growing daughters, thought that you would see how you liked living with the Frenchman who himself had a wife in France and children?*
A. *Well, that is one way of putting it.*
Q. *You think what you have done here was perfectly moral and fine?*
A. *I think it was moral under the circumstances, yes.*
Q. *Do you feel at all that the inculcation of decent moral principles is important in the raising of a girl?*
A. *I certainly do.*
Q. *Is it one of your principles that the only way to know a man is to live with him?*
A. *For me, yes.*
Q. *And that is in your opinion a moral and ethical principle, is it; yes or no?*
A. *For me, yes.*
Q. *That, however, would not be a good principle for anyone else in the world but you?*
A. *I didn"t say that.*
Q. *I am trying to get your standard, as the person who wants to have the custody of children. Is that principle that you expressed a principle applicable, not only to yourself, but to other women as well; yes or no?*
A. *To full-grown adults, yes, but not when they are young—to full-grown adults who are mature and who know something about life and who understand people. Then I think they are free; otherwise they have no right.*
Q. *What is your definition of a full-grown adult?*

A. *I feel a full-grown adult . . . I don't think any woman is a full-grown adult until she reaches the age of over twenty-eight.*
Q. *Then it is your standard and moral principle that a woman over the age of twenty-eight is following proper ethical standards who chooses to sleep and have intercourse with a man other than her husband; is that right?*
A. *If she wishes it, it is right.*

* * *

A. *I think it is wrong for young girls to go out and have intercourse with men. I do.*
Q. *But not after twenty-eight?*
A. *You know, people vary. There are some people of twenty-eight who never grow up and there are some people who are younger that are matured.*
Q. *Then for some persons it would be all right to go out and do what you did at a age considerably younger than twenty-eight?*
A. *I wouldn't want my children to do it, no.*
Q. *At any age?*
A. *I wouldn't want them to do that until they were absolutely fully grown. As a matter of fact, I wouldn't want my daughters to do that until they reached the age that I gave you, or over.*

Principle Five

Witnesses Tend To Minimize Or Enlarge Facts

Once a witness has decided on the events and the facts that he feels support the conclusions there is tendency to minimize those facts which do not support the position and enlarge upon those which support the position. The advocate can make use of the this tendency by encouraging the witness to magnify or diminish some aspect of his account so as to arrive at an improbable, impossible, or patently absurd conclusion. One good technique is to formulate questions in the negative. For example, "You don't really mean you could see the accident?"? This suggests the disbelief or incredulity and will encourage the witness to exaggerate his response. If encouraged to do it enough, the witness will ultimately lead to an impeachable position or lose credibility in the eyes of the jury.

Significance Of The Signed Papers: Cross-Examination In The Baccarat Case

In the so called Baccarat case Lord Russell used this technique along with others to attack the credibility of Sir William Gordon-Cumming. Gordon-Cumming had been a guest at a country manor and was accused by several other guests of cheating at cards. The resolution of the matter was that he signed a pledge never to play cards again in exchange for the matter being kept quiet. Later the incident was disclosed by some of the guests and Gordon-Cumming sued for slander. The defense was that he had cheated and in effect admitted doing so by signing the pledge.

There are several interesting items to watch for in the cross-examination by Russell. He does a wonderful job of establishing that both a Lord and a General had urged him to sign and that five people had accused him of cheating without really confronting the witness with the issue. Russell is thus able to create great tension which will result in the denouement later on. He uses equal skill in establishing repetition of meetings leading up to the signing thus showing indirectly the time for deliberation that Gordon-Cumming had.

About a third of the way into the examination he asks "why did you as an innocent man sign that paper?" I think the question was a bad one. The issue is how he might have handled the situation without resorting to a "why" question?

Q. *By Sir Charles Russell: After the singing of the document, did you say you proposed to go to the races the next day, and did General Owen Williams say to you, "Certainly you cannot; you must leave the first thing in the morning"?*

A. *By Gordon-Cumming: He suggested that I should leave the house as soon as possible, and I did leave first thing.*

Q. *Now I put one question which I ask you anxiously to consider. Do you suggest, as has been suggested by learned counsel today, that Lord Coventry and General Owen Williams advised you to sign that paper, and asked you to leave the house believing you to be an innocent man? Did they say they believed you?*

A. *I am totally unable to say.*

Q. *And as you stand there now, are you unable to say?*

A. *I am perfectly unable to say. I have had no conversation with either of them since, except on one occasion, and they never expressed any opinion as to my innocence or guilt.*

Q. *So you are quite unable to say whether, in advising you, they were advising you as an old friend whom they believed to be innocent?*

A. *I had a communication from them the gist of which was, to the best of my recollection, that there was no possibility of believing other than my guilt from the fact of there being five to one against me. I received that letter two days after leaving Tranby Croft.*

Q. Then the suggestion made on your behalf that these gentlemen could not possible be guilty was not yours?

A. I do not understand.

Q. Your first interview in which anything was communicated to you as to this serious charge was before dinner on the evening of Wednesday, the 11th?

A. On Wednesday.

Q. It was on this occasion you expressed a desire to have an interview with the Price?

A. It was.

Q. That interview you had in the presence of himself, Lord Coventry, and General Owen Williams, after dinner. At what hour?

A. I should say about half-past ten or eleven.

Q. Then you retired, and the last and final interview was when Lord Coventry and General Owen Williams gave you the paper which you signed?

A. Yes.

Q. All that would be about half-past eleven?

A. Yes.

Q. Did you think that in signing that paper you were doing a dishonouring act or not?

A. I felt I was doing a foolish one.

Q. Did you think it was a dishonouring act?

A. At the time I had no thought, but I have thought since that it was.

Q. Since the case of Lord de Ros, a good many years ago now, have you ever heard of a gentleman and a man of honour signing a paper in which he pledges himself not to play cards as a consideration for silence on an accusation of cheating?

A. No I have not.

Q. You read the paper?

A. Yes.

Q. More than once?

A. No.

Q. *You discussed it?*
A. Yes, I discussed it.
Q. *You pointed out to Lord Coventry and General Williams that it was virtually an admission of guilt?*
A. I said it was virtually an admission, and they agreed that it would be.
Q. *There was no name appended to it at the time it was put before you?*
A. No.
Q. *The other signatures to it were not there?*
A. No.
Q. *Sir William Gordon-Cumming, why did you, as an innocent man, sign that paper?*
A. Because it was put to me by these two friends of mine, on whom I placed implicit reliance, that I had no chance of clearing myself; that however often I reiterated my innocence, I had no chance of proving it against five witnesses. I was told a horrible scandal would follow, in which my name, my regiment and everything would suffer, unless I signed that paper.
Q. *You were told that the scandal would be all over the place?*
A. Yes.
Q. *The horrible scandal would be that you, an officer in the Guards, had been accused by five witnesses of cheating at cards?*
A. Probably the word scandal was used by General Williams—a scandal to which the name of the Prince of Wales and of other persons would be attached.
Q. *How?*
A. It would not be desirable that the name of the Prince of Wales should be associated with a game of baccarat with an officer who had been accused of cheating by his hosts, or by the people of the house in which the Prince of Wales was staying.
Q. *I think you told me that it was an innocent game?*
A. It was a scandal for a man in my position.
Q. *And to avoid that scandal you signed that paper?*
A. Yes, to avoid the scandal I signed that paper, and I have never ceased to regret that I did so.
Q. *Now I ask you again, do you not know that, rightly or wrongly,*

these friends of yours were advising you as they thought best in your interests as a guilty man?

A. I was not aware on what grounds they gave their advice.

Q. Do you think they were honestly advising you?

A. I think that nothing could have been worse than the advice they gave me, and nothing could have been more unwise than my following it.

Q. I was not asking you whether the advice was good or bad. Did you not know—did you not believe that it was the advice of men who were advising you in your interest and in the belief that you were guilty?

A. No; I do not think they believed it at the time.

Q. You did within twenty-four hours?

A. That is a different thing, I had signed the paper in twenty-four hours.

Q. Were you not warned by General Williams that you were not to meet the Prince of Wales?

A. No; it was by letter—not warned, but requested.

Q. Before I read this letter, am I right in saying that you signed the promise on the advice of Lord Coventry and General Williams on their advice alone?

A. Yes.

Q. No one else advised you?

A. No.

Q. You do not suggest that the Prince of Wales did?

A. I did not see the Prince after the one interview.

Q. I now read two letters—the first from you to General Williams:

"Thursday September 11th.—Dear Owen,—I hope you will take an opportunity of telling the Prince of Wales how entirely I was guided in my action yesterday by his advice and yours and Coventry's." Why did you speak of the advice of His Royal Highness?

A. Because I believed that the document was submitted to the Prince of Wales before being sent to me.

Q. "While utterly and entirely denying the truth of allegations brought against me, I thoroughly see now, for my own sake as well as that of others, it is essential to avoid an open row and the scandal arising *therefrom. It is difficult for anyone, however innocent he may know himself to be, and however unstained his character may be, to come well out of an accusation brought by numbers against one alone, and I shrink, therefore, from doing as perhaps I ought, and court a full and thorough investigation. What a cruel blow it is to me to know that any men, even if almost strangers to me, should tell me that I have deliberately cheated them at cards, or to feel that men like His Royal Highness and Coventry, against whom never a word has been said, and who have been called upon to advise me on such a charge, possibly believe, from the fact of my signing that paper, that I am in any way unfitted to associate with you and men like you. Of course my word is passed as regards cards; but it was quite unnecessary, for I should never, under any circumstance, have touched them again. As regards the money I won on the week, I feel it impossible for me to take it. I believe it was mainly won from the Prince, but Sassoon need know nothing as to whether I received it or not. His Royal Highness will doubtless insist upon paying it, but I should wish to be disposed of in any way in which he may think fit either to a hospital or for a charity. I intend to fulfill my engagements in Scotland and elsewhere as if this had not occurred though with a very sore heart. This I owe to myself. Again thanking you and Coventry, I am yours, sincerely, W. GORDON-CUMMING."*

You wrote that letter just read and left it to be given to General Owen Williams on the morning of your departure?
A. I did.
Q. This is the answer: *"Tranby Croft. September 11th, 1890: Dear Cumming,—I have shown the letter I received from you this morning to the Prince of Wales and Lord Coventry.—(Signed) O.W."* Then followed this memorandum, signed by the Prince, by Lord Coventry and by General Williams: *"We have no desire to be unnecessarily hard upon you, but you must clearly understand that in the face of the overwhelming evidence against you it is useless to attempt to deny the accusation. So long as you comply with the conditions you have signed, silence will be strictly maintained as far as we are concerned. In this we have dealt with you as old friends and in your interest, but we must plainly tell you that we consider we have*

acted quite as leniently as we possibly could under the painful circumstances of the case. As a matter of course, you will receive a cheque from Mr. Sassoon for the money owing you, in which proceeding we all agree, and it will then rest with you to dispose of it as you think fit." Have you disposed of it?

A. The money is in my possession.

Q. As a fact the cheque has been paid into the bank?

A. But the money is in my possession.

(After adjournment.)

Q. I put to you (yesterday) Sir William Gordon-Cumming, the letter of September 11th—the day on which you left Tranby Croft—signed by the Prince of Wales, Lord Coventry and General Williams. Did you get another note from General Williams, and is this your letter acknowledging it?

A. It is in my handwriting.

Q. The letter is as follows:—"Harriet Street, Lowndes Square—Dear Owen,—Your letter received to-day. I had hoped that you, at all events, would have seen your way to give me the benefit of any doubt in the matter, but it seems this is not be. This secret is in the hands of far too many to remain one long, and I have little before me to make life worth having. I suppose that in the meantime I must try and live as of old.—Yours always the same, WILLIAM GORDON-CUMMINGS."

Now the letter that you had already received, Sir William Gordon-Cumming, and which I read yesterday, stated two things—that it was useless for you to attempt to deny the accusation and that they had dealt with you as old friends and in your own interest, concluding, "We must plainly tell you that we have acted as leniently as we could." Had you any doubt after the receipt of those communications that they believed you guilty, or that they were acting, so far as they could, to shield you?

A. I did believe that Lord Coventry and General Williams thought me guilty.

Q. And the prince?

A. *And the Prince.*
Q. *And that they had acted as they did, wisely or unwisely, in your interest, and to shield you as far as they could?*
A. *And in their own.*
Q. *In your interest and in their own?*
A. *Yes.*
Q. *What interest had General Williams of his own to shield?*
A. *Neither General Williams nor Lord Coventry, as I said yesterday, wished their names to be connected with any scandal, such as would have ensued in connection with this case.*
Q. *But as far as General Williams was concerned, what would be the scandal except his being, or having been the friend of a man accused of cheating at cards?*
A. *I do not say that General Williams was not actuated by friendly motives towards me.*
Q. *What interest had Lord Coventry to shield?*
A. *I really cannot say.*
Q. *Upon the occasion of the interview with the Prince of Wales, was one word said as to your signing the memorandum?*
A. *The memorandum had not come up then. No question of that kind had been entered into.*
Q. *Kindly answer "Yes" or "No". Is your answer "No"?*
A. *Repeat your question please.*
Q. *At the interview with the Prince of Wales, at which Lord Coventry and General Williams were present, was one word suggested as to your singing any undertaking?*
A. *No.*
Q. *The interest of the Prince of Wales, as I understood you to suggest yesterday, was in not liking to have his name mixed up with a scandal of that kind?*
A. *Precisely.*
Q. *The scandal being that a man of position, as my learned friend has properly said, and a distinguished person, had been accused by five witnesses of cheating?*
A. *Precisely.*
Q. *The scandal being that a man of position, as my learned friend*

has properly said, and a distinguished person, had been accused by five witnesses of cheating?—

A. Certainly.

Q. Now, at all events, we have got to a time when, if you had ever thought it, you could no longer entertain the respect of these men whose friendship you had enjoyed. You had reached that point?

A. I beg your pardon.

Q. When you received these letters, you had reached the point of knowing that you no longer retained the respect, as an honourable man, of these men whose friendship and esteem you valued?

A. If I had been guilty of the offence, yes.

Q. Of course you know—though it was perhaps a comparatively unimportant matter—that you were regarded by these five persons as having been guilty of dishonourable conduct?

A. Apparently, as they accused me of being so.

Q. Why did you not, even then, take steps to assert your innocence and to vindicate yourself by bringing yourself face to face with your accusers?

A. Because I considered that, having taken that very fatal and foolish step of signing the document, it would be impossible to succeed, as many people would think me guilty, whether I was or not.

Q. Does that mean that you regarded signing the document, and believed that it would be regarded by others, as an admission of your guilt?

A. No.

Q. Let me remind you, Sir William Gordon-Cumming, that you have said that the document was put before you and that you then said—in your own language—that it would be regarded as a virtual admission of your guilt, and that you were told by Lord Coventry . . .

A. Excuse me, Sir Charles; I think I said that it would be considered by some as an admission of guilt.

Q. I do not think you said "considered by some". However, you said that it was tantamount to an admission of guilt, and that you were told by Lord Coventry and by General Williams that it was so?

A. They assented to my statement that it was so.

Q. Then what has altered the position of things from 18th September, except the fact that somehow or other this very melancholy story has become public property?

A. After signing the paper and committing the act of gross folly, as I characterized it yesterday, and after a reflection of four-and-twenty hours, I saw the mistake I had made. But on the assurance by letter from General Williams that by no possibility could it come out, except to the persons immediately concerned, I lived for some time in a fool's paradise, hoping and believing that that would be the case.

Q. Then, although in the eyes of these once-valued and esteemed friends, you were a dishonoured man, you were content to remain so if secrecy were continued?

A. It does not follow that because these five people believed me guilty I was guilty. I knew perfectly well that I was not.

Q. Pray attend to my question?

A. I have answered your question.

Q. I assure you have not, Sir William Gordon-Cumming. Although you knew—rightly or wrongly—that in the eyes of these gentlemen, whose respect and esteem you valued, you were a dishonoured man you were content to you so?

A. I was not content to remain so.

Q. Attend, attend! You were content to remain so, so long as secrecy was maintained?

A. I had no alternative.

Q. Then I ask you again the question to which I have not yet got an answer. What has since taken place which has altered the position as it was when those letters arrived in September, except the fact that this story has become public property?

A. The mere fact of its becoming public property was quite sufficient for me.

Q. Was that the only reason?—Are you asking me my reasons for taking these proceedings?

Q. I am asking the question which I have put to you. I will now repeat it for the third or fourth time, and I hope you will kindly attend. You have told me that when you received those letters in September, you then became aware of the fact that you were regarded-rightly or wrongly—by these esteemed friends as a dishonoured man, and you *have said in effect that you were content not to take proceedings provided the secrecy was maintained . . .*

Sir Edward Clarke, Attorney for Gordon-Cumming: *Those are not the words of the witness.*

Sir Charles Russell: *In effect.*

Sir Edward Clarke: *When my learned friend says "in effect." I know what he means.*

Sir Charles Russell continued: *My question is, what is the altered condition of things except the breach of the secrecy and the story becoming public property?*

A. *The thing had become such public property that I thought the matter would be at once taken up by my Clubs, by my regiment, and by my friends.*

Q. *That is your answer, and that is the answer I expected you to have given long ago. Did you get a letter from General Williams on September 13th?*

A. *I cannot recollect how many letters I got from General Williams. I think I did get another letter.*

Q. *And did you answer his letter on 15th September?*

A. *If I received a letter from General Williams I probably answered it. The letter produced is my letter.*

Q. *I will take it from you not producing General Williams' letter that you have not got it?*

A. *I can recollect what was in it now that I have seen my answer to it. I have not got the letter, but I recollect it very well.*

Q. *What did you do with it?*

A. *Burned it.*

Q. *You are entitled to say what was in the letter, if you like?*

A. *It was a very friendly letter, expressing extreme regret at what had occurred, saying that he was glad he was there to suppress a horrible scandal, and saying that the matter would remain a secret, and that not another word would be said about it. That is as nearly as I can recollect.*

Q. *And this is your answer, dated September 15th, Monday: "My dear Owen,—Thanks for your letter of the 13th. You can well understand how deeply I feel the great kindness and friendship you have shown* me in the matter. I have taken your advice about . . .—Yours ever very truly, William Gordon-Cumming.

A. Will you kindly say what is the last word in that letter, Sir Charles?
Q. "Thanks for your letter of 13th. You can well understand how deeply I feel the great kindness and friendship you have shown me in the matter. I have taken your advice about Mar.
A. Precisely.
Q. Was that advice that you were not to meet the Prince of Wales at Mar?
A. It was.
Q. I think you told us yesterday that you have not met the Prince since?
A. I have not.
Q. You know also that, in order that there should be as far as possible no suspicion raised, Lord Coventry and General Owen Williams have, if they have met you casually at the clubs, recognized you in the ordinary way?
A. Certainly.
Q. But you have never met either of them in Society since?
A. In the clubs and on the race-course. Nowhere else, except once at General Williams's house.
Q. That is this very year?
A. Yes.
Q. I am coming to that. At the interview with Lord Coventry and the Prince of Wales and General Owen Williams you disclaimed the intention of taking the money which you had won on September 8th and 9th?
A. No; I never suggested it.
Q. Not at the interview?
A. I did not.
Q. Here is the cheque for the money you received. I think it was paid into your bankers?
A. Precisely.
Q. Into your general account?
A. Into my general account.
Q. Then when you said you had this 228 [pounds] still, you meant that you had the balance at our banker's still?
A. Yes.

Q. *You paid it into the bank and then drew your cheques in the ordinary way?*
A. *Precisely.*
Q. *I do not think you even acknowledged the receipt of the cheque?*
A. *Receiving it and paying it in would constitute a receipt.*
Q. *True, in law; I quite agree. The end of September passes, the whole of October, the whole of November, and up to the month of December, you had done nothing?*
A. *In what way?*
Q. *In any way towards your vindication, or your reinstatement in the good opinion of your friends?*
A. *I had done nothing of any sort or kind.*
Q. *And did you, then, at the end of December—on December 27th— receive an anonymous telegram from Paris?*
A. *A letter.*
Q. *Have you got it?*
A. *Yes.*
Q. *It is in French, but I will read it, translating as I go. It is dated "Paris" and it says—"They are beginning to talk much here of what passed at Newmarket this summer and of your sad adventure. If you come to Paris or to Monte Carlo, be very reserved and do not touch a card. They have talked too much about it" and the signature is "Someone who pities you"?*
A. *Precisely.*
Q. *I may just ask you, in passing, is the place from which this was written 4 Place de la Concorde:*
A. *Yes.*
Q. *Is that a club that you belong to?*
A. *Yes, it is.*
Q. *Upon receiving this anonymous letter, did you at once send it to General Owen Williams?*
A. *I did.*

The jury found for the defendants.

Principle Six

The Indirect Attack Is Best Against The Strong Or Vigorous Witness

Often the advocate is confronted with a witness who is comfortable in the witness chair and exhibits a strong and vigorous ability to parry even the most clever thrusts. He is usually confidant and erudite as well as quick witted. The indirect approach is best against this witness.

In using an indirect attack against a witness the advocate must lead the witness to the belief that the witness is the more clever of the two. The witness must be allowed to score points at the advocate's expense, and led into admissions that on their face are unimportant. This form of strategy is best exemplified in the use of irony-a technique when used by a master is brilliant cross-examination. A technique when used by a master against this sort of witness can lead to brilliant cross-examination. It is the trope of irony. The best description of this method I have found appears in the Book of J by Harold Bloom.

"Irony" goes back to the Greek word eiron, "dissembler" ", and our dictionaries still follow Greek tradition by defining irony first as Socratic: "a feigned ignorance and humility designed to expose the inadequate assumptions of others, by way of skilled dialectical questioning."

It takes a simple form with the lawyer who assumes the "just a country boy" role feigning ignorance or sophistication with a witness until the witness works his way into a mistake. It means taking several hard blows and suffering humiliation but can be very effective in the hands of the right person. Edward Carson was a master of it and it has never been demonstrated more effectively than in his cross-examination of Oscar Wilde.

Wilde had been accused of being a sodomite by the Marquis of Queensberry as a result of Wild's involvement with Queensberry's son. Wilde brought suit against Queensberry and the cross-examination that follows was conducted on behalf of Queensberry by Carson. As a result of the disclosures at this trial criminal charges were brought against Wilde and after being convicted was sentenced to jail.

This excerpt takes place well into the first trial. Carson had been the butt of a good many jokes by Wilde and he finally turns his attention to Wilde's friendship with Alfred Taylor who Queensberry alleged had served as a procurer of young men for Wilde.

Q. BY CARSON: *'Did he use to do his own cooking?'*
A. BY WILDE: *'I don't know. I don't think he did anything wrong.'*
Q. *'I have not suggested that he did,'* said Carson.
A. *'Well, cooking is an art.'*
Q. *'Another art? Did he always open the door to you?'*
A. *'No. Sometimes he did; sometimes his friends did.'*
Q. *'Did his rooms strike you as being peculiar?'*
A. *'No, except that he displayed more taste than usual.'*
Q. *'There was rather elaborate furniture in the rooms, was there not?'*
A. *'The rooms were furnished in good taste.'*
Q. *'Is it true that he never admitted daylight into them?'*
A. *'Really?' I don't know what you mean.'*
Q. *'Well, was there always candle or gaslight there?'*
A. *'No.'*
Q. *'Did you ever see the curtains drawn back in the sitting-room?'*
A. *'When I went there to see Taylor, it was generally in the winter about five o'clock-tea-time-but I am under the impression of having seen him earlier in the day when it was daylight.'*
Q. *'Are your prepared to say that you ever saw the curtains otherwise than drawn across?'*

A. 'Yes, I think so.'
Q. 'It would not be true, then to say that he always had a double lot to curtains drawn across the windows, and the room, day or night, artificially lighted?'
A. 'I don't think so.'
Q. 'Can you declare specifically that any daylight was ever admitted into the room?'
A. 'Well, I can't say as to that.'
Q. 'Were the rooms strongly perfumed?'
A. 'Yes, I have known him to burn perfumes. But I would not say the rooms were always perfumed. I am in the habit of burning perfumes in my own rooms.'

[There some questions by Carson regarding the fact that Taylor sometimes dressed as a woman and whether Wilde knew about it.]

A. 'He is a man of great taste and intelligence, and I know he was brought up at a good English school.'
Q. 'Is he a literary man?'
A. 'I have never seen any created work of his.'
Q. 'Did you ever discuss literature with him?'
A. 'He used to listen. He was a very artistic, pleasant fellow.'
Q. 'Was he an artist?'
A. 'Not in the sense of creating anything. He was extremely intellectual and clever, and I liked him very much.'
Q. 'Did you get him to arrange dinners at which you could meet young men?'
A. 'No.'
Q. 'Now, did you not know that Taylor was notorious for introducing young men to older men?'
A. 'I never heard that in my life.'
Q. 'Now, did you know that Taylor was being watched by the police?'
A. 'No, I never heard that.'
Q. 'Has he introduced young men to you?'
A. 'Yes.'

Q. *'How many young men has he introduced to you?'*
A. *'Do you mean of those mentioned in this case?'* Wilde queried.
Q. *'No,'* said Carson; *'young men with whom you afterwards became intimate.'*
A. *'About five.'*
Q. *'They were young men whom you would call by their Christian names?'*
A. *'Yes. I always call by their Christian names people whom I like. People I dislike I call something else.'*
Q. *'Were these young men all about twenty?'*
A. *'Yes; twenty or twenty-two. I like the society of young men.'*
Q. *'What was their occupation?'*
A. *'I do not know if these particular young men had occupations.'*
Q. *'Have you given money to them?'*
A. *'Yes. I think to all five—money or presents.'*
Q. *'Did they give you anything?'*
A. *'Me? Me? Oh, no.'*
Q. *'Among these five did Taylor introduce you to Charles Parker?'*
A. *'Yes'*
Q. *'Did you become friendly with him?'*
A. *'Yes.'*
Q. *'Did you know that Parker was a gentleman's servant out of employment?'*
A. *'No.'*
Q. *'But if he were, you would still have become friendly with him?'*
A. *'Yes. I would become friendly with any human being I liked.'*
Q. *'How old was he?'*
A. *'Really, I do not keep a census.'*
Q. *'Never mind about a census, Tell me how old he was?'*
A. *'I should say he was about twenty. He was young, and that was one of his attractions.'*
Q. *'Was he a literary character?'*
A. *'Oh, no!'*
Q. *'Was he intellectual?'*
A. *'Culture was not his strong point. He was not an artist.'*
Q. *'Was he an educated man?'*

A. 'Education depends on what one's standard is.'
Q. 'Where is he now?'
A. 'I haven't the slightest idea. I have lost sight of him.'
Q. 'How much money did you give Parker?'
A. 'During the time I have known him I should think about £4 or £5.'
Q. 'Why? For what reason?'
A. "Because he was poor, and I liked him. What better reason could I have.'
Q. 'Did you ask what his previous occupation was?'
A. 'I never inquire about people's pasts.'
Q. 'Nor their future?'
A. 'Oh, that is not problematical.'
Q. 'Where did you first meet him?'
A. 'At Kettner's. I was introduced by Mr. Taylor.'
Q. 'Did you become friendly with Parker's brother as well?'
A. 'Yes. They were my guests, and as such I became friendly with both of them.'
Q. 'On the very first occasion that you saw them?'
A. 'Yes. It was Taylor's birthday, and I asked him to dinner, telling him to bring any of his friends.'
Q. 'Did you know that one, Parker, was a gentleman's valet, and the other a groom?'
A. 'I did not know it, but if I had I should have not cared. I didn't care twopence what they were. I liked them. I have a passion to civilize the community.'
Q. 'What enjoyment was it to you to entertain grooms and coachmen?'
A. 'The pleasure to me was being with those who are young, bright, happy, careless, and free. I do not like the sensible and I do not like the old.'
Q. Taylor accepted your invitation by bringing a valet and a groom to dine with you?'
A. 'That is your account, not mine.'
Q. 'Were they persons of that class?'
A. 'I am surprised at your description of them. They did not seem to have the manners of that class. They seemed to me pleasant and

nice. They spoke of a father at Datchet as a person of wealth—well, not of wealth, but of some fortune. Charlie Parker told me that he was desirous to go on the stage.'
Q. 'Did you call him "Charlie"?'
A. 'Yes.'
Q. 'What did you have for dinner?'
A. 'Well, really I have forgotten the menu.'
Q. 'Was it a good dinner?'
A. 'Kettner's is not so gorgeous as some restaurants, but is was Kettner at his best.'
Q. 'With the best of Kettner's wines?'
A. 'Yes, certainly.'
Q. 'All for the valet and the groom?'
A. 'No, for my friends-for Mr. Taylor, whose birthday it was.'
Q. 'You did the honours to the valet and the groom?'
A. 'I entertained Taylor and his two guests.'
Q. 'In a private room, of course?'
'A. Yes, certainly.'
Q. 'Did you give them an intellectual treat?'
A. 'They seemed deeply impressed.'
Q. 'During the dinner did you become more intimate with Charles than the other?'
A. 'I liked him better.'
Q. 'Did Charles Parker call you "Oscar"?'
A. 'Yes, I like to be called "Oscar" or "Mr. Wilde".'
Q. 'You had wine?'
A. 'Of course.'
Q. 'Was there plenty of champagne?'
A. 'Well, I did not press wine upon them.'
Q. 'You did not stint them?'
A. 'What gentleman would stint his guests?'
Q. What gentleman would stint the valet and the groom?
A. "Really, Mr. Carson!'

[Carson through a series of questions managed to make Wilde admit young men had visited him at the Savoy Hotel.]

Q. *'Did any of these men who visited you at the Savoy have whiskies and sodas and iced champagne?'*
A. *'I can't say what they had.'*
Q. *'Did you drink champagne yourself?'*
A. *'Yes. Iced champagne in a favourite drink of mine-strongly against my doctor's order.'*
Q. *'Never mind your doctor's orders, sir!'*
A. *'I never do.'*
Q. *'Did improprieties take place there?'*
A. *'None whatever.'*
Q. *'When he came to tea, what was he doing all the time?'*
A. *'What was he doing? why, having his tea, smoking cigarettes, and, I hope, enjoying himself.'*
Q. *'What was there in common between this young man and yourself: What attraction had he for you?'*
A. *'I delight in the society of people much younger than myself. I like those who may be called idle and careless. I recognize no social distinctions at all of any kind; and to me youth, the mere fact of youth, is so wonderful that I would sooner talk to a young man for half-an-hour than be-well cross-examined in Court!'*
Q. *'Do I understand that even a young boy you might pick up in the street would be a pleasing companion?'*
A. *'I would talk to a street arab, with pleasure.'*
Q. *'You would talk to a street arab?'*
A. *'Yes with pleasure, if he would talk to me.'*
Q. *'And take him to your rooms?'*
A. *'Be it so.'*
Q. *'Did you write him any beautiful letters?'*
A. *'I don't think I have ever written any letters to him.'*
Q. *'Have you any letters of his?'*
A. *'Only one.'*

Carson read the text of the following letter, which was alleged to have been written by Parker to the witness.

50 Park Walk Chelsea

Dear Oscar,

Am I to have the pleasure of dining with you this evening? If so, please reply by messenger or wire to the above address. I trust you can, and we can spend a pleasant evening.

Yours faithfully,
CHARLIE PARKER

Q. 'In March or April of last year did you go one night to visit Parker at 50 Park Walk, about half past twelve at night?'
A. 'No.'
Q. 'Is Park Walk about ten minutes from Tite Street?'
A. 'I don't know, I never walk.'
Q. 'I suppose, when you pay visits, you always take a cab?'
A. 'Always.'
Q. 'And, if you visited, you would leave the cab outside?'
A. 'If it were a good cab!'
Q. 'When did you see Charles Parker last?'
A. 'I don't think I have seen him since February of last year.'
Q. 'Did you ever hear what became of him?'
A. 'I heard the he had gone into the army-enlisted as a private.'
Q. 'You saw in the papers of the arrest of Taylor and Parker?'
A. 'Yes, I read that they were arrested.'
Q. 'You know that they were charged with felonious practices?'
A. 'I knew nothing of the charges.'
Q. 'That when they were arrested they were in the company of several men in women's clothing?'
A. 'I read in the newspapers that two men in women's clothes, music-hall artists, drove up to the house and were arrested outside.'
Q. 'Did you not think it a somewhat serious thing that Mr. Taylor, your great friend, and Charles Parker, another great friend, should have been arrested in a police raid?'
A. 'I was very much distressed at the time, and wrote to Mr. Taylor, but the magistrates took a different view of the case because they

dismissed the charge. It made no difference to my friendship for him.'
Q. 'Was the same Taylor lunching with you on Tuesday last?'
A. 'Not lunching. He came to my house to see me.'

[Carson now began to go through a virtual catalogue of young men that Wilde had developed a social relationship with. He came then to the name Fred Atkins and began to question Wilde about him. It turned out he and Wilde had gone to Paris together.]

Q. 'You dined with him?'
A. 'Yes.'
Q. 'Gave him an excellent dinner?'
A. 'I never have anything else. I do everything excellently.'
Q. 'Did you give him plenty of wine at dinner?'
A. 'As I have said before, anyone who dines at my table is not stinted in wine. If you mean, did I ply him with wine, then I say "No!" It's monstrous and I won't have it!'
Q. 'I have not suggested it.'
A. 'But you have suggested it before.'
Q. 'After dinner, did you give him a sovereign to go to the Moulin Rouge?'
A. 'Yes, I went that night, I think, to a French theatre, and when I got back to the hotel, Atkins had gone to bed.'

[Carson next turned his attention to Ernest Scharfe]

Q. 'Did you know he was a valet and is a valet still?'
A. 'No. I have never met him in Society, though he has been in my society, which is more important!'
Q. 'Why did you ask him to dinner?'
A. 'Because I am so good natured! It is a good action to ask to dinner those beneath on in social station.'

[Next the name of Sidney Mavor who spent the night as Wilde's guest at the Ablemarle Hotel.]

Q. 'And did you find pleasure in his society that night?'

A. *'Yes, in the evening and at breakfast. It amused and pleased him that I should ask him to be my guest at a very nice, charming hotel!'*

A picture of Mavor was shown to Wilde.

A. *'Ah! taken at a period earlier than that at which I knew him!'*

Next he was shown a cigarette case.

A. *'No. really, I could not! I have given so many I could not recognize it.'*

[Finally the name of sixteen year old Walter Grainger and disaster. Grainger was a servant and had waited on Wilde from time to time.]

Q. *'Did you ever kiss him?'*
A. *'Oh, dear no! He was a peculiarly plain boy. He was, unfortunately, extremely ugly. I pitied him for it.'*
Q. *'Was that the reason why you did not kiss him?'*
A. *'Oh! Mr. Carson: you are pertinently insolent.'* [*Author's note: Some believe this should read, 'impertinent and insolent'*]
Q. *'Did you say that in support of your statement that you never kissed him?'*
A. *'No.' It is a childish question.'*
Q. *'Did you put that forward as a reason why you never kissed the boy?'*
A. *'Not at all.'*
Q. *'Why, sir, did you mention that this boy was extremely ugly?'*
A. *'For this reason. If I were asked why I did not kiss a door-mat, I should say because I do not like to kiss door-mats. I do not know why I mentioned that he was ugly, except that I was stung by the insolent question you put to me and the way you have insulted me throughout this hearing. Am I to be cross-examined because I do not like it? It is ridiculous to imagine that any such thing could have happened in the circumstances.'*
Q. *'Then why did you mention his ugliness, I ask you?'*

A. *'Perhaps you insulted me by an insulting question.'*
Q. *'Was that the reason why you should say the boy was ugly?'*
A. *'You sting me and insult me and try to unnerve me—and at times one says things flippantly when one ought to speak more seriously. I admit it.'*
'Oh, yes, it was a flippant answer.'

Principle Seven

Never Try And Impeach An Apparently Truthful Witness

It seems to be self evident that an advocate should not try to impeach a truthful witness Unfortunately one need only go to the courthouse on a daily basis to see the spectacle occur with frightening frequency and with the same inevitable result.

The advocate is confronted with testimony of a witness about whom there is no doubt as to their integrity, honesty and utter lack of interest in the case. The advocate then seeks to do battle with the witness and attempt to convert what is clearly high moral ground into something else and make the witness appear to be what clearly he is not.

The attempt always fails and the testimony of the witness is only enhanced and their integrity and honesty flows over to the side calling them in a disproportionate way. But the fact that the witness is honest can be turned to the advocates' advantage. In this case cross-examination should be thought of as providing the jury with as much that is beneficial to your case as is possible.

The honest neutral witness will have something in their knowledge that will help your case. The clever advocate must find it. It may simply be that the witness admits that a set of facts provide insufficient information on which to base a conclusion. This may prove useful later when a less honest witness, with no greater basis of information, does draw a conclusion. This resulting discrepancy can then be used during summation and the jury will be called on to accept the honest witness' version.

A masterful example of using the honest witness to your advantage is found in the cross-examination of Dr. Willcox by Marshall Hall in the Seddon case. (Marshall Hall went a few steps too far and the result ultimately hurt him but it is still a fine example of the proposition.) It was the defense in that case that the deceased female victim had died from epidemic diarrhea, aggravated by chronic arsenical poisoning. The prosecution alleged she had died of acute arsenical poisoning administered by the defendant.

Before the cross-examination of Dr. Willcox, the doctor who had diagnosed the acute arsenical poisoning as the cause of death, Hall had read a Royal Commission study which reported that:

1. Arsenic does not penetrate into the hair nearest the scalp (proximal hair) until some weeks after the arsenic has been taken.
2. The arsenic does not migrate to the hair away from the roots (distal hair) for months or even years.
3. The arsenic remains in the hair as it grows.
4. Hair grows about five to six inches a year.

Based on these findings the Commission concluded that it was possible to determine how long ago arsenic had been ingested by its location in the hair and its distance from the scalp.

Dr. Willcox had found arsenic at the end of a strand of the victim's hair about twelve inches long. For the arsenic to have been there it meant the victim ingested the arsenic long before coming to live with the Seddons. Hall recognized the honesty of the witness and used the honesty to obtain concessions that might have resulted in an acquittal of the defendant. Unfortunately he failed to recognize when to stop and by going too far undid his success.

Q. *[By Marshall Hall] In the proximal end of the hair you found one-eightieth of a milligram?*
A. *[By Dr. Willcox] Yes.*

Q. *What did you find in the distal end of the hair?*
A. *One three-thousandth—about a quarter as much.*
Q. *Is the finding of the arsenic in the hair corroborative of acute arsenical poisoning, or of chronic arsenic taking?*
A. *If arsenic is found in the hair it indicates that probably the arsenic had been taken for some period.*
Q. *Apart from all other symptoms or any other questions, if you only find arsenic in the hair, you would take that as being a symptom of a prolonged course of arsenic?*
A. *Of a course of arsenic over some period.*
Q. *And the minimum period would be something about three months?*
A. *I think that.*
Q. *In the proximal portion, but . . . you would not expect to find it in the distal ends in three months, would you?*
A. *Not in large amounts.*
Q. *Not in the amount you have got here . . . ? This minute quantity in the distal end might possibly mean some arsenic might have been taken, perhaps a year or more ago . . . . A year or more ago?*
A. *More than a year ago.*

This was a good place for Marshall Hall to stop. Instead he hammered home the point seeking to be sure the jury understood completely the significance of the situation. Unfortunately it gave Willcox more time to think of the situation in his own mind. He was convinced Barrow had died of acute arsenic poisoning and what In driving his point across, Marshall Hall also pointed out that the victim's hair had been washed prior to being examined and therefore was not contaminated by blood of the dead victim. Willcox may have left the matter alone had Hall stopped after the first concession but the lengthy examination had the effect of giving rise to his curiosity. After being released returned to the hospital and, along with a colleague, took hair from a healthy patient, soaked it in the blood from Barrow (the victim in the murder trial), washed it and examined it, and found arsenic there. He returned to the stand and explained the situation and undid Marshall Hall's brilliant cross-examination.

The cross-examination of an honest witness was done beautifully. It did not stop soon enough in this case but that is a minor criticism since the reasons for not stopping were equally valid.

Principle Eight

Always End The Cross-Examination On A High Note

The most effective cross-examination always ends on a triumphant high note. The advocate should be ever watchful for a good place to end. If the last thing the jury hears from a witness is a lie or contradiction, or the witness is shown to be incredible in the eyes of the jury that is a good place to stop and one that will leave the jury with a poor impression of the witness.

Jurors are usually instructed that if they disbelieve any of the testimony they may disregard all of it. Thus, if the last impression is a negative one, they will probably reject it.

Knowing when to stop is a difficult decision. Often times you will reach a very high note early in the examination which would be an ideal place to end, but there are matters that must not be left alone and you simply cannot end there. In these situations it is often possible to continue to cover the additional points and then return to the earlier victory and attempt to recreate it through reiteration.

In some cases there are no high points, but a great many minor ones. In these instances it is often worthwhile to reach the end of the examination and then take a moment to recapitulate the contradictions or errors and end with something like "And in spite of this you are nevertheless asking the jury to accept your version of the events? Yes. I have no further questions.

Darrow's Accuser Is Tripped Up

When Clarence Darrow was accused of attempting to bribe a juror his defense was handled by Earl Rogers. Bert Franklin was the chief prosecution witness and the juror allegedly bribed was named Lockwood. Rogers cross-examined Franklin and made a serious rookie mistake by asking that treacherous "why" question. This excerpt from the cross-examination is instructive to show how much trouble you can get into with the "why" question and how a brilliant advocate like Rogers extricates himself and forces the issue to end on a high note.

Q. You"d known Lockwood for years, hadn't you?
A. Yes, sir . . . .
Q. Worked with him as deputy sheriff, didn't you?
A. Yes, sir.
Q. Knew him to be a good officer?
A. Yes—a good officer.
Q. Knew him to be an honest man?
A. Yes.
Q. He was a friend-he was your friend—you counted him as your friend?
A. Yes.
Q. A good man to have beside you in danger-in trouble?
A. Yes sir . . . .
Q. You told Mr. Darrow you thought, you knew, Lockwood as an honest man?
A. Yes sir.
Q. Why if you thought he was honest did you think you could bribe him?
A. No man's that honest.
Q. You thought you could tempt him with his own destruction?
A. Well—I thought he had his weak spot. I thought the offer of enough money might influence him, yes.
Q. You knew he had a mortgage on his little ranch?
A. Oh yes.

Q. *You knew how much love and work he'd put into it, how he and his wife loved it and hoped to spend their declining years there?*
A. *I guess so.*
Q. *So you, his friend, his old comrade in arms, you dangled enough money, $4,000 in cash, enough to pay off the mortgage, in front of him to seduce him from his honesty, to betray his honor—you did that?*
A. *I did—yes.*
Q. *Then in the end when you saw you were in a trap, you thought you'd take your friend up to the policeman on the corner and say he had solicited you for a bribe—you did say that to the district attorney, didn't you?*
A. *Yes, I thought I might make it look as though he started it.*
Q. *So your quite ready to charge an honest man, your lifelong friend, with a dastardly crime, an innocent man as he was, to save yourself?*
A. *I was only doing the best I could to get out of the straits I was in.*
Q. *And are still in, aren't you, Mr. Franklin?*

[Rogers brought to examination around to Darrow's complicity.]

Q. *Now, Bert, the district attorney began asking you to implicate Darrow almost at once, didn't he?*
A. *He asked me if Darrow had been in on it, yes.*
Q. *And you said he hadn't?*
A. *That's right.*
Q. *You said to them that Darrow was never in on the bribery?*
A. *Yes.*
Q. *That Darrow had never given you a corrupt dollar?*
A. *Yes.*
Q. *That Darrow knew nothing that was going on?*
A. *That's right.*
Q. *That Darrow was innocent as a baby and it he hadn't appeared at Third and Los Angeles Streets that day they"d never have thought of it.*
A. *I said he was innocent, I don't remember the last part. I said he was innocent as a baby.*

Q. *Inexplicably Rogers asks:* Why did you say all those things if they weren't true Bert?
A. To protect that man there [he points at Darrow] to protect him. Because he'd sold me a bill of goods, Darrow had. He'd made me believe in him-even when I was shocked that he'd plan jury bribery.

[A damaging moment well earned by Rogers. How does he retrieve it?]

Q. *By Rogers:* No, no, let me ask this. Didn't the district attorney begin at once to assure you that you wouldn't be in any trouble if you played ball? Didn't he assure you of that?
A. Sure.
Q. Bert, the district attorney told you he didn't want you. We want Darrow, isn't that what he said? We don't want you, we don't care anything about you. We want Darrow.
A. They said if Darrow had been in this they wanted me to tell them.
Q. And you said he hadn't?
A. At first I did.
Q. That was a lie?
A. Well.
Q. Then you said he was in it?
A. Yes.
Q. Which one was a lie—one or the other was a lie—you lied sometime, Bert, didn't you?
A. I didn't tell the truth when I said Darrow didn't know about it.
Q. But how can we tell? How can we be sure which time you lied? They told you they wanted to get Darrow.

[In effect Rogers was able to retrace his steps to the admission of lying that Franklin had confessed to before. Resurrected it and contrived a place to end on a high note in spite of the fact he had failed to end at the proper time and had blundered by asking the "why" question.]

Part Seven
Thinking On Your Feet

Principle One

Sizing Up A Witness Requires On-The-Spot Decision Making

All the preparation in the world will not relieve the advocate from having to make on the spot decisions with respect to cross-examination. He will be constantly faced with ever changing situations which require spontaneous judgments. The advocate must recognize openings in a witness' testimony and make immediate decisions as to whether the opening should be exploited and, if so, how and when. He must consider how to use the information he has against a witness without time for reflection and often while he is involved in another line of questioning.

The timing of the cross-examination, and the pace and rhythm of it, all require spontaneous decision making. The cross-examiner must have the intuition to decide when he has exploited a subject sufficiently, when to abandon a potentially harmful line of questioning. He must be able to regulate the questions so as to create a sense of drama, and to orchestrate the situation so that it reaches its climax at the most effective moment, and do it while he is involved in another line of questioning.

The trial lawyer must also cope with attempts by the opposition to upset his pace and rhythm with objections and speeches, and he must have the presence of mind to recover from harmful events without showing damage.

How the advocate develops the skills necessary for "thinking on his feet" will vary from individual to individual. Experience and repetition are essential.

In this respect, there are two areas of practice the advocate must master if he is to become successful at thinking on his feet. The first is a mastery of the rules of evidence and the law dealing with methods of impeaching a witnesses. The second is an ability to read the witnesses and understand what motivates them.

The rules of evidence set forth the basis for impeaching a witness. These rules in turn give the advocate the legal framework within which all his strategy must be defined. The trial lawyer, when challenged, must be able to convince a judge his line of questions come within an acceptable rule of evidence. This means fitting the argument within one or more of the rules governing the admissibility of evidence or the cross-examination of a witness.

The rules provide the concepts upon which the credibility of a witness may be attacked. Having an impeccable knowledge of these rules will give the advocate the framework for obtaining from the judge a favorable ruling to the objections of the opposition.

The rules provide three broad categories by which a witness may be attacked. and each of these categories contain three subjects.

1. **Knowledge of critical events**

With respect to his knowledge of the events that are the subject of the trial, the witness may be attacked on the following points:

> A. *His ability to see or hear the events.* Was the witness in a position to see or hear? Does the witness have some infirmity that would impair his ability to witness the events?
> B. *His ability to remember what he saw.* How good is the memory? Is it accurate and consistent?
> C. *His ability to communicate.* Does the witness possess the skills to convince the jury of his credibility.

2. **The relationship of the witness to the case.**

A. *Does the oath mean anything to the witness?* The oath comes into play when the witness is shown to have lied throughout the case leading up to the trial and now wishes the jury to believe that by taking an oath to tell the truth he has suddenly changed his spots. This happens frequently with police informants or co-conspirators that have received immunity or lesser sentences in exchange for testifying.

B. *Is the witness biased?* A simple example is to show that the witness is a relative of a party and therefore may lie or color the testimony because of the relationship.

C. *Has the witness committed some act inconsistent with the testimony?* This occurs where the witness said or did (or failed to say or do) something outside the courtroom that is inconsistent with his courtroom testimony.

3. **The character of the witness.**

Challenges to character include: prior criminal convictions, prior bad acts not amounting to a criminal conviction, and reputation in the community for truth and veracity. There is one additional means of attack with respect to opinion evidence and that is the learned treatise exception to the hearsay rule. If a witness is permitted to give an opinion, the opinion may be impeached through the use of a learned treatise on the subject. This usually applies to experts. (See Part Eight for a full discussion).

Having a firm understanding of these concepts for attacking the credibility of the witness will arm the advocate with reasonable categories within which to launch his assault. However, the rules of evidence are only a legal framework which permits a strategy. Defining and implementing the strategy spontaneously requires an understanding of human nature and an ability to recognize certain weaknesses.

Witnesses may simply be mistaken in their testimony. This may occur for several reasons some of which may be unintentional and other intentional. Witness may be wrong because they are lacking in physical skills. He may be physically unable to have done, seen, or heard that which he has testified to. Of course, the lack of physical skills may be internal or external. An external may include line of sight, lighting conditions, speed and all other physical obstacles. Example of the lack of internal skills are blindness, deafness, color blindness, or being crippled.

Even if the witness has no physical disability there must still be mental acuity. The witness must have memory skills, the skills of perception, the ability to comprehend, and the ability to rationally articulate the facts.

All of these abilities may exist to lesser or greater degree in any witness, and the cross-examiner's main task is to determine where the deficiency lies and then to demonstrate it to the jury.

Inaccurate perception may result from: insufficient attention; poor experience upon which to make associations; poor mental retentiveness; inadequate imagery for the purpose of picturing an object; ability to separate that which is observed from that which is inferred; and the effect of suggestion by which other elements may be brought into the story.

Experiments have shown that psychology students, informed they were to be tested with respect to powers of observation, and then been confronted with a dramatic situation lasting no more than a brief time have given differing opinions as to what transpired. Indeed their reports may vary as much as seventy percent with respect to the details. And the various elements may vary even more. For instance an event lasting one minute may be described by some as being ten minutes and others as being only seconds.

Nevertheless, the immediate application of this new knowledge by the trial advocate still is difficult. The cross-examiner must make a threshold decision as to whether a witness is a liar, a perjurer, honest, mistaken, or has a direct or indirect interest in the outcome of the case, and must do so with those skills that he develops through experience and intuition.

It is often extremely useful to observe a witness during the direct examination. The advocate should note whether the witness is on guard or relaxed. Either posture may indicate something to hide or nervousness about quality and vulnerability of the testimony. The kind of language used may help in deciding what approach to take. If the witness uses flowery, exaggerated language, it may suggest exaggeration of the facts. A sober and straight forward recitation may suggest something different. Some witnesses will respond in a very closemouthed way while others will be voluble and help you formulate an approach. Some are cocky; others hesitant. It is important to note whether the witness is quick to see where you are going in the questioning or slow to see the point. Some witnesses will digress while others will stick to the issue.

Whether the witness is precise or vague with respect to dates, times, places, or persons will give the advocate good information. A witness may be precise because he has been well rehearsed or because he is honest and truthful and has a good capacity for memory and communication. The vague witness may have the same characteristics but simply wasn't in a position to be as certain. It is the art of the cross-examiner to determine which is which and to pursue the advantages for the benefit of his side. The advocate should also be careful to observe whether the story told by the witness sounds too pat or memorized as opposed to being natural and plausible.

Principle Two

The Whole Is Not Always Equal To The Sum Of The Parts

A witness may tell a convincing story that, taken as a whole, suggests a credible tale. Viewed in its entirety, it meets all the criteria for the jury's reaching a decision in favor of the side offering the witness. Usually the story is rich in detail, the witness has a good grasp of the facts, and the communication is convincing. It is quite often true, however, that, if the story is broken down into its components and each one scrutinized outside the context of the others, the story can be shown to be implausible or unbelievable.

Testimony by a police officer about a person's sobriety while driving a car is a good example of this. The officer will inevitably testify that he saw the car weave or otherwise commit some traffic infraction; that the driver was unsteady on his feet; smelled of alcohol; had watery or bloodshot eyes; and had slurred speech. If the cross-examiner takes each of these items separately, he should be able to obtain a concession from the officer that each one may be evidence of something other than insobriety. Cars are driven improperly all the time by drivers who are sober so the fact the car was weaving doesn't mean the driver was drunk. People may be unsteady on their feet for many reasons besides drunkenness. Since the alcohol in so-called liquors, (vodka, bourbon, etc.) has no odor the alleged smell of alcohol was really that of other constituents of a drink that may contain alcohol. A strong or weak smell may not indicate the amount of alcohol, in any event he should concede that he (the policeman) cannot testify from the odor how many drinks had been consumed. He will also concede that slurred speech and watery or bloodshot eyes are likewise something that may exist in a sober person.

Breaking the story down in this way gives the advocate the opportunity to argue to the jury that there is insufficient evidence upon which to find drunkenness beyond a reasonable doubt and that the policeman was giving an opinion based on insufficient information. Before the advent of mandatory chemical tests gave scientific support to the officer's opinion, this line of questioning proved quite effective. The principle is especially effective with respect to an expert in the field of psychiatry and psychology.

The tactic of destroying the whole of the testimony by attacking each of its components was used most effectively by Clarence Darrow in the famous Scopes trial. Scopes was a school teacher in Tennessee and taught the theory of evolution contrary to the laws of the state and was prosecuted. Scopes was defended by Darrow and the state was represented by William Jennings Bryan. Bryan was a strong advocate of the creationist as opposed to evolutionist theory, and in a rather strange move agreed to take the stand and allow his views on creationism to be cross-examined by Darrow. Darrow's strategy was to attack Bryan's literal interpretation of the bible. Here are excerpts from that cross-examination.

Darrow: You have given considerable study to the Bible, haven't you, Mr. Bryan?
Bryan: Yes, I have. I have studied the Bible for about fifty years.
Q. Do you claim that everything in the Bible should be literally interpreted?
A. I believe everything in the Bible should be accepted as it is given there; some of the bible is given illustratively. For instance: 'Ye are the salt of the earth.' I would not insist that man was actually salt or that he had flesh of salt, but it is used in the sense of salt as saving God's people.

Q. When you read that the whale swallowed Jonah, how do you literally interpret that?
A. When I read that a big fish swallowed Jonah, I believe it, and I believe in a God who can make a whale and can make a man and make them both do what he pleases. One miracle is just as easy to believe as another.
Q. You mean just as hard?
A. It is hard to believe for you, but easy for me.
Q. Do you believe Joshua made the sun stand still?
A. I believe what the Bible says.
Q. I suppose you mean that the earth stood still?
A. I don't know. I am talking about the Bible now. I accept the Bible absolutely.
Q. Do you believe at that time the entire sun went around the earth?
A. No, I believe the earth goes around the sun.
Q. Do you believe that the men who wrote it thought that the day could be lengthened or that the sun could be stopped?
A. I believe what they wrote was inspired by the Almighty, and He may have used language that could be understood at that time—instead of language that could not be understood until Darrow was born.
Q. Now, Mr. Bryan, have you ever pondered what would have happened to the earth if it stood still suddenly?
A. No.
Q. Don't you know it would have been converted into a molten mass of matter?
A. You testify to that when you get on the stand; I will give you a chance.
Q. You believe the story of the flood to be a literal interpretation?
A. Yes sir.
Q. When was that flood?
A. I would not attempt to fix the day.
Q. But what do you think that the Bible itself says? Don't you know how it was arrived at?
A. I never made a calculation.
Q. What do you think?

A. I do not think about things I don't think about.
Q. Do you think about things you do think about?
A. Well, sometimes.
Q. How long ago was the flood, Mr. Bryan?
A. Two thousand three hundred and forty-eight years B.C.
Q. You believe that all the living things that were not contained in the ark were destroyed?
A. I think the fish may have lived.
Q. Don't you know there are any number of civilizations that are traced back to more than five thousand years? You believe that every civilization on the earth and every living thing, except possibly the fishes, were wiped out by the flood?
A. At that time.
Q. You have never had any interest in the age of the various races and peoples and civilizations and animals that exist upon the earth today?
A. I have never felt a great deal of interest in the effort that has been made to dispute the Bible by the speculations of men or the investigations of men.
Q. And you never have investigated to find out how long man has been on the earth?
A. I have never found it necessary.
Q. Don't you know that the ancient civilizations of China are six thousand or seven thousand years old, at the very least?
A. No, but they would not run back beyond the creation, according to the Bible, six thousand years.
Q. You don't know how old they are; is that right?
A. I don't know how old they are, but probably you do. I think you would give the preference to anybody who opposed the Bible.
Q. Well, you are welcome to your opinion. Have you any idea how old the Egyptian civilization is?
A. No.
Q. Mr. Bryan, you don't know whether any other religion ever gave a similar account of the destruction of the earth by the flood?
A. The Christian religion has satisfied me, and I have never felt it necessary to look up some competing religions.

Q. Do you know how old the Confucian religion is?
A. I can't give you the exact date of it.
Q. Do you know how old the religion of Zoroaster is?
A. No, sir.
Q. What about the religion of Confucius or Buddha? Do you regard them as competitive?
A. No, I think they are very inferior. Would you like for me to tell you what I know about it?
Q. No. Do you know anything about how many people there were in Egypt thirty-five hundred years ago or how many people there were in China five thousand years ago?
A. No.
Q. Have you ever tried to find out?
Q. No sir; you are the first man I ever heard of that has been interested in it.
Q. Mr. Bryan, am I the first man you ever heard of who has been interested in the age of human societies and primitive man?
A. You are the first man I ever heard speak of the number of people at those different periods.
Q. Where have you lived all you life?
A. Not near you.
Q. Did you ever read a book on primitive man? Like Tyler's Primitive Culture, or Boas, or any of the great authorities?
A. I don't think I have read the ones you have mentioned.
Q. Have you read any?
A. Well, I have read a little from time to time. But I don't pursue it because I didn't know I was to be called as a witness.
Q. You have never in all your life made any attempt to find out about the other peoples of the earth—how old their civilizations are, how long they have existed on the earth—have you?
Q. No sir, I have been so well satisfied with the Christian religion that I have spent no time trying to find arguments against it. I have all the information I want to live by and to die by.
Q. Do you think the earth was made in six days?
A. Not six days of twenty-four hours.

Q. Doesn't the Bible say so?
A. No sir.
Q. Mr. Bryan, do you believe that the first woman was Eve?
A. Yes.
Q. Do you believe she was literally made out of Adam's rib?
A. I do.
Q. Did you ever discover where Cain got his wife?
A. No sir; I leave the agnostics to hunt for her.
Q. Do you think the sun was made on the fourth day?
A. Yes.
Q. And they had evening and morning without the sun?
A. I am simply saying it is a period.
Q. The creation might have been going on for a long time?
A. It might have continued for millions of years.
Q. Yes. All right. Do you believe the story of the temptation of Eve by the serpent?
A. I will believe just what the Bible says. Read the Bible and I will answer.
Q. All right, I will do that. 'And I will put enmity between thee and the woman and between they seed and her seed; it shall bruise they head and thou shalt bruise his heel. Unto the woman he said, 'I will greatly multiply they sorrow and they conception; in sorrow thou shalt bring forth children; and thy desire shall be to thy husband, and he shall rule over thee.' That is right, is it?
A. I accept it as it is.
Q. And God said to the serpent, 'Because thou hast done this, thou art cursed above all cattle, and above, every beast of the field; upon they belly shalt thou go and dust shalt thou eat all the days of they life.' Do you think that is why the serpent is compelled to crawl upon its belly?
A. I believe that.
Q. Have you any idea how the snake went before that time?
A. No sir.
Q. Do you know whether he walked on his tail or not?
A. No sir. I have no way to know.

Principle Three

Embroidery Of The Facts Is Often The Downfall Of The Witness

Some witnesses simply cannot let well enough alone. They are like the patient that believes if one pill is good for them then several must even be better. They often lack conscience and imagination and believe that they can embroider the facts to make the story even more plausible. When this happens, the alert cross-examiner will find the weak link and allow the witness to embroider to their heart's content. The inevitable result is that the witness finally puts himself into an indefensible position from which he cannot extricate himself. This tactic requires great skill in recognizing the symptoms and making an on-the-spot decision to pursue the matter.

A wrong decision, however, can be disastrous. It is important that the advocate probe the testimony gently at first to see if, in fact, this is the embroiderer and not an honest witness that remembers information incrementally. If the advocate is wrong in his judgment and the witness is, in fact, truthful, the result of allowing great latitude may simply be to reinforce the testimony. The cross-examiner should be able to discover the true nature of the witness through the asking of questions on collateral matters. Thus, if he discovers in the course of probe that the witness does indeed exaggerate when led to do so, he may safely undertake a line of questions on more important matters which will be designed to give the witness free reign to his imagination.

Erskine's Cross Of Thomas Dunne

In England, about the time of America's independence, Thomas Erskine, a great trial lawyer and defender of individual liberties was involved in the treason trial of Thomas Walker. The government relied most heavily on the testimony of an informant named Thomas Dunne. The following extract shows not only the tactic of allowing the witness to embroider to his own detriment but also how a witness may be impeached in the most difficult area of impeachment—a challenge to the witness' ability to adhere to the oath.

At the time of this case, the nature and circumstances surrounding the taking of the oath by a witness was a more serious undertaking than it tends to be in today's trials. Thus, to show any minor discrepancy by a witness was to seriously damage that witness' credibility in the eyes of the jury. Of course, the technique of attacking a witness with respect to his ability to adhere to or respect the oath should be subject of even greater interest in an age of undercover agents and co-conspirators who have made contradictory statements throughout the case. Types such as these usually maintain that the jury should believe their courtroom testimony rather than what they have said out of court by court by arguing that they were not under oath when they were outside the courtroom. This tactic raises some interesting avenues of impeachment concerning their fundamental honesty. Here is how Erskine did it in one case.

Question by Erskine: What is your Christian name?
Answer by Dunne: Thomas Dunne.
Q. Why do you call it your Christian name?
A. I was brought up by that.
Q. Were you ever christened?
A. I hope so.
Q. Then you forgot the circumstances formerly—do you hear me?
A. Yes.

Q. You forgot that circumstance once of your being christened?
A. Have I? How long since?
Q. Do you remember ever having been asked that question?
A. I remember you asked my name and I answered you that my name was Thomas Dunne.
Q. Were you ever asked at any other time and by anybody else?
A. Very well, and suppose I choose to tell this or that.
Q. But you happened to be upon your oath at the time I am speaking of?
A. I am speaking now that my name is Thomas Dunne, and upon my oath I am speaking. I know what you are upon, Mr. Erskine; I tell you in this place that I defy you, though the learned Mr. Erskine has come down here to insult me.
Q. I will resume my question again. Were you never asked, when you were sworn to speak the truth, whether you had been christened or not, and what answer did you give?
A. No, never in my life.
Q. Do you mean to swear that such a question was never put to you in a court of justice, when you came forward to convict one of those innocent men?
A. Innocent?
Q. That His Lordship and the jury are to try. Was that question ever put to you, and did you give it any and what answer? [Dunne was slow to answer] I am in no hurry; His Lordship will have the goodness to wait for you—if you will speak the words over again—were you never asked when sworn upon the gospels to speak the truth, whether you were christened or not?
A. I never was asked whether I was christened or not.
Q. Never was what?
A. I never was asked whether I was christened.

Principle Four

Ask A Crucial Question When The Witness Is Ebullient

One important aspect of thinking on one's feet is the ability to formulate a tactic and a strategy on the spot. This often means pursuing a line of questions while considering a new line of questions and then putting the witness into a mood that will give the new line of questions the most telling effect.

Making the witness feel good about himself is one good approach to this tactic. This can entail allowing the witness to puff himself up and often at your expense. When a witness reaches that plateau of basking in the warmth of his own skills, his ability to perceive danger in a question or to respond in a dissembling way may be at its lowest.

The issue is not to ask a question because it occurs to you, but rather having perceived a possible weak spot, to maneuver the witness into a situation where the question will have the best effect. In other words, you let the witness's own sense of security contribute to his undoing.

The following example involves a lawsuit in which the plaintiff alleged he had been wrongfully discharged from employment, had been unable to obtain other work and was therefore entitled to damages. The defenses counsel sensed that if given the opportunity the plaintiff exaggerate, and his exaggeration would grow in proportion to how good he felt about himself.

While there is no devastating single question in this segment, the overall effect of the examination can be sensed. The witnesses' own ebullience led him to the position of either having lied about his attempts to gain other employment and mitigate his damages or demonstrating that he was so incompetent that literally thousands of potential employers had found him unfit.

Q. *After you were discharged, you did not look for work, did you?*
A. *Oh, yes. I certainly did.*
Q. *But you didn't look for work every day, did you?*
A. *I most certainly did—every day.*
Q. *But you didn't see more than one or two people a day, did you?*
A. *Oh, many more than that.*
Q. *Well, how many more?*
A. *I'd say as many as eight to ten people every day.*
Q. *You didn't ask them all for employment, did you?*
A. *I did. I asked each one for a job.*
Q. *But you didn't go looking for a job every day, did you?*
A. *I told you before. I went out every day hunting for a job.*
Q. *Please multiply eight by five and tell me what you get.*
A. *Forty.*
Q. *Good. Now be good enough to multiply forty by fifty and tell me what you get.*
A. *That comes to two thousand.*
Q. *Now take half of two thousand to that, what will the final sum come to?*
A. *Three thousand.*

Principle Five

The Lying Witness Cannot Invent Lies As Quickly As The Lawyer Can Invent Questions

Once the advocate can catch the witness in one lie, it becomes relatively easy to undo the witness completely. It is important not to confront the witness with the lie immediately. To do so often allows the witness to offer an explanation or confess that he was wrong and take some of the sting from the error.

One tactic is to ignore the lie as if you failed to notice it or are unaware of it and go on to something else. This had the effect of lulling the witness into a false sense of security. The witness should then be led to several other statements which have as their foundation the lie you ignored. Having laid this foundation, the cross-examiner then returns to the lie and confronts the witness with it. At this point, the witness will not be able to invent lies quickly enough to cover his tracks because of the supporting statements made in the course of the testimony. The entire testimony will come falling about this head.

Nizer And The Blacklister

After World War II America went through a period of hysteria about anyone with a communist past. Often the damage, using nothing more than rumor, innuendo, and false accusations, utterly destroyed a person. It resulted in blacklists (especially in the entertainment industry) that destroyed a career without a person's ever being charged with a crime or given the chance to face his accusers.

One of these incidents involved an entertainer named John Henry Faulk and an organization called Aware. The chief witness against Faulk and the alleged communist activities was Vincent Hartnett. Louis Nizer's account of part of his cross-examination of Hartnett helps demonstrate the principle of how quickly testimony may unravel once the first lie is exposed.

During the second day of cross-examination I noticed that Hartnett would occasionally take a pink card out of his pocket, write something on it, put it back in his breast pocket, and proceed to answer my questions. At first I thought he was making notes for his counsel for redirect examination. Even this would be strange behavior by a witness. It is the lawyer who usually carries this burden, while the witness is preoccupied enough responding to hostile questions. But soon I observed that before Hartnett made these notes on his colored card, he had looked at the doors of the courtroom which were almost directly opposite him. On one occasion as I followed his eyes to the door, then to the clock on the wall, and then saw him unclip his fountain pen and write a note on a card, I interrupted cross-examination of a subject I was pursuing:

Q. *Incidentally, you have made notes of people coming into the courtroom even while you have been on the stand, haven't you, and the time they have come into the courtroom, on those pink slips?*
A. *Yes.*
Q. *Did you write down the time they entered the courtroom?*
A. *I did.*

Since comment on this incident had to await summation, I indulged in the only communication possible at the time—a long, meaningful look at the jury.

Now, several days later, Bolan was conducting redirect examination of Hartnett. he decided to exploit this incident to his own purpose.

Q. On cross-examination Mr. Nizer asked you if you were recording the names of the people who came into the courtroom during your testimony. Do you recall that?
A. I do.
Q. Who were the names of the people you wrote?
A. Elliot Sullivan, who was sitting next to Mrs. Faulk; John Randolph, Alan Manson, Jack Gilford, were some of them.

This stuck me as extraordinary. Was attendance at a public trial to be included in some future report by Hartnett, as evidence of procommunism? Hartnett had considered an artist's attendance at a funeral of an alleged pro-communist, activity which required listing in his reports. Now, apparently being present at a trial of Aware and Hartnett was proof of disloyalty to our country and warranted a notation with the precise time of entry. Aside from the neurotic illogic of the whole thing, for the crowded courtroom often held many members of Aware, I was particularly struck by Hartnett's reference to the fact that one of these visitors sat down next to Mrs. Faulk. What an exquisite extension of the doctrine of guilt by association. Now it was guilt by proximity. I marked his answer on my pad with several penciled stars, to remind me that this was worthy of recross-examination in depth. I needed no reminder. I had already decided to take a gamble which the prudent rules of cross-examination would have ruled out. But there are times when caution is the great risk, and besides, my anger was getting the better of me. Now the time for recross had come. Once more, I faced Hartnett, although we had thought we were through with him.

Q. You have said that when you were on the witness stand, when somebody came into the room you wrote down the name, and in answer to your counsel's question you gave the name of one person, Mr. Sullivan, and you added he sat right down next to Mrs. Faulk. Did you say that?

A. *I did.*
Q. *Do you see Mrs. Faulk in the court now?*
A. *I believe she is the lady over there, I am not sure.*
THE COURT: *Which lady?*
MR. NIZER: *Will you stand up?*

(*A woman rose in the courtroom.*)

MR. NIZER: *What is your name, please?*
THE WOMAN: *Sofer. S-o-f-e-r.*

There was a roar of laughter in the courtroom which rose and rolled on as the full realization of his blunder took over. I imagined the hilarity was also tinged with ridicule. The jury too revealed the shock underneath its own burst of mirth. Against this emotional background of derision, I shouted.

Q. *Is that the way you identify people when you also choose—Objection was sustained.*
Q. *Would you like to have a second chance at ... identifying her? ... Can you identify Mrs. Faulk in this courtroom now?*
A. *A certain lady was pointed out to me, described by Mr. Sibley as being Mrs. Faulk.*
Q. *Which one is that?*
MR. BOLIN: *He said Mr. Sibley of the New York Times pointed out—*
MR. NIZER: *Mr. Bolan, I am not asking you to testify.*
THE COURT: *Now wait a minute, Mr. Bolan. We want the answer from the witness.*
A. *It looked like her, Your Honor. I mistook her then.*

Hartnett's reflex was typical. When he was caught in an egregious, embarrassing error, he immediately shifted the blame to someone else—Sibley, a New York Times reporter had misled him! Of course, this wasn't true. Sibley took the stand later, to deny vehemently that he had ever pointed out Mrs. Faulk to Hartnett or anyone else. He did not relish Hartnett's clutching at him to lift himself out of a hole. Hartnett, instead of taking his loss in a manly manner, revealed a persecution complex—a reporter had done him in by false identification.

What better way could we conclude with Hartnett than this incident? Its dramatic effect could not be adequately measured. It not only belied Sullivan's sitting down next to Mrs. Fault (an unlikely event, if for no other reason than that the courtroom was usually crowded, and it would have been a coincidence if a seat next to her happened to b e unoccupied); but it also was a shocking demonstration of the inaccuracy with which Hartnett fingered artists and marked them for destruction. An experiment had been improved right in the courtroom, and Hartnett had revealed himself to be inaccurate, reckless, and irresponsible—and he had not even had the grace to admit his error. He immediately indicted someone else for his blunder.

Principle Six

The Witness May Be Hiding A Personality Disorder

Because the memory is a creative process the cross-examiner must have the skills to recognize what part of the witnesses' testimony is accurate and which is the product of creativity. The advocate that can point out to the jury those parts of the testimony that have been created by the witness he has gone a long way in discrediting the witness.

Demonstrating to the jury the fact that a witness is lacking in credibility often requires that the advocate expose some or all of the symptoms that play a role in personality disorders. To do this the advocate must have a good understanding of the various disorders, how they manifest themselves, and what line of questioning will expose the witness and call his credibility into question.

Often the advocate can discover such a disorder in the pretrial investigation by discussing the personality of the witness with people who are familiar with him; taking depositions; or from an understanding of the events surrounding the involvement of the witness in the case. Other times the advocate must recognize the symptoms during the direct examination or cross-examination of the witness.

A witness who suffers a personality disorder is vulnerable because a series of probing questions that play on the disorder will usually provoke a response by the witness that most jurors will recognize and raise some doubts on his credibility.

Personality Disorders and Their Symptoms

Generally there are twelve types of personality disorders. Eleven are distinct, classifiable types and the twelfth is a catch-all category in which disorders not fitting one of the other categories are placed.

*** *Paranoid Personality Disorder.* Beginning in early adulthood this person tends to interpret actions by others as insulting or menacing. A person subject to this disorder suspects others will harm or take advantage of him. Motives of friends are always questioned. He sees innocent remarks or events in a malignant way, and thinks of revenge for perceived rejection. He is reluctant to be trustful or confide in others, and will strike back with little provocation being quick to see a slight, and usually questions the fidelity of a spouse or sexual partner.

*** *Schizoid Personality Disorder.* this person doesn't care about relationships of a social nature and is restricted in emotional experience and expression. this person rejects relationships and is not part of a family and chooses solitary activities. His failure to show strong emotion can be confused with stoicism. He usually appears aloof or indifferent and is slow to exchange a nod or smile.

*** *Schizotypal Personality Disorder.* This disorder manifests itself in strange ideas, dress and actions along with a lack of interpersonal relatedness. A person affected by this disorder may display several of the following symptoms: social anxiety; beliefs outside the norm and having a relation to magic that include strange experiences such as sensing a poltergeist, talking to oneself and having slovenly appearance; anti-social affected speech patterns; paranoia; and the adoption of mannerisms inappropriate to the situation.

****Antisocial Personality Disorder.* This disorder is often encountered in criminal cases and cases involving violence, such as child abuse. Before the age of 15, the person with this disorder will exhibit such conduct as truancy, running away from home, involvement in fights (sometimes with a weapon), sexual aggression, cruelty to people and animals, deliberate destruction of property including fire setting, lying and stealing with or without confrontation with the victim.

After the age of 15 this personality may be unable to maintain employment or be law abiding. violence is part of his world, including physical fighting or the abuse of someone under his control. He has no regard for truth or financial responsibility, cannot plan ahead, is careless of his or other's safety, is a poor parent, finds it impossible to remain monogamous, and does not feel remorse for his shortcomings.

*** *Borderline Personality Disorder.* This disorder is permeated by mood changes, poor self-image, and unstable relationships. This person dissipates relationships through devaluing them or overdoing them. Often he displays overindulgence in sex, spending, substance abuse, or minor criminal behavior. Insecurity and feelings of boredom are often present, as are recurrent suicidal threats, changes in personal identity, and impulsive anger.

*** *Histrionic Personality Disorder.* Here the pattern is too much emotion and attention-seeking. this person is in constant need of praise or approval, Usually inappropriately sexual in behavior or appearance, he is overly concerned with physical attractiveness. Always wanting to be the center of attention, he will be overly demonstrative and exaggerate emotional expression which shifts rapidly. His speech lacks detail and he is self centered.

*** *Narcissistic Personality Disorder.* Grandiosity, a lack of empathy, and hypersensitivity to the opinion of others marks this disorder. Criticism often evokes rage, shame, or humiliation in this person. He exploits others and has a grandiose sense of self-worth. He believes his problems are unique and spends a great deal of time fantasizing about success. He requires constant attention and admiration and feels entitled to it.

*** *Avoidant Personality Disorder.* A person subject to this disorder displays social discomfort, timidity, and a fear of being evaluated negatively. Criticism or disapproval is painful. He chooses relationships only if assured of being liked, but eschews close relationships, avoids tasks involving great social demands, and fears embarrassment or being found lacking in a social situation.

*** *Dependent Personality Disorder.* This person is unable to make everyday decisions and relies on others to do so. He is not a self-starter and will agree with someone he believes is wrong, rather than risk rejection. He accepts unsavory tasks to gain approval, and feels helpless when left alone. the end of relationships can have a devastating effect on him and he cannot bear the thought of abandonment or disapproval.

*** *Obsessive Compulsive Personality Disorder.* This person exhibits inflexibility and perfectionism that interferes with his ability to complete a project. Rules, lists, details, organization preoccupies him. things must be done his way and work takes a disproportionate amount of his time. He is indecisive, over conscientious, and inflexible regarding matters of ethics and morality. His generosity is tied to personal gain and he retains personal objects long after they've served their purpose.

*** *Passive Aggressive Personality Disorder.* A passive resistance to social or performance demands generally describes this disorder. Procrastination, churlishness, deliberate delay, unjustifiable complaining, avoidance of fulfilling obligations are all aspects of this disorder. A person with this problem believes he never gets enough credit for his work, resents suggestions about performance, and obstructs others by failing to cooperate, while criticizing the others especially those in authority.

*** *Personality Disorders Not Otherwise Specified.* These are disorders of personality functioning not otherwise included in the other groups. Examples include Impulsive Personality Disorder, Immature Personality Disorder, and Sadistic Personality Disorder.

SOME COMMON THREADS

What concerns the cross-examiner with respect to personality disorders is the manifestation of these disorders and their relationship to the credibility of the witness. If the personality disorder has played a role in the witness's testimony then probing that disorder should cause the witness to react in an unflattering way. In order to do this the advocate must understand how to recognize the disorder and what there is about the disorder that may lead the witness to lose credibility with the jury by behaving in a way the jury either does not understand or distrusts.

There are common aspects to many personality disorders the advocate should be aware of. If the witness can be forced to display these to the jury it will effect his credibility and cast doubt on his testimony.

- *Paranoia.* If the witness is sufficiently threatened that he begins to see aggression in the most benign question the jury will begin to doubt all of the testimony.
- *Fear of rejection or overweening desire to please.* The jury may conclude that these emotions drove the witness to exaggerate or color his testimony.
- *Strong reaction to any slight, real or imagined.* The advocate can force this witness into apparently unjustified anger and loss of control.
- *Inappropriate social responses.* Here the witness begins to smile when a serious countenance is called for, or laugh when he should be sober.
- *Basing logical conclusions on illogical premises.* He is sure the light was green because a spirit has confirmed that fact to him since the incident.
- *Becoming churlish and defensive when challenged.* Often this witness will lose control and vent his anger on the advocate.
- *Having a history of violent relationships.* These can be determined through investigation and when used to confront the witness may elicit a negative reaction.
- *Lying when the truth is not harmful.* This is a common problem and when it occurs the cross-examiner should be able to destroy the witness.
- *Frequent mood swings.* If the advocate detects a mood swing by the witness while he is on the stand it should be exploited to the advocates advantage.
- *Strong reaction to criticism.* Once exposed this trait can be made to grow in intensity to the point that the witness becomes belligerent.
- *Can be easily led to a contrary opinion.* This trait will give the

jury the impression that the witness will change sides depending upon who is doing the flattering and his credibility will be harmed.

Principle Seven

How The Question Is Asked May Effect The Truth Of The Answer

Often, the form of the cross-examiner's question may affect the truth of the witness's answer. If the witness believes from the way the question is asked that the advocate is ignorant of certain events the witness may feel encouraged to elaborate or embellish in ways he otherwise might not. If the witness is led to believe that the question is not of great importance and is being asked only as a matter of course when, in fact, it is a critical question, the witness may treat it in a flippant way.

The tactic is important when the advocate is confronted with a witness who is biased, a smart aleck, mistaken or lying. In these cases the witness is usually more inclined to embellish his story if he believes he can get away with it. It is also particularly useful with the wary witness whom the advocate wishes to have commit to as many details as possible, thus making it more difficult to backtrack when confronted with impeaching material.

Witnesses whose testimony is influenced by mistake, bias, faulty memory or deceit, or who have an interest in the outcome of the case, will often adjust their testimony by degrees depending on their perception of the strength of their position. This position, as they perceive it, is often based on what they believe the cross-examiner knows or does not know, or how clever they believe the cross-examiner to be.

Exploiting this tendency serves the purpose of leading the witness into one or more exaggerations or omissions that either conflict with other evidence or can be impeached with other witnesses or evidence.

The tactic of influencing the witness with your tone of voice, or apparent ignorance, or possession or lack of crucial information accomplishes several goals. It can lead the witness into a false sense of security with respect to his ability to match wits with you. It can lead the witness into a false sense of security regarding the information the cross-examiner has in his possession and it can discomfort the witness by suggesting the existence of information that the witness is unaware of.

The feigned ignorance of Socratic irony used so effectively by Carson against Oscar Wilde and Murphy against Binger is a prominent example of this tactic. But there are other less elaborate examples. The question the advocate feels is important can be asked out of sequence in an offhand way, as if it were of no importance. Or the advocate can ask the question in an uncertain or misguided was suggesting his own failure to grasp the subject matter. A tone of voice suggesting incredulity or disbelief may cause the witness to volunteer additional details to support his position that only serve to did the hole deeper before he is pushed in. The advocate can conduct inartful cross-examination on the subject early in the examination during which the witness scores several points which serves to commit the witness ever more forcefully to a position before the real impeachment takes place.

You can, for example, suggest that you have information when in fact you do not and, in so doing, make the witness hedge his bets on a subject he is not sure of. This can soften a witness's position when he would otherwise be more adamant if he knew you did not actually have information to impeach him with.

The opposite of this tactic is to imply to the witness that you do not have impeaching information when in fact you do. The witness will often feel that he can enlarge or minimize a situation, confident that you will be unable to contradict his position. In this case, you lull the witness into a false sense of security that heightens the effect of the impeaching material when you present it. It makes it quite impossible for the witness to fashion contradictory statements when confronted.

Thus, the same question seeking the same information may elicit a different response depending on the tone of voice used, the sequence of the questioning, and the body language you employ. For example, a question put in an incredulous tone such as "do you mean to tell the court that . . . ?" while holding a deposition in a way that the witness can see that it is a deposition may make the witness hesitate. In fact the deposition may be from another case having nothing to do with the witness.

Another side of this technique is for the advocate to show the witness enough ignorance to encourage the witness to exaggerate a position only incrementally. This is done by addressing a subject out of sequence, in an offhand way, for the purpose of obtaining just a minor concession from the witness, without letting the witness realize that the advocate has in his possession material that will contradict whatever the witness says. After returning to the main topic for a period of time the advocate then makes another minor excursion into the real topic in the hope that the witness, emboldened by his success in other matters, will once again make a minor concession that may solidify his position. This should continue so long as progress is being made and until the witness is so firmly committed to his position that when faced with impeaching material he will find it impossible to extricate himself.

In some cases the witness will not embellish his statement but he can be made to reiterate it with growing assertiveness by the advocate adopting various tones of voice in his questioning. The advocate may pose the question in terms of "you don't expect us to believe such and such do you?," or, "did you really say such and such on your direct examination?" In these cases the witness will usually grow indignant and respond with something such as "I certainly did!" Then when faced with the impeaching testimony the witness will be hard pressed to claim bad memory or mistake, since the advocate can point out that he was given several chances to correct the statement and, in fact, emphasized it.

Principle Eight

Prior Inconsistent Acts Or Statements By The Witness Must Be Demonstrated To The Jury

Any prior act by the witness, either of omission or commission, that is inconsistent with the testimony should be demonstrated to the jury on cross-examination. Acts of commission are acts in which the witness is shown to have acted, said or written something inconsistent with the present testimony. At the trial, he may testify that the traffic light was green and had told a friend or acquaintance that the light was red. The use of these kinds of inconsistent statements or acts are somewhat routine and should occur to every cross-examiner.

The kind of acts that are, from time to time, missed by the advocate and somewhat more difficult to demonstrate to the jury are inconsistent acts or statements resulting from omission. In this situation, the lawyer attempts to demonstrate that the witness failed to act or write something consistent with the testimony. This may involve an example where the witness was in a situation in which he had the opportunity to tell someone the light was green and it would have been logical to do but he failed to mention it.

Of these two, the former is the more effective in terms of convincing the jury. It is always a dramatic moment when counsel, armed with a prior inconsistent statement of the witness, confronts him. (Presumably after laying a foundation which does not the permit the witness to extricate himself from the trap.)

It is somewhat more difficult to drive home to the jury the point that a witness did not say or do something that a reasonable person would have done in light of the present testimony. It is in many ways akin to proving a negative and is most difficult.

Early in American history Aaron Burr was accused of treason. The plot was one of taking over a newly acquired piece of American territory next to the Mississippi. The chief witness against Burr was General Eaton who testified Burr had attempted to enlist his aid in the plot with promises of money and power. The defense knew that shortly after Eaton had met with Burr he had visited Washington and had conferred with the President and had suggested Burr for a diplomatic post.

Here was a situation where the defense counsel (Burr himself and Luther Martin) set out to attack Eaton's credibility by showing his failure to act.

Question by Martin Luther: Had you not visited the Capital shortly after you had learned of the prisoner's treasonable plans?
Answer by Eaton: I had.
Q. Well, did you at the time denounce the plot to the authorities?
A. No.
Q. Why not, pray?
A. Because I feared to place my testimony against the weight of Mr. Burr's character.
Q. Indeed! Well, you had held a conference with the President on that occasion concerning Mr. Burr, had you not?
A. Yes.
Q. Just what was the nature of that conference?
A. I urged the President to appoint Mr. Burr to a foreign mission, either Paris, London or Madrid.
Q. What! Impossible! Surely you never could have recommended a man whom you knew to be a traitor to his country for an important post in the country's service? That is utterly incredible!
A. I did so only to rid the country of a dangerous citizen.

Q. *Really! So that was your purpose, was it? Did you confide this highly moral argument to the President or did you seal it in your patriotic bosom?*
A. I did not confide it to the President.
Q. *Exactly. That is all!*

Martin had demonstrated that Eaton was either lying about the plot or was derelict in his duty in disclosing it and recommending Burr for an important position. Now it was Burr's turn.

Question by Burr: *Did you not attempt for some years to collect a certain claim from the United States government?*
Answer by Eaton: I did.
Q. *Well, what was the nature of that claim?*
A. It was for money owed me by the government for official expenses in Tripoli.
Q. *Did you not present that claim to Congress?*
A. I did.
Q. *Did Congress reject or allow it?*
A. My claim was not allowed.
Q. *It did not allow it, eh? Well, was it not true that certain very injurious strictures had been passed upon your conduct while your claim was under discussion in the House of Representatives?*
A. Yes, I was criticized.
Q. *Unjustly?*
A. Yes, of course.
Q. *But the end of it all was the rejection of the claim, was it not?*
A. It was not allowed.
Q. *That is, it was not paid, was it?*
A. Not then.
Q. *Not then? Then when? Some time ago? How long since: Was it before or after you swore to the deposition against the defendant in this case?*
A. After.
Q. *Indeed! Just about how long after you signed that widely published deposition was your claim adjusted?*
A. Three weeks afterward.

Q. *Really! Well, what was the sum then paid you?*
A. *That is my own private concern.*
Q. *No, sir! That is public business! What sum did you so opportunely receive from the Treasury funds?*
A. *$10,000.*

PRINCIPLE NINE

Test The Witness's Ability To See, The Exactitude Of his Memory, And His Ability To Articulate What He Knows

The credibility of any witness depends upon his ability to have seen the events that he describes and how well he remembers them. Even given the ability to see and remember his credibility may come into issue because of his inability to communicate the facts to the jury or, because of the way in which communicates the facts.

Sometimes the way in which the story is communicated will give the cross-examiner a clue as to the veracity of the story. It may indicate that words of the narrative are not words that this witness would normally use, suggesting that the preparation of the witness has gone beyond the bounds of propriety.

THE TRIANGLE FIRE CASE

The Triangle Waist Company case involved a fire in a manufacturing facility on the top three floors of a ten story building near Greenwich Village, New York City. A great many people died in the fire and the district attorney brought charges against the tenants of the building on the grounds they had illegally locked an exit door to prevent pilfering. The door would not open during the fire and thus resulted in the death of one Margaret Schwartz. The issue came to rest mostly on the testimony of one Kate Alterman.

The example which follows of the cross-examination of Ms. Alterman by Max Stueur is used by most modern commentators as an exception that proves a rule. Max Steuer violated several rules of cross-examination the most important of which was allowing the witness to repeat her direct testimony not once but several times. Most commentators go on to point out that, while it worked for Steuer in this particular case, it should not be attempted in everyday practice. However, this analysis misses the point. It is a brilliant display of how to attack the credibility of a witness on the basis of the ability of the witness to communicate what they saw.

Q. Did you have a sister working in the place?
A. No, sir.
Q. When did you come from Philadelphia?
A. I came about the 20th of November, the 18th or 20th of November, I do not remember the date.

CROSS-EXAMINATION BY MR. STEUER:

Q. And you have been here ever since?
A. No, sir, I left after the fire.
Q. Oh, you mean that you came about the 18th or 20th of November before the fire?
A. Yes, sir.
Q. I mean when did you come here to testify?
A. The day of the trial.
Q. When was that?
A. On two weeks ago Monday.
Q. And you came from Philadelphia?
A. Yes, Sir.
Q. And you have been here ever since that time?
A. Yes, sir.

Q. And you were not put on the stand here until you are the last, is that the idea?
A. I don't know whether I was kept to the last, or first, but I was not on the witness stand.
Q. You know you have been kept for over two weeks from Philadelphia?
A. Yes, sir.
Q. Where have you been living? In the Bronx.
Q. And your home is in Philadelphia?
A. Yes, sir.
Q. With Whom?
A. With my parents, now.
Q. And your parents reside there in Philadelphia and you have been away from your parents for two weeks now?
A. Yes, sir.
Q. You have been willing to go on the witness stand every day since you have been here, haven't you?
A. Yes, sir.
Q. And you went away from Court each afternoon and came down next morning?
A. Yes, Sir.
Q. Spent the day down here in one of the offices in the building?
A. Yes, sir.
Q. Before you came down here this last time, to come down every day for two weeks, when did you see anybody from the District Attorney's office before that?
A. Saturday.
Q. You were down here Saturday, too, were you?
A. Yes, sir.
Q. And did you go anywhere with Mr. Rubin and Mr. Bostwick? [The prosecutors]
A. Yes, sir.
Q. They took you up to the building, did they?
A. Yes, sir.
Q. And they went along?
A. Yes, sir.
Q. And they pointed out to you where the Washington Place door is?

A. *I had to point it out to them.*
Q. *You were taken right over to the Washington Place door, weren't you?*
A. *I took them to the Washington Place door.*
Q. *They didn't know where it was?*
A. *I don't know whether they knew or not, but they asked me to show it to them.*
Q. *Well, they took you all around the floor, didn't they?*
A. *I took them all around the floor.*
Q. *You took Mr. Bostwick and Mr. Rubin all around the floor?*
A. *Yes, sir.*
Q. *You had never gone there before in all the two weeks you were in New York, had you?*
A. *No, sir.*
Q. *And how was the appointment made for Saturday?*
A. *Mr. Rubin told me to come, he wants to see me. He showed me the plan and asked me to show on the plan where I saw Margaret last; I couldn't show him very well on the plan for I picked it in my mind the place as it was before the fire, and he couldn't make out very well with me there, and he took me to the place and he told me to show him exactly the place.*
Q. *All that you have told us about that, was that she was right up against the door, isn't that so?*
A. *She was right near the door.*
Q. *Well, now, that was right alongside of the Washington Place door?*
A. *She was right near the door with her hands at the knob.*
Q. *With her hands at the knob?*
A. *At the knob.*
Q. *But you couldn't tell him that before you went up to the loft?*
A. *Well, I don't believe I told him—I think I told him, I am not sure, though, for when I gave my statement first I was sick that time.*
Q. *And so you did not make it the same way as you are making it now?*
A. *I made it the same way, just the same way.*
Q. *Did you tell then that she was with her hand on the knob?*

A. *I don't remember exactly whether I told the knob, or not, for it was nine months ago.*
Q. *Did you ever have a sister that visited you at that place?*
A. *Never did.*
Q. *Have you got a sister at all?*
A. *I have sisters, yes, sir.*
Q. *How many?*
A. *I have five sisters.*
Q. *Does one of your sisters live in New York?*
A. *No, sir, they never did.*
Q. *Are you the only one that was working in New York?*
A. *Yes, sir.*
Q. *Now, I want you to tell me your story over again just as you told it before?*
A. *What kind of a story do you mean?*
Q. *You told us before that you had gone to the dressing room, do you remember that?*
A. *Yes, sir, before I heard the cry of the fire.*
Q. *And then it was in the dressing room that you heard the cry of fire?*
A. *Yes, sir.*
Q. *Now tell us what you did then when you heard the cry of fire?*
A. *I went out from the dressing room, went to the Waverly side windows to look for fire escapes, I didn't find any. Margaret Schwartz was with me, afterwards she disappeared. I turned away to get to Greene Street side, but she disappeared, she disappeared from me. I went into the toilet room, I went out from the toilet rooms, bent my face over the sink, and then I went to the Washington side to the elevators, but there was a big crowd, and I saw a crowd around the door, trying to open the door; there I saw Bernstein, the manager's brother, trying to open the door but he couldn't; he left; and Margaret was there, too, and she tried to open the door and she could not. I pushed her on a side. I tried to open the door, and I could not, and then she pushed me on the side, and she said, "I will open the door," and she tried to open the door, and then the big smoke came and Margaret Schwartz I saw bending down on her knees, her*

hair was loose and her dress was on the floor a little far from her, and then she screamed at the top of her voice, "Open the door! Fire! I am lost! My God, I am lost, there is fire!" And I went away from Margaret. I left, stood in the middle of the room. That is, I went in the dressing room, first, there was a big crowd, I went out of the dressing room, went in the middle of the room between the machines and examining tables, and then I went in; I saw Bernstein, the manager's brother, throwing around the windows, putting his head from the window—he wanted to jump, I suppose, but he was afraid—he drawed himself back, and then I saw the flames cover him, and some other man on Greene Street, the flames covered him, too, and then I turned my coat on the wrong side and put it on my head with the fur to my face, the lining on the outside, and I got hold of a bunch of dresses and covered up the top of my head. I just got ready to go and somebody came and began to chase me back, pulled my dress back, and I kicked her with the foot and she disappeared. I tried to make my escape. I had a pocketbook with me, and that pocketbook began to burn, I pressed it to my heart to extinguish the fire, and I made my escape right through the flames—the whole door was a flame, right to the roof.

Q. I looked like a wall of flame?
A. Like a red curtain of fire.
Q. Now, there was something in that that you left out, I think, Miss Alterman. When Bernstein was jumping around, do you remember what that was like? Like a wildcat, wasn't it?
A. Like a wildcat.
Q. You did leave that out, didn't you, just now, when you told us about Bernstein, that he jumped around like a wildcat?
A. Well, I didn't imagine whether a wildcat or a wild dog; I just speak to imagine just exactly.
Q. How long have you lived in Philadelphia?
A. Before?
Q. Yes?
A. For nine years.
Q. Was that the only time you were in New York?
A. Yes, sir.

Q. *Altogether you spent in New York how many months?*
A. *Four months.*
Q. *And during all those four months were you working in this same place?*
A. *Yes, sir.*
Q. *Was that the only time you worked in New York?*
A. *The only time, yes, sir.*
Q. *When you were at work where did you sit?*
A. *At work? On the Washington side, the third table.*
Q. *You mean the third table from the Washington Place side?*
A. *Yes, sir.*
Q. *And about where on that table did you sit?*
A. *About where? Well, how many machines from the end?*
Q. *Yes.*
A. *I couldn't tell you exactly.*
Q. *I don't want to be exact. Just give us an idea so that we can picture it here?*
A. *Well, about six machines, probably, or five machines—I don't know exactly.*
Q. *From the Washington Place windows?*
A. *No, sir, from the other side. From the Washington Place side was about seven or eight machines.*
Q. *Well, at any rate that would put you pretty near to the middle of the table, wouldn't it?*
A. *Yes, sir, pretty near, crossing the door.*
Q. *Now, you heard the signal or bell for the shutting off of the power, didn't you?*
A. *Yes, sir.*
Q. *Then you got up and left your table, is that it?*
A. *Yes, sir.*
Q. *And was it at that time that you went into the dressing room?*
A. *Yes, sir.*
Q. *That was the only time you went to the dressing room, was it?*
A. *Yes, sir.*
Q. *And of course I am speaking of that afternoon—I meant that afternoon?*

A. *Of that day, yes, sir.*
Q. *Now, could you tell us again what you did after that time?*
A. *After going out from the dressing room?*
Q. *Yes?*
A. *I went to the Waverly side windows to look for fire escapes. Margaret Schwartz was with me, and then Margaret disappeared. I called her to Greene Street, she disappeared, and I went into the toilet room, went out, bent my face over the sink, and then I wanted to go to the Washington side, to the elevator. I saw there a big crowd, I couldn't push through. I saw around the Washington side door a whole lot of people standing; I pushed through there and I saw Bernstein, the manager's brother, trying to open the door; he could not, and he left. Margaret Schwartz was there, she tried to open the door and she could not. I pushed Margaret on the side, tried to open the door, I could not, and then Margaret pushed me on the other side, and she tried to open the door. But smoke came and Margaret bent on her knees; her trail was a little far from her, just spreading on the floor far from her, and her hair was loose, and I saw the ends of her dress and the ends of her hair begin to burn. I went into the small dressing room, there was a big crowd, and I tried—I stood there and I went out right away, pushed though and went out and then I stood in the center of the room between the examining tables and the machines. There I noticed the Washington side windows—Bernstein, the manager's brother trying to jump from the window; he stuck his head out—he wanted to jump, I suppose, but he was afraid—then he would draw himself back, then I saw the flames cover him. He jumped like a wildcat on the walls. And then I stood, took my coat, covered my head, turning the fur to my head, the lining to the outside, got hold of a bunch of dresses that was lying on the table, and covered it up over my head, and I just wanted to go and some lady came and she began to pull the back of my dress; I kicked her with the foot and I don't know where she go to. And then I had a purse with me, and that purse begin to burn, I pressed it to my heart to extinguish the fire, and I ran through the fire. The whole door was a flame, it was a red curtain of fire, and I went right on to the roof.*

Q. *You never spoke to anybody about what you were going to tell us when you came here, did you?*
A. *No, sir.*
Q. *You have got a father and a mother and four sisters?*
A. *Five sisters. I have a father, I have no mother—I have a stepmother.*
Q. *And you never spoke to them about it?*
A. *No, sir, I never did.*
Q. *They never asked you about it?*
A. *They asked me and I told her once, and then they stopped me, they didn't want me to talk any more about it.*
Q. *You told them once and then they stopped you and you never talked about it again?*
A. *I never did.*
Q. *And you never talked to anybody else about it?*
A. *No, sir.*
Q. *And what you told us here today you didn't study that and tell it that way, did you?*
A. *No, sir.*
Q. *You didn't study the words in which you would tell it?*
A. *No, sir.*
Q. *Do you remember that you got out of the center of the floor—you remember that?*
A. *I remember I got out through the Greene Street side door.*
Q. *You remember that you did get to the center of the floor, don't you?*
A. *Between the tables, between the machines, and examining table, in the center.*
Q. *Now, tell us from there on what you did; start at that point now instead of at the beginning?*
A. *In the beginning I saw Bernstein on the Washington side, Bernstein's brother, throwing around like a wildcat; he wanted to jump out from the window, I suppose, but he was afraid; and then he drawed himself back and the flames covered him up; and I took my coat, turned it on the wrong side with the fur to my face, and the lining on the outside, got hold of a bunch of dresses from the examining table, covered up my head, and I wanted to run, and then a lady came along, she begin to pull my dress back, she wanted to pull my*

back, and I kicked her with my foot—I don't know where she got to—and I ran out through the Greene Street side door, which was in flames; it was a red curtain of fire on that door; to the roof.
Q. You never studied those words, did you?
A. No, sir.

RE-DIRECT EXAMINATION BY MR. BOSTWICK:

Q. Now, Miss Alterman, each time that you have answered Mr. Steuer's question you have tried to repeat it in the same language that you first told it here in Court, have you not?
A. Yes, sir.
Q. And you remember every detail of that story as well as if it happened yesterday?
A. Yes, sir.
Q. And it is all true?
A. All true, yes, sir.

RE-CROSS-EXAMINATION BY MR. STEUER:

Q. Can you tell that story in any other words than those you have told it in?
A. In any other words? I remember it this way, just exactly how it was done.
Q. Will you please answer my question? Could you tell it in any other words than the words you have told it in here three and one-half times?
A. Probably I can.

BY MR. BOSTWICK:

Q. As a matter of fact you did on Saturday, didn't you?
A. Yes, sir.
Q. And as a matter of fact you did in that statement use different words than you have stated now?
A. Yes, sir.

Q. And you could repeat over whatever you told me on Saturday, in those other words?
A. Yes, sir.
Q. And you could repeat over your statement that you made, in other words?
A. Yes, sir.
Q. Will you state to the jury why you tried to repeat that last time what you told Mr. Steuer in the same language that you used the first time you told Mr. Steuer?
A. Because he asked me the very same story over and over, and I tried to tell him the very same thing, because he asked me the very same thing over and over.
Q. And did you think you had to tell it in the same words?
A. No, I didn't think, I just told the way he asked me to say it over and over, and I told him in the same words.
Q. I have not spoken to you since recess, have I?
A. No, sir.
Q. Not a word?
A. No, sir.

BY MR. STEUER:

Q. You say you can tell the jury the same words you used in your written statement?
A. Probably I can. My written statement was nine months ago.
MR. BOSTWICK: I offer the statement to the jury.
Q. Tell us the words in the statement, please?
THE COURT: Answer the question.
A. Shall I tell you just as in the statement?
Q. Yes, the words in the statement.
A. Well, I gave a very long statement, I believe, to Mr. Rubin.
Q. Now, start with the words in the statement, please, and not an explanation, Miss, if you can. Tell us just how you started the statement, and then give us the words that are in the statement?
A. Well, it would be 4.45 on Saturday, I think that I started this way, I

am not quite sure, I don't remember just how I started the beginning of the statement, I can't do it to you.
Q. Do you remember the words of the statement now, or don't you?
A. I don't remember the beginning of the statement, how I began it.
Q. Mr. Bostwick asked you before whether you could tell again in the same words of the statement, and you said yes. Now I suppose you did not understand that question that way, did you?
A. No, sir, I did not.

Principle Ten

Every Witness Should Be Damaged Or Neutralized On Cross-Examination

The threshold decision with every witness is should the advocate cross-examine at all? As has been discussed many factors go into making this decision. The most fundamental of which is has the witness hurt your case and is cross-examination the only means at your disposal for dealing with the damage?

If, after careful consideration, the decision is that the damage caused can only be dealt with through cross-examination then it is incumbent upon the advocate to cross-examine in such a way that the witness is damaged or neutralized to some degree.

At the end of any cross-examination, the advocate must have one or more items from the examination that he can use to his advantage with other witnesses or in his summation. There are many levels of success in any cross-examination. The advocate must realize that he can only attain the possible with each witness and it is not necessary to score some significant victory in order for the examination to be a success. Victories in trials are more often than not of an incremental nature. This may be a small point with a witness that goes unnoticed when made but which gains great significance as the trial progresses. It is a victory shaped in this way that is the rule. The devastating cross-examination of one witness that destroys the opponent's case is more the stuff of fiction.

All too often the advocate, when faced with a witness that has done damage to his case makes up his mind that his only option is to destroy the credibility of the witness or the testimony. In fact, this is rarely accomplished and to stake everything on that throw of the dice is foolhardy and unnecessary. The goals in most cases must be much more modest; and, the effective cross-examination ultimately relies on a combination of casting some doubt on the witness and the testimony, and using another witness or evidence and summation to render the testimony ineffective.

The advocate must be patient and carefully assemble his final structure from the bits and pieces given him throughout the trial. He must be aware that he has a wide range choices with regard to goals that he can achieve with each witness. He must be able to make a decision with respect to what he may realistically achieve with the witness, and he must do this while attending to all the others matters in the courtroom that demand his attention. He must formulate strategy and tactics while fighting the battle.

If cross-examination impeaches a witness or the testimony in a flagrant way, and the witness is caught in an obvious lie or contradiction, or is shown to have an interest in the case that transcends all other factors, the examiner has connected for a home run. It is a good feeling and one worth savoring but the truth is that the game is made up more of a great many little things. The bunt, the hit and run, the single, or taking the extra base. In the great majority of cases, the advocate must be content with just getting single or advancing the runner with a sacrifice rather than scoring the home run.

It is in these situations that the advocate must concentrate much of his intuition and be able to make a decision about when to go for the home run or when a triple or double may be possible or whether he must settle for the bunt or sacrifice. In any case, the advocate must always get the bat on the ball. He should never strike out. Once the decision to cross-examine is made, he must end the cross-examination having achieved something that will help him on closing argument.

As the cross-examination proceeds, the advocate must continually monitor what is taking place and make rapid decisions and evaluations regarding what his realistic goal may be with the witness and create a strategy for incorporating the goal into his case; achieve the goal; and then end the cross.

The goals of damaging the witness and neutralizing the witness must be viewed differently and the approach to the witness will vary depending upon which of the two are being sought.

Damaging the witness can consist of totally discrediting the witness or his testimony. This may consist of showing the witness to be a perjurer hired by the other side to testify, or showing that the witness was factually unable to see what he has testified to. Damaging the witness can also be of a more modest nature. This consists of scoring some points with respect to showing that the witness is vulnerable in one or more areas of impeachment.

The witness may be shown to be biased. He may have faulty recollection or was unable to clearly see what he has testified to. His ability to communicate to the jury may be used to the advantage of the advocate. There may be prior acts or omission that are inconsistent with the testimony in court. The witness may be in the position of admitting to telling lies outside of court and now having to justify his truthfulness in court.

There are few witnesses against whom some progress cannot be made in causing some damage on one or more of these subjects. All of these areas may be used to one degree or another cast doubt on the witness.

The concept of neutralizing the witness is more subtle and requires more finesse on the part of the advocate. The goal here is to extract from the witness some admission, concession or statement that you will use at a later time. Either with another witness or in closing argument that will serve to diminish his impact on the jury by suggesting that he was really a neutral witness and testified for both parties.

This method of cross-examination requires the advocate to create an atmosphere of friendliness with the witness and avoids at all cost any sense of confrontation. Once the mood is established and the witness has relieved himself of the fear of an attack by the cross-examiner, questions can then be put that will serve to aid the advocate later on.

Obtain a concession from the witness that some aspect of your case in theory can be true. The question usually takes a form such as "Wouldn't you agree, Mr. Jones, that such and such might possibly have happened in this way?" No matter how reluctantly the witness gives a positive answer the advocate must accept it and move on. Later, during closing argument the lawyer may be able to deflect some of the witness's testimony by suggesting that even he agreed that your version could be true and by implication the jury will not be faulted if they agree.

Validate something favorable another witness has said. "Mr. Jones a prior witness has testified that it was too dark to see who fired the shot? Do you disagree with that?" The witness may only be able to say that he has no knowledge of the fact. Nevertheless, it has served the purpose of reiterating the favorable testimony and later may be pointed to in the context of the witness is not contradicting the fact.

This same validation process may be applied to a witness whom you expect to call. Anticipating testimony from a future witness, you may ask the witness on the stand if what the future witness will testify may be true. Again the witness may merely claim insufficient information but the matter has been put before the jury without contradiction. Some juror may use it during deliberation to buttress an argument that he has for your side. The validation process may take place by getting the witness to admit to membership in one or more organizations in which a future witness on your side may be active. This serves to suggest that the opposition at least has common interests with your witness and the credentials of the one being cross-examined may be used to validate the testimony of the other.

The witness can be used to repeat favorable testimony from other witnesses to once again bring the matter to the attention of the jury. This can be done by pointing out the testimony to the witness and asking him if he agrees or disagrees with it. This witness usually has no knowledge of the subject whatsoever and says so. The advocate then asks additional questions with respect to some other favorable testimony and receives the same answer. Later, in summation, it can be pointed out to the jury that this witness didn't disagree the statement. This must be done with a great deal of subtlety. Jurors are quick to resent being told something during argument that is deceptive and this particular technique requires great finesse.

There are several goals that the advocate may achieve with the witness that will help neutralize the witness. Something the witness testifies to, no matter how seemingly insignificant, can be used by the advocate as an argument in support of his position. This may be nothing more than a simple concession that a certain event could have happened or that a certain fact could be true. It may be a concession that one of your witnesses has a good reputation. Or that a statement of one of the other witnesses could be erroneous. These concessions do not have to be significant. At the time they may seem completely insignificant to the jury but can be used by the advocate during summation to buttress some point that he wishes to make.

Another tactic to formulate a series of questions that may be susceptible to several interpretations and extract from the witness the admission of their possible validity and then adopt the interpretation you wish when you characterize the testimony in closing argument.

A concession may be obtained that has no bearing at all on the direct testimony which may come to have a greater significance when similar information, albeit construed differently, is brought out in your case in chief.

The lesson to be learned is that, once the advocate undertakes cross-examination, he must continually adjust his goals with respect to the witness until he finds one that can be accomplished. Having done this the advocate must content himself with this modest success and end the examination.

Part Eight
The Expert Witness

Principle One

The Expert Is Easier To Cross-Examine Than Is Usually Supposed

As the complexity of issues being tried in our courts has increased, so has the use of experts to explain complex information to the juries. The law generally recognizes that special knowledge of a scientific, technical or specialized nature that will aid the jury in coming to a conclusion may be presented to the jury in the form of an opinion.

A person may be qualified as an expert on a subject when he possesses special knowledge, skill, experience, training, or education on a that subject. Clearly this definition of *expert* goes far beyond the idea of professional and people who hold an advanced degrees from a university.

In addition to testifying about a particular subject and giving opinions with respect to a subject; the expert may give an opinion on the subject solely on the basis of information seen or heard at the trial or made known to him during or just before the trial. In forming the opinion the expert witness may rely on facts or data that may not be admissible into evidence. And, the law allows the expert to give an opinion on the very issue the jury is expected to decide.

For all these reasons the use of expert witnesses is tricky. The problems are magnified when the side presenting the expert is given the opportunity to ask the expert a hypothetical question and elicit an opinion. Such a question, however, must contain matters that have been put into evidence. This tactic is often used by a lawyer to make a closing argument to the jury; using a witness—who has been approved as an expert by the court—to give an opinion regarding its validity.

These provisions of the law are susceptible to great abuse. Often the qualifications of a so-called expert are based on a triumph of form over substance, activity over action, and movement over direction. A person may get an advanced degree, join several professional organizations, publish articles that amount to no more than a rehash of existing information, and take on the aura of an expert without having any real expertise in the field.

It is the important task of the cross-examiner to reduce expert testimony to proper its proportions. Because the damage that can be done by the expert witness is so great, the importance of damaging the expert's testimony through cross-examination is even greater.

Fortunately the law has counterbalanced the leeway given to the use of experts by giving the cross-examiner special weapons for the cross-examination. These weapons more than compensate for the power given the expert and, when used correctly, make the expert witness one the easiest witness to cross-examine.

ORDINARY RULES OF CROSS-EXAMINATION STILL APPLY

As important as these special tools are, the advocate must never lose sight of other considerations that apply to all witnesses. Asking the 'why' question with the expert will land you in a great deal more hot water and much more quickly that with any other type of witness. It is vitally important that the witness be limited to 'yes' or 'no' answers. Controlling the witness also takes on greater significance because the expert is always on the lookout for an opportunity to expand on the opinion.

Another common error that lawyers make is forgetting that the expert can be impeached in any of the ways the non-expert witness can be impeached. The expert can be questioned with respect to his memory, his opportunity to perceive that which he testifies to, and his ability to communicate the information. The expert can be impeached with respect to his oath, his bias, or interest in the outcome of the case. It can be shown, for example, that the expert is being paid to testify in a certain way and that if he had another opinion he would not have been hired to testify. And as with any other witness, the expert may be impeached for prior criminal convictions. (This area of impeachment also includes other bad acts and character reputation). Of course, as with all other witnesses, any attack in these areas must have some good-faith basis. The point is that experts are not immune from this impeachment by virtue of their being declared experts.

ADDITIONAL CONSIDERATIONS

The advocate must take into account some additional considerations in the cross-examination of the expert. The advocate should make the expert admit that his opinions have been wrong before, and that he has been in situations where colleagues of equal or greater rank have disagreed with his opinion. The advocate should also point out that one of those opinions—either of the witness or that of the other expert—had to be wrong.

It is important to avoid lapsing into the jargon of the witness's field of the expertise. The advocate may think that using the jargon shows his own grasp of the information. The problem here is that jargon leaves the jury out of the discussion which could prove disastrous. The advocate must be careful to put himself in the jurors' shoes and ask the expert questions that the jurors would ask and in language they would use.

Advocates must also be careful never to confuse the statement of a scientific fact with an opinion. Recognizing the difference is important because the statement of a scientific fact should be questioned only if it is objectively wrong and can be proven to be so (for instance an anatomical question in which the doctor misidentifies a bone). An opinion, on the other hand, is always subject to attack because it is an opinion and may not be held by others with equal or greater expertise.

The advocate should make the expert admit that his opinion would be better if based on first-hand knowledge. In addition, the cross-examiner should get the witness to admit that the information he relies on in most cases is the very information possessed by the cross-examiners witnesses. The advocate should also force the expert to admit that he would be in a better position to render an opinion if he heard both sides of the story.

The advocate should never assume that the expert's qualifications cover the precise area involved in the dispute. An advocate who believes that the expert's specific training is in an area that is not the one best qualified to render an opinion in the case should bring this concern to the jury's attention without attacking the witness directly.

A very effective technique of cross-examining the expert is attacking the individual facts upon which the opinion is based. Before doing this, it is important that the advocate make the expert commit to his position as much as possible so that he has little room to qualify his previous answer when faced with contradictions or other opinions.

Most good trial lawyers will use the hypothetical question to put before the jury all the facts in evidence that are favorable to their side. In this situation, the lawyer presenting the witness will pose to the expert witness a question that asks the witness to assume the truth of the facts and to give an opinion based upon those facts. This procedure allows the lawyer to state his case in its most favorable light. It is the opportunity to have two closing arguments. This advantage for the proponent can be used to equal or greater advantage by the cross-examiner. The advocate should use the cross-examination of the hypothetical to repeat his own favorable testimony more than once. He should confront the expert with each element of the hypothetical and extract a concession that the opinion might change given a changed circumstance, especially with respect to a changed circumstance consistent with the cross-examiner's version of the events.

Another technique that can be used to advantage in certain circumstances is asking the expert to repeat the hypothetical. Unless it has been put in writing and provided to him, it is unlikely he will be able to do so.

Finally, the cross-examiner must know how to impeach the witness with learned treatises that are accepted as authority. This is the single most important tool in the advocate's arsenal when cross-examining the expert. The advocate must develop techniques to qualify the material as authoritative. Other witnesses can do this if the expert refuses to concede the fact, but this is time consuming and expensive. If the advocate asks the witness the proper preliminary questions regarding what constitutes authority in his field there should be little difficulty obtaining a concession with respect to the authority of the impeaching material.

The advocate should not view the task of cross-examining the expert with trepidation. He should anticipate the experience with relish. The cross-examination process calls upon his skills in a special way, but as long as he understands the possibilities and remembers that the expert must come to the advocate's playing field and play by the advocate's rules using the advocate's ball, he will find the task much easier and more enjoyable.

Principle Two

The Expert Should Be Impeached With The Same Tools Used On Any Other Witness

When confronted with the prospect of cross-examining the expert the advocate will often concentrate on the special aspects of expert testimony, forgetting all the other principle of cross-examination. This is a grave mistake. Before considering the special tools that can be used in examining the expert the advocate should sort through—and use—the catalogue of techniques to be used with any other witness.

The expert is different than other witnesses only because he is allowed to offer opinion testimony. This does not mean that he cannot be impeached and his credibility attacked in the same manner as any other witness. In fact, the common areas of impeachment can prove quite fertile when applied to the expert.

The advocate should carefully probe the expert's possible bias not only with respect to the facts and parties involved in the case but also with respect to any bias the expert may have with respect to competing opinions in his field of expertise. The expert's ability (or inability) to communicate, perceive, and remember are all legitimate areas of cross-examination. Any prior acts of inconsistency are grounds for impeachment. This is especially true with respect to previous writings that may contradict the expert's present position.

The advocate should explore the possibility that the expert has committed prior criminal acts before confronting the witness. Irving Younger told a story of being on the bench and having a doctor appear before him numerous times as an expert for the defense in personal injury cases. According to Younger the doctor testified more than twenty times before a plaintiff's lawyer finally asked if he had ever been convicted of a felony. The answer was 'yes'. No one had ever bothered to investigate the possibility that the doctor had been convicted of a felony! (In this case it was tax evasion). Prior counsel had always assumed a doctor testifying as an expert would not have a felony conviction.

The advocate must also keep in mind the fact that the jury members will throw out the expert's opinion only if they are made aware of the expert's weaknesses in language and terms that are *understandable to them*. A jury that hears a fight between the expert and the advocate in jargon filled language will most likely give the benefit of the doubt to the expert.

Joseph Murphy had one of the first opportunities in the federal court system to cross-examine an expert in psychiatry. The story is as follows.

In 1948, the House Un-American Activities Committee was in the business of ferreting out communists in the government. Whittaker Chambers told the committee about several people who had been part of the Russian underground apparatus in Washington in the late thirties. One was Alger Hiss, who vehemently denied the charge and challenged Chambers to make the statements outside the privilege of the committee. Chambers did so. Hiss sued him for slander. A grand jury indicted Hiss for lying to the committee and he was prosecuted and, after two trials, he was convicted. In the second trial, Hiss's attorney called Dr. Carl Binger of Harvard to testify as to the personality of Whittaker Chambers. Binger based his testimony on his observation of Chambers on the witness stand and from reading some of Chamber's writings.

In what was a landmark decision Judge Goddard decided to permit Hiss to call Dr. Binger to the stand as an expert for the purpose of offering testimony as to Chambers' mental condition. Binger's testimony was to be based on his observation of Chambers during the time Chambers was a witness and from a reading of some of Chamber's writings.

Binger was asked a hypothetical question by Hiss's lawyer which ended with the magic language of what was the doctor's opinion "within the bounds of reasonable medical certainty" of the mental condition of Whittaker Chambers.

Binger answered that Chambers suffered from a condition of psychopathic personality embodying amoral and asocial behavior. The condition according to Binger caused the person to ignore traditional notions of morality and to disregard the good of society or individuals. The resulting behavior was usually destructive to both.

Symptoms were chronic and persistent lying, deceit, substance abuse and addiction, abnormal sexuality, begging, failure in stable attachments, accusing falsely and having a defect in the formation of a conscience.

Binger further testified that the psychopathic condition was somewhat between psychotic and neurotic, and that it was difficult to tell how many people suffered from it because the person having it was quite clever at hiding or masking it. He pointed out that they lived in a fantasy life claiming nonexistent friendships and were isolated and egocentric.

Dr. Binger spent most of the testimony comparing the symptoms of psychopathic personality with Chamber's known behavior outside the court, his writings, and Binger's observation of him on the witness stand.

Allowing Dr. Binger to testify caused Murphy a great many problems. Once a witness is qualified as an expert and allowed to give opinion testimony he may draw any conclusion he wishes and the attorney must at his peril try and find a whole in the result. Since Binger was basing his opinion on Chamber's behavior and testimony from the witness stand, Murphy did not have the benefit of seeing the conclusions and supporting information before he was required to cross-examine. Nor did he have adequate opportunity to call his own expert to rebut Binger's findings.

Murphy decided that his best chance for success was to cast himself in the role of the jury and ask those questions a jury would ask rather than those another expert might ask. This proved to be fertile ground because psychiatry was not as well accepted then as it is now. And even now there is a natural tendency on the part of lay people to distrust a discipline that purports to read into our everyday lives and behavior some sinister meaning and lack of mental health.

Murphy used most of the techniques known for cross-examination with devastating effectiveness. His main cross-examination technique was the use of Socratic irony. He placed himself in the position of feigning ignorance of the matters the doctor was testifying to and asking Binger to help himself and the jury to understand exactly what all this exalted learned really meant to the average person.

First he cast doubt on the doctor's qualifications. He extracted from Binger the fact that while Binger had graduated from medical school over thirty-five years earlier he had been certified as a psychiatrist for only three years.

Murphy then moved to the area of Binger's own mental state. He asked him if he had been psychoanalyzed. Binger said he had and when he attempted to point out that all certified psychiatrists had to undergo the procedure Murphy quickly established control. He insisted that the doctor answer his questions "yes" or "no."

Once Murphy had cast some doubt on Binger's qualifications, pointed out to the jury that the doctor had himself been psychoanalyzed, and established control of the witness, he turned his attention to breaking the testimony down into small parts which analyzed separately sounded at best trifling and weak and at worst downright silly.

Could various symptoms relied on by the doctor be valid symptoms of the behavior of a normal person? Yes, but . . . . Just a "yes" or "no" answer please, doctor. Wouldn't a diagnosis depend on all that Chambers had written rather than just the isolated articles read by Binger? And wasn't it true the doctor had not read everything? And didn't the doctor rely particularly upon a work Chambers had translated, and had the doctor ignored another work that Chambers had translated?

Murphy isolated every symptom relied upon by Binger and showed that each one could exist in a perfectly healthy human being. He pointed out the ones that obviously did not fit Chambers and forced Binger to agree that they did not exist in Chambers. Binger was put in the position of defending those symptoms which supported his conclusion by saying they had to be viewed in the totality of the picture and rejecting from the totality those symptoms that he did not find. Thus, since Binger concluded that Chambers was a chronic liar he included this symptom as one the supported his findings. Since he did not find panhandling in Chambers he decided its absence did not change the conclusion.

Murphy was then able to cast Binger in the light of (1) finding significance in a symptom if it supported his diagnosis and (2) rejecting as unimportant those that did not, all the while contending that no single item was dispositive but rather the totality had to be considered.

Murphy took some of the more eccentric symptoms, such as slovenly dress or unkempt appearance, and applied them to historical figures. Wasn't it true, he asked, that Will Rogers was not exactly a fashion plate? Yes, Binger agreed. Did that mean Rogers may be neurotic? No, not that in itself.

Murphy asked Binger how many lies he had counted that he believed Chambers had told over the years. Reluctantly Binger gave a total that on its face seemed significant. Murphy averaged the number over Chambers lifetime and pointed out there were about ten a year and most of an insignificant nature. Was that psychosis or neurosis?

Murphy then extracted a concession from Binger that his diagnosis was capable of contrary diagnosis by another expert and that Binger had found himself at odds with other psychiatrists, sometimes being correct and other times being proved wrong.

Surely Dr. Binger wasn't suggesting that his discipline was exact and that every expert would agree with him in his diagnosis. In fact the good doctor himself had been wrong the past.

Since Binger had relied in large measure on his observation of Chambers on the witness stand for his diagnosis, this became a particularly fertile ground for Murphy. Once again he forced Binger to identify specific actions and idiosyncrasies displayed by Chambers that Binger felt were indicative of the personality disorder. There items were such things as patterns of speech such as saying "it should have been," or "it might have been." Murphy pointed out these sayings had been used by Hiss in his testimony over twenty times more often than by Chambers.

Murphy got Binger to describe some action of Chambers during testimony, such as looking the ceiling before or during an answer, that he took as a symptom, and then pointed out that Binger himself had used the same mannerism more often than Chambers.

The genius of Murphy's cross-examination was that he questioned Binger in terms a lay-person would use. He asked the questions any lay person might ask of someone who was presuming to decided whether decisions and behavior that in one respect or another were found in most people amounted to mental disease.

Murphy approached Binger much the same as he would have approached any witness. In his ironical way he asked simple, unambiguous questions the jury could understand; he never lost control of the witness; he attacked the whole by attacking the parts. Using techniques of cross-examination he would have employed with any witness, Murphy reduced Binger's testimony to no value. Hiss lost the case.

Principle Three

The Superstructure Should Be Brought Down With An Attack On The Nuts And Bolts

The cross-examination principle, discussed earlier in this book, of attacking the bits and pieces that form the basis of the opinion is particularly effective with expert witnesses. The advocate must always ask himself whether or not the opinion (the superstructure) is supported by the details of the story (the nuts and bolts). This concept is extremely important when cross-examining the expert because of the subjective quality of the opinion. If the objective factors relied on for the opinion can be called into question, or if they can be shown to be inadequate, it is unlikely that the opinion will withstand scrutiny.

The advocate should keep in mind that experts in any field tend to be somewhat arrogant. They are rarely required to support their opinion with a detailed defense of the premises upon which the opinion is based. They tend to take it for granted that their opinion will be accepted as gospel. They are confident that the attorney will not be able to master the field as well as the expert has and that the advocate cannot possibly understand the subject as well as they do.

The expert usually fails to realize, however, that the advocate need not be an expert in a particular field to be able to expose fallacies, cast doubt on testimony, or make the witness appear the fool. Good cross-examiners can accomplish these goals without expertise in a particular field. Confronted with an experienced cross-examiner who is armed with an awareness of the subject matter and a knowledge of the authoritative literature on the subject, the expert will usually not have much of a chance.

A good lesson in the techniques of cross-examining an expert if found in the famous case of plagiarism in which the song "Rum and Coca-Cola" was alleged to have been stolen from another song. The background of the case is easily explained:

Morey Amsterdam, a comedian of some renown, visited the island of Trinidad and upon his return published a song called "Rum and Coca-Cola." A composer and musical expert named Maurice Baron sued on the grounds that the tune had been plagiarized. Louis Nizer, who represented Baron, was faced with cross-examining Dr. Sigmund Spaeth, the expert called by the defendants. Nizer felt that if he could not cast some doubt on Spaeth's testimony, he would lose the case.

Q. Dr. Spaeth, in the course of your professional activities you have become known as a tune detective, is that right?
A. That title has been applied to me, yes.
Q. And you have performed in theaters as a tune detective giving entertainment and demonstrating that art of being a tune detective?
A. At one time, yes; a good many years ago.
Q. In some vaudeville theaters?
A. Only for guest performances, yes.
Q. And then you also appeared on the radio, on commercial and sustaining programs showing how you do your tune detective work?
A. That is right. I might say I did one week at Radio City Hall under Roxy as a tune detective. I have done it for entertainment and for instruction.
Q. Well, also for pay.
A. Well, sometimes yes, sometimes not.
Q. And in addition to Radio City Music Hall, you have appeared in smaller vaudeville theaters, haven't you?
A. Occasionally, yes.
Q. Will you mention some of them please?

A. Well there was one in Casper, Wyoming. I cannot remember the name of the theater.
Q. Who else was on the bill with you?
A. I have not the slightest idea.
Q. Was there an acrobat act on?
A. I don't know, because the way—
Q. All right. You don't know.
A. I don't know. I could give you the bill on Radio City Music Hall.
Q. But I did not ask you that.
A. That is one I remember. Theaters I do not.
Q. And you were booked through a regular professional agent?
A. No, I was not.
Q. You did it yourself?
A. Yes.
Q. How long did your act take?
A. It varied, depending on how much time they wanted for that.
Q. Well, in other words, how much room they had for the act?
A. That is right. If they asked me to do five minutes I could do five minutes, which generally meant one tune like my famous discussion of "Yes! We Have No Bananas." That was a stock stunt. It became almost the song of the year. Every program I would have to bring on "Yes! We Have No Bananas."
Q. Incidentally, "Yes! We Have No Bananas" you traced through three prior classical works?
A. Mostly classical.
Q. And you traced them by taking a bar or two or snatch of melody here or there and traced that back to some old work, is that right?
A. That is right.
Q. And then by taking three snatches of melody from old works you pieced together "Yes! We Have No Bananas"?
A. It became a famous song because I made an entertaining little stunt of taking these snatches of old songs in it; an entertaining stunt. Let us put it that way.
Q. Will you mention some of the commercial sponsors you had on your radio programs?

A. Texas Company, International Silver for a program that was called "Fun in Print."

Q. No, I asked you the programs you had.

A. Another one was Rheingold beer, also on Schaefer beer.

Q. Those were paid engagements in which you performed these musical stunts, is that right?

A. Yes, that is right. I was on salary with the American Piano Company and they paid me a salary as a promotion man, and part of my work was to go with their electric player piano, the Ampico, and on stages of all kinds and other places to do such demonstrations and also to use the records.

Q. So you were booked into various vaudeville theaters in which they did not pay you for the vaudeville, but your compensation came from the piano company?

A. It was on salary.

Q. It was a public relations salary?

A. It was a public relations salary.

This preliminary questioning slid almost imperceptibly into the contradictions between his direct testimony and his books. He was so reluctant to give an affirmative answer that at one point the Court observed: "This expert would make a wonderful virtuous girl, he has such great reluctance to saying 'yes.'"

* * *

Spaeth had torn apart our charts which showed that 36 out of 38 notes were identical in the two songs. He gave a lecture and wound up with a chart he had drawn which showed only 12 out of 38 were the same. His conclusion was: "Thirty-six parallels would constitute practically an identity, whereas twelve represents only a very ordinary similarity."

How had he turned identity into nonidentity? By insisting that we had ignored accent and beat and particularly the bar lines. Here is an illustration of his ingenious technique beribboned with erudition: "There are only seven notes altogether in the diatonic scale, but of those seven only six have been used in these two tunes. So if you put those six notes in any position you choose you can always create identity, and the actual identity is the fact that there are six notes, common to the two tunes. No more.

"Therefore, if one note is even slightly out of position so far as a real parallel of the melodies is concerned, which means a parallel by having parallel bar lines, parallel beats—melodies run on beats of time, and tones that come on those important beats are parallel."

My task was to destroy this theory that parallel bar lines were the acid test of fair comparison. Could we demonstrate that Spaeth in his own books had ignored the bar lines in concluding that one tune was a literal transcription of the others? Could we get him to admit that you could have a flagrant plagiarism even though the beat was different, and the bar lines didn't match? After a long preliminary struggle this is how we fared:

Q. I ask you to look at it now on page 43 of your book *The Common Sense of Music*, and I ask you whether the middle section of "Yes! We Have No Bananas" is the same as the notes in "I Dreamt I Dwelt in Marble Halls."
A. Well, you see the melody notes. They are really identical. That is an identical melodic line which is syncopated in "Yes! We Have No Bananas" and this is on 6/8 time.
Q. I do not want the melodic line. I am asking a specific question. Are the notes the same in both?
A. "Yes! We Have No Bananas: is started out with two extra notes. Outside of that the notes are identical.
Q. And the rhythm you say was changed?
A. The rhythm is changed, yes.
Q. To what extent was it changed?
A. It is a 4/4 rag time in one song and 6/8 in the other.
Q. Now Mr. Spaeth, if the notes are spread on a different number of bars and the rhythm is different would you call these two songs a literal transcription of one another?

A. A literal transcription of one another is a very different thing from a parallel. I would call it a literal parallel.
   This was a good enough admission, but not I was not ready to accept anything less than unconditional surrender.
Q. I didn't ask you that. I asked whether you would say one as a literal transcription from the other despite those differences?
A. No, not necessarily. It could easily be a coincidence.
COURT: That was not the question. The question was a literal transcription.
WITNESS: I still do not know. If you mean in "Bananas" the literal four-bar strains, a literal transcription from the four bars in "I Dreamt I Dwelt in Marble Halls," I would say no.
Q. Reading from your book: "The middle section of 'I Dreamt I Dwelt in Marble Halls' is literally transcribed in the corresponding portion of 'Yes! We Have No Bananas.'" Did you write that?
A. I must have, if it is in print.
Q. And what has caused you to change your mind today that that is not a literal transcription? Can you tell us?
A. Yes, very easily. Because there are two additional notes and still every note of "I Dreamt I Dwelt in Marble Hall" is in there, and that is why, without having referred to my book, I was quite ready to play ball and say it is not literal, because I have two extra notes in "Yes! We Have No Bananas."
Q. I am not here to play ball or to play games. I am here to get the truth. Now I ask you, sir, when you wrote that even though there was a difference of rhythm, and a difference of two notes, that nevertheless, you describe these two as one being a literal transcript from the other. Was that a correct statement when you wrote it?
A. I would say when I wrote it that is what I considered it.
Q. Let us see if we understand the fact. A few notes may have been added in one that did not exist in the other, and the fact that the rhythm has been changed does not, in your opinion, amount to so much that one cannot still be called a literal transcription of the other; is that correct?
A. Well, that is a hard question to answer.

Q. Then answer.
WITNESS: May I play it on the piano?
Q. No, I don't want music. I want an answer. I want music in words.
A. It is difficult to answer in words, because we are talking about a snatch.
Q. You cannot answer that question?
A. The notes in the snatch of "The Bohemian Girl" are all literally repeated in the snatch from "Yes! We Have No Bananas," which, however, has a couple of additional notes, in the strain, which are not in the earlier tune, but there are certain parallel notes quite obvious. It might have been a coincidence, it might have been deliberate—I don't know.
COURT: The question is whether, and I should like to have an answer myself, whether the degree of difference between the snatch of "Bohemian Girl" and the snatch of "We Have No Bananas," namely the change of rhythm and the addition of those two notes, constitute a change of such magnitude as to prevent you from call one a transcription of the other?
WITNESS: I would agree that it would not prevent me from calling one a transcription of the other.

Different witnesses react differently to cross-examination embarrassment. Spaeth grew more determined under pressure. At one point he complained to the court: "Mr. Nizer is asking me questions that do not make sense."

No witness could announce his distress more vividly than to accuse his tormentor with being ineffectual. And Spaeth appeared visibly distressed.

Q. Isn't it a fact that you called "Yes! We Have No bananas" a deliberate, flagrant plagiarism?
A. Never in my life have I referred to it that way.

A few moments later:

Q. . . . Did you ever call this fox trot melody a flagrant plagiarism?

A. That I cannot remember. If I wrote anything like that in this book it is possible. I wrote that when quite a young man, in 1925.
Q. Now that you have become more mature, would you still say that?
A. You see, in a court of law—
Q. Listen to my question. I read on page 37: "This was flagrant plagiarism if you will, but it certainly brought Chopin into the American home." Do you stand by that?
A. Yes, if you will.

Then I struck directly at his basic theory that the bar lines must match in order to make a comparison of notes fair.

Q. Now I ask you to look at the bar lines of these two compositions on page 37 of your book which you have called a flagrant violation and ask you whether they coincide.
Q. The bar lines do not coincide.
Q. So even though the bar lines are different, you still refer to them as flagrant plagiarism?
A. I have already explained the word "flagrant" and I used that little phrase "if you will."

Finally he made a complete admission about the validity of our chart.

Q. Now you stated that except for the fact that our chart omitted this second note, there would be very considerable similarity.
A. I would say considerable similarity in any case, yes.

I showed him the compositions that he claimed were ancestors of "L'Annee Passee" and more similar to it than "Rum and Coca-Cola," and forced him to admit that there he had ignored differences in beat, accent, rhythm, bar lines, and notes far greater than between the two songs in our case. In each instance at first he proclaimed denial or distinction, but always an illustration from one of his own books, brought him back into line. It was a battle of attrition, made all the more effective by the final collapse on each point. His refusal to cede a point until all alternatives had been rejected and nothing was left to him but an admission, taxed the patience of the Court. It brought such comments as:

COURT: Dr. Spaeth, if you would subside and not run ahead of the question—
COURT: If you say it only once, Dr. Spaeth, we might get it.
WITNESS: It is a very clear musical point here, Mr. Nizer.
COURT: There is no musical point involved here at all except an inability to say yes or no.

In order to create dozens of "ancestors" for "L'Annee Passee," Spaeth had emphasized that its melody was composed virtually of three notes:

Q. Now you have referred to the three notes that predominate in "L'Annee Passee." What are those three notes?
A. The G is the most important, and the two adjoining notes, A and F. You have more of those three than anything else.

I wanted him to admit that one could trace three notes in any composition to prior ancestors and therefore this was not significant. Here I appealed to his pride. If I could get him to do his vaudeville routines, I thought it would prove my point. He readily obliged by pointing out that "Three Blind Mice" was composed of three notes, Nos. 3, 2, and 1 in the scale, and he hummed excerpts from a famous lullaby, "Mary Had a Little Lamb," to demonstrate that they were based on the same three notes; "Yankee Doodle" used them, but in another order. He claimed that, with his skill and experience, he could trace three or four notes or a strain in any given piece of music to some prior work.

But, of course, he could not do it by tracing a number of bars as distinguished from three notes, and he admitted that "the number of bars having similar melodic strains" between "L'Annee Passee" and "Rum and Coca-Cola" were eight! So his "ancestors" based on three notes were not ancestors at all for eight bars. He had disproved his own thesis.

* * *

There is a psychological principle which you can demonstrate with a parlor game. It rarely fails. You tell someone that you are gong to make him say the word "No" despite his resolve not to do so. No matter what you say he must not use the word "No," or he loses. You will tell him a brief story and then ask some questions, which he must answer quickly, but of course you warn him again, the word "No" must not pass his lips. then you begin the story that will be the basis of the questions. "Once in Peiping, there lived an old Chinese who had a wife and seven children. In the back of the house was a garden—" You stop the recitation and suddenly say, "You are smiling. You know this. You've done it before." Invariably the answer is, "No, really I haven't." The first word out of his mouth is the word "No." Sometimes the comical effect is heightened by the exclamation "No, no, no," so that the only word he has uttered, within a few seconds after your warning to him, is "No," repeated several times.

Psychologically a person can only stick to a story he has adopted if he can concentrate on doing so. But if he can be taken unaware by any device which breaks his concentration on the particular point, he will betray his true feelings about the immediate matter broached to him. I have on many occasions applied this principle in cross-examination. I tried it with Spaeth.

Of course "Rum and Coca-Cola" was virtually identical to "L'Annee Passee," but Spaeth denied this and raised every possible facile distinction between the two. If I could catch him off guard by diverting his concentration maybe we could induce him to contradict his own contention. This is now it was done. I questioned him at length about a Spanish song, "El Cafecito," which he had put in evidence to show that it was very similar to "L'Annee Passee." When his mind was thus riveted on the Spanish song and its similarity to "L'Annee Passee" and he was fighting off my suggestions that they were not similar, I suddenly shifted:

Q. *I now ask you is "El Cafecito" also similar to "Rum and coca-Cola" or not?*

A. *There must be come similarity, because "Rum and Coca-Cola"— Well, I won't go on after that.*

I stared long and silently at the witness, not moving an inch. Neither did he. Then finally I said in as soft a voice as I could muster: "You would not want to finish that sentence, would you?"

He replied: "Well, I will chiefly say that the chief similarities are with 'L'Annee Passee.'"

Much later when I was driving to a conclusion, I revived his broken sentence and asked him if he hadn't really meant that if "El Cafecito' was similar to "L'Annee Passee," it must be similar to "Rum and Coca-Cola" because of the striking similarity between the two? He denied it.

Principle Four

Contrast The Expert With The Witness Who Has First Hand Knowledge

The advocate should force the expert to admit that his opinion would be better if it were based on firsthand knowledge. For instance, the advocate should make the accidentology expert admit that his opinion would be more exact or reliable if he had witnessed the accident instead of trying to recreate it through the measurements of skid marks, accident reports of investigating police officers, and the statements of witnesses.

This technique can be used in most cases where the expert is called upon for a subjective conclusion based upon so-called objective facts. An example of this is the situation in which a psychologist or psychiatrist is called upon to give an opinion as to a testator's state of mind when he drew a will. Here the advocate should bring the doctor to the position where it is apparent to the jury that the expert is relying on the testimony of people who witnessed the testator during the time he made and signed the will. Having brought the doctor to this position it is easy for the advocate to point out to the jury that the expert has admitted that his best information is that possessed by the very witnesses the advocate will call to support the advocate's position. By implication, the expert has said that these witnesses would be in a better position to know the real state of the testator's mind.

A good example of this kind of cross-examination is found in George Medalie's cross-examination of Dr. Smith Ely Jelliffe with respect to Jelliffe's findings that Joseph Harriman should not be prosecuted for bank fraud because of diminished mental capacity. Harriman was examined by Dr. Jelliffe, who found a complication of diseases that served to impair Harriman's memory, judgment, and ability to transact business. The cross-examination warrants study for the way in which Medalie pointed out to the jury that Jelliffe's conclusions do not coincide with those having firsthand knowledge.

To appreciate this cross-examination, one must keep clearly in mind the fact that the issue to be determined related solely to Harriman's comprehension of the charges made against him.

Q. "I would like again to come back to what you said to Harriman on the subject of the accusation, and I would like you, because it is important, to search your memory for what was said. Is your memory normal? I think we will agree it is. Isn't it?"
A. "I don't know. That is for you to decide."
Q. "Very good. Now, how did you go about putting his mind on this painful subject of a accusation of crime against him, who had been regarded, as you know, as a distinguished citizen?"
A. "I said, in substance—repeated some of the statements that were made in Mr. Leisure's letter to me, of information."
Q. "What did you say to him? I now want what you said to Mr. Harriman."
A. "I am now trying to tell you."
Q. "Do not say that it was Mr. Leisure's letter; say what you said."
A. "Well, I have already told you that I cannot repeat verbatim what was said."
By the Court.
Q. "We do not want verbatim. We want the substance of what you said."
A. "That is what I have tried—"
Q. "You have not told us yet."
A. "Yes, the substance was that certain transactions took place."
Q. "That means nothing. What did you tell him?"

A. "I told him that he was being accused of doing certain things."
By Mr. Medalie.
Q. "What things?"
By the Court.
Q. "What things?"
A. "Namely, that certain slips were signed by him, and that certain transfers were made from one account to another, and I went over each one of them that were mentioned, and I have already testified that he did not remember the details of any of them and was not—said that he did not give orders to have that done, and, I have already testified, he said that he had officers that he paid fifteen to twenty-five thousand dollars a year to, to attend to those details, and he expected that they would attend to them, and he had no knowledge of them. I have already said that three or four times."

The point of the examination was then made as follows:

By Mr. Medalie.
Q. "Doctor, I would like to put it this way: It is clear, then, that he knew that you were talking about the Harriman National Bank?"
A. "Yes, he knew that he had been president of the Harriman National Bank, and—"
Q. "And he knew that that was what you were talking about?"
A. "Yes, he did."
Q. "He knew that you were talking about a securities company account?"
A. "He did."
Q. "He knew that you were talking about the accounts of certain depositors?"
A. "He did not know whether they—those accounts—that they were accounts; he was not aware of those. That was a function, he said, of his underlings."
Q. "Do you mean to say that he said that he did not know of those accounts, or that he did not know of the transfers to those accounts?"
A. "I don't know that he said—I never asked him if he ever heard of those accounts. He didn't know of the transfer of those accounts."

It was quite clear at this point that Harriman had been fully aware of the charges made against him and that, in his conversation with the doctor, he had simply denied his guilt.

Dr. Jelliffe had testified that he believed Harriman to be incompetent because he was unable to confine himself to a single subject. Throughout the cross-examination of the witness he indicated a similar tendency to stray from the subject of the examination. There was a perceptible ripple of laughter in the courtroom when the witness was asked:

Q. "Did you observe any perceptions of repetition of ideas on his part, when you asked him about other matters—if you asked him about one thing he would go off to another subject and stick to the other subject?"
A. "Yes, he did that quite frequently." . . .
Q. "Now, doctor, when I ask you a question, will you please stick to the question I ask you and not go off to something else?"

The examination then touched on the tests which the doctor had made.

Q. "I want to be sure of this. I want your help. Did he say that he never heard of the National Exhibition Company? You remember that name, don't you?"
A. "I don't remember the National Exhibition Company."
Q. "Didn't Mr.—?"
A. "I don't remember it offhand now."
Q. "I would like to ask another thing about Mr. Harriman. Has he the habit of repetition?"
A. "Very much so."
Q. "And talking at length about the same thing over and over again, so that you can't stop him at the end of one sentence?"
A. "I would not characterize it that way, no."
Q. "Was it almost that?"
A. "No, not almost that, but he repeats very frequently."
Q. "Is that a characteristic of aging persons who are normal?"
A. "Is that a characteristic of aging persons?"
Q. "Yes."
A. "Of what?"
Q. "Aging normal people."

A. "They very frequently do something like that, yes."
Q. "The mere fact that a man does it is no evidence of his imbecility, insanity or deterioration, of itself?"
A. "Of itself alone, no."
Q. "In other words, if a witness were on the stand in the courtroom and did that kind of thing, you would not say that he was mentally deteriorated?"
A. "No, on that basis of fact, no."
Q. "Did you question Mr. Harriman about entries made in April, 1931, to the amount of $1,600,000?"
A. "No, not specifically about $1,600,000. I only made reference to the $300,000 amount that I have already—"
Q. "Of December, 1931?"
A. (Continuing.) "—that I have testified to. Except as I have already said, that a very large amount of stock had accumulated."
Q. "Were you informed by Mr. Leisure that what Mr. Harriman was accused of specifically in the indictment was transferring the liability of the Harriman Securities Company to individual depositors of the bank without their knowledge? Did you know that at that time?"
A. "I believe on the date of my letter, which was of April 5th, there had been no indictment handed down, so—"
Q. "Well, did you know that that was a fact which the Government claimed or which bank examiners claimed?"
A. "I think the phrase that was used in the letter was that the Government will make such and such a claim."
Q. "Yes. Now what I am getting to, the particular claim, did you know that the claim that was to be made by the Government was that Harriman had transferred or caused to be transferred the Securities Company liability to depositors, without their knowledge? Did you know that?"
A. "I gathered that in a general sense from the letter, yes."
Q. "Well, did you call Harriman's attention to that?"
A. "Not specifically in those words."
Q. "Well, why didn't you?"
A. "I have already told you what I asked him about."

Q. "But I want to know why you did not. Why in examining him for the purpose of finding out what he understood didn't you ask him that?"
A. "I have already told you that he told me he knew nothing at all about the transaction."
Q. "Didn't you attempt to bring his mind to specific things in connection with it, in the face of his denial?"
A. "I think I have already testified to that, yes."
Q. "Never mind what you have already testified to; I want to know what you did."
A. "I think I have already told you."
Q. "Did you call his attention to the fact that the Government claimed that he had saddled these liabilities on the books on the depositors, who knew nothing about it?"
A. "I think I said that the Government was making a claim that there was $300,000 that had been transferred from one account to the other and asked him to explain it and he was unable to explain it."
Q. "You mean he said he could not explain it, knew nothing about it?"
A. "He gave me no explanation whereby I could get any further information."
Q. "What he actually did was to tell you that he knew nothing about it?"
A. "Yes, he said he new nothing about it, he had had no information about it. He made the further remark such as I have already testified to, that he had underlings, that he had salaried men that he paid large amounts of money to, and they took care of the details."
Q. "Is it unusual for sane men charged with crime to invent a false defense which involves a pretense of absence of knowledge or information as to the matters with which they are charged?"
A. "I think it could be done, yes."
Q. Well, don't you know from experience that that is quite frequent?"
A. "No."
Q. "You do not know that?"
A. "No, I have not had much experience of that nature."
Q. "Then you do not feel able to say whether that is a normal device of

an accused person who is sane, to falsely set up a defense of no knowledge or information?"
A. *"I can conceive that it might be done, yes."*

The defendant's indulgence in repetition was dealt with as follows:

Q. *"Do not patients with physical ailments love to tell it to the doctor? Perfectly sane people do that kind of thing?"*
A. *"Surely."*
Q. *"And in fact do to friends and relatives until friends and relatives sicken of hearing it?"*
A. *"Unquestionably."*
Q. *"And perfectly sane people do it?"*
A. *"Unquestionably."*
Q. *"That is in line with the general idea, 'Let me tell you about my operation'?"*
A. *"Unquestionably."*

After considering several items included in the doctor's notes, none of which were especially significant, the examination was concluded as follows:

Q. *"When did you see him after that?"*
A. *"I have not seen him except in court."*
Q. *"Well, did you see him when Dr. Gregory examined him recently?"*
A. *"I beg your pardon; yes, I saw him with Dr. Gregory on two occasions."*
Q. *"That is Friday and Saturday of last week?"*
A. *"Yes, sir."*
Q. *"Did you observe any improvement in him since June 29th?"*
Q. *"Well, not since June 29th, but certainly since March 24th."*
Q. *"A substantial improvement?"*
A. *"I would say in a sense, yes, but in another sense, no. That is, superficially and speaking in general, his narrative with Dr. Gregory was more sustained, it was clearer, it was repetitious in the same sense that I have already mentioned. He also had made jocular allusions. He also told some funny stories, some of which I do not think he would like to have repeated in court."*

Q. *"You mean the kind of story one tells to his intimates?"*
A. *"The kind of stories which, in view of the occasion, being examined by an alienist, one would hardly expect a man to tell, in view of the seriousness of the situation. In other words, distinctly out of color, in view of the whole seriousness of the whole matter, the kind of story that a person might tell you, might say at a club or a whole lot of fellows together."*
Q. *"Or a whole lot of directors together?"*
A. *"But hardly the kind of story you would expect the Judge to hear—"*
Q. *"We don't need to hear them. We know what those stories are, in a general way."*
A. *"I beg you pardon, you have not heard these stories."*
Q. *"At clubs, boards of directors meetings, aggregations of lawyers, eminent physicians, jurists and statesmen, the same kind of stories."*
A. *"Oh, yes, sir, under certain circumstances but hardly the right thing under those circumstances."*
Q. *"You mean it was not appropriate?"*
A. *"Very distinctly inappropriate."*
Q. *"Well, a lot of normal people do inappropriate things, don't they, without affecting their mental worth or ability?"*
A. *"I think a great many people that pass for normal do just that sort of thing."*
Q. *"Can't we very well eliminate that or wouldn't we if it were not Harriman?"*
A. *"Not in view of the whole situation."*
Q. *"Did you ever hear that Abraham Lincoln used to do that sort of thing?"*
A. *"Dr. Brill is quite an expert on Abraham Lincoln stories. Better ask him about that."*
Q. *"And that Daniel Webster used to do that kind of thing?"*
A. *"I have heard he did."*
Q. *"Regardless of whether—"*
A. *"But I don't believe that Daniel Webster in such a situation as Mr. Harriman was in would ever tell the same things that he told Dr. Gregory."*

Q. *"You mean that he might not have done so on the floor of the Senate, but might have done so in the Cloakroom or in the corridor?"*
A. *"Yes, sir. He certainly would not do it if he was being examined as to his mental competency."*
Q. *"Did you make Mr. Harriman aware of the fact that his mental competency was being examined into?"*
A. *"That I don't know, what Mr. Harriman was aware of; absolutely I don't think he was very keenly aware of what it was all about, because Mr. Harriman immediately became the salesman with Dr. Gregory. You would have thought he was more of a bond salesman going to sell Dr. Gregory something."*
Q. *"Is that a sign of abnormality?"*
A. *"It was in my opinion distinctly under the circumstances."*
Q. *"And is it not a fact that alienists and neurologists, like all other physicians, try as far as possible to put a patient at his ease, so that the patient is not overpowered with the importance of the occasion?"*
A. *"I think that is a fairly just statement, yes, sir."*
Q. *"In other words, the patient is made to feel that it is just a personal, friendly, helpful visit."*
A. *"That is what we attempt to do, put them at their ease as much as possible."*
Q. *"Didn't you ever tell a patient a perfectly appropriate and proper story or describe some incident to make the patient feel at ease?"*
A. *"It depends upon the patient."*
Q. *"You do that occasionally, don't you?"*
A. *"Occasionally, yes, sir."*
Q. *"Now let me understand this: Mr. Harriman is considerably improved today over what he was on March 24th?"*
A. *"I would say somewhat improved. I would not say considerably."*
Q. *"He walks a little better?"*
A. *"Not much."*
Q. *"He conducts a sustained conversation?"*
A. *"Somewhat sustained conversation, sometimes he does and sometimes he doesn't."*
Q. *"When he talked to Dr. Gregory he kept on talking?"*
A. *"Yes, sir."*

Q. "On the subject of the bank and its condition?"
A. "Yes, sir, he kept on talking about the subject of the bank and how the bank grew up, and how he was a poor boy, etc."
Q. "Did he say anything on that occasion that struck you as abnormal or as indicating mental incompetence, either on Friday or Saturday last?"
A. "Well, I think he overemphasized the idea that there was a plot to do him, to put him on the spot, that he had been picked out as a special victim, and that they were going to get him."
Q. "You mean the bankers, the Government or the public, which?"
A. "The bankers."
Q. "The Clearing House?"
A. "Yes."
Q. "The Clearing House wanted to close his bank?"
A. "No, the Clearing House wanted to get him."
Q. "Haven't you heard that sort of thing before? Haven't read it in newspapers, as coming from financiers and industrial leaders who were out of business or were put out of business and claimed a plot of that kind?"
A. "I have."
Q. "Haven't you heard, for example, that a prominent—"
A. "I get letters once a week—"
Q. "Wait a minute."
A. (Continuing.) "—more or less, of people who make just that sort of complaint."
Q. "Haven't you heard recently that a great industrialist claimed that the banks wanted to put him out of business?"
A. "I have read it in newspapers, yes."
Q. "Do you regard him as incompetent?"
A. "I do not know whether he ever said it or not. I only read it in the newspapers. But I know what this man said and I know the manner in which he said it, and I know particularly the evidence which he gave to sustain his statement. He told in detail how it was that they wanted to do this for him, and the relationship, the proof was so trivial, that there was no relationship; between them."
Q. "What is it that he said the Clearing House wanted to do to him and how he attempted to prove it?"

A. "My best recollection is he said the story goes back to 1907 when there were difficulties of a certain nature, that is in the financial world; that he had offered to help somebody of financial standing in the community; he even said at one time that he offered to give him five hundred thousand dollars and at another time he said he did give him five hundred thousand dollars, and then some time later, in 1927, 1928, and 1929, and just before the crash when speculation was so active that the brokers would bring their certifications to the Clearing House of the amounts of money that they might want to borrow in the course of the day, and that he with others or that some others persuaded him to be spokesman that the Clearing House should not get so much gravy, as he expressed it."

The Court. "So much what?"

The Witness. "So much gravy."

Q. "Meaning profit?"

A. "That is to say, that a brokerage house would bring in an uncertified—or a certain amount that they thought they might have to borrow in the course of the day two hundred thousand, three hundred thousand, four hundred thousand dollars; they had put a certain percentage on that and at the end of the day the percentage charge was the actual amount of money that they did borrow, whereas some of the people in the Clearing House, as I understood it, see, wanted to charge them the actual amounts that they wrote in blank at the beginning of the day. Now Mr. Harriman stood as a spokesman out against that kind of procedure at that time, and said that they should only be charged for what they actually borrowed, and he stood on the floor and made his argument and they had a vote and they lost, and that was the reason they wanted to put him on the spot."

Q. "Did he tell you how they put him on the spot?"

A. "Not specifically, no."

A. "Did you ask him?"

A. "No."

Q. "Was he referring to the fact that the Clearing House had a new man to put in as president and that he was relieved of the post of president?"

A. "That was not taken up, no."

Q. *"Didn't you know that was the fact?"*
A. *"In general, yes."*
Q. *"That is, that in June or July, 1932, through Clearing House influence Mr. Cooper was made president and Mr. Harriman was left with a nominal, ornamental position of chairman of the board of directors?"*
A. *"I think I read something like that in the newspapers, yes."*
Q. *"Did it sound like a normal grievance to you, with a knowledge of that fact—the kind of grievance that a loser might normally have, even though wrong in this statement?"*
A. *"He had a grievance, yes."*
Q. *"Anything unusual in normal sane people having unjustified grievances with a trivial basis of fact?"*
A. *"All I can say is the material given to me and the way and the manner in which it was given to me impressed me as distinctly anomalous and abnormal and not justified.*
Q. *"I want you to forget about Harriman for a minute and generalize with me again. Doesn't your experience and observation show that a normal or at least a competent person will have an unfounded grievance where he is the loser, that has only a trivial basis in fact?"*
A. *"Very frequently that is true, yes."*
Q. *"Is the thought of self-destruction necessarily evidence of incompetency?"*
A. *"The thought of it? No."*
Q. *"Are efforts in that direction necessarily evidence of incompetence?"*
A. *"In general, yes."*
Q. *"You say that unreservedly?"*
A. *"Unreservedly, yes. There might be very few exceptions, but I have never met them."*
Q. *"You would say that everybody that you have seen who has attempted suicide was mentally incompetent?"*
A. *"Every person that I have ever met that I know of, see, anything at all about, I found them to be incompetent, yes."*
Q. *"By incompetent you mean unable to take care of their own affairs, unable to give any normal judgment on the ordinary processes of life?"*

A. "No, I don't mean that absolutely. I mean that with reference to the act that they performed."
Q. "Well, outside of the act they performed?"
A. "But that is the act."
Q. "I know. Having attempted to commit suicide, would you say that such a person is not competent to manage his own affairs—that is, give a business judgment, decide on whether to borrow money or lend money, decide on whether to make a lease or not made a lease, decide on whether to move or not to move?"
A. "During the time that he is committing that act, no, he is not."
Q. "And when it is over with?"
A. "He might return again to such a condition that you have described, yes, or he might not. It depends on the particular kind of illness that he suffers which brings about the suicide."
Mr. Medalie. "That is all."

The decision of the Court was that Mr. Harriman was of sound mind and should stand trial. About a year later, after a five-weeks' trial, he was convicted and sentenced to four and a half years in the United States Penitentiary at Lewisburg, Pa., where he is now confined. He filed a notice of appeal, but six weeks later withdrew it and decided to serve his term.

Principle Five

Do Not Allow The Witness To Expand On The Opinion

Any cross-examination that allows an expert to expand on his opinion and theory will be disastrous. Allowing the expert to expand is more potentially damaging than allowing a non-expert witness to do so because the expert is usually more articulate and has the training in forensics to seize every opportunity to elaborate on the opinion. Because the court has allowed him to give an opinion the expert is already armed with the presumption that his testimony carries more weight than that of other witnesses. Permitting the expert the opportunity to expand on his theory may allow him to clarify some point in his direct testimony that was unclear or open to two interpretations. Worse it may allow him to bring out something that was omitted from the direct testimony.

A cross-examination technique that often works with the expert, especially the arrogant expert, is the use of mock ignorance or Socratic irony. This is the "Gosh doctor, I don't understand any of this and I'm way out of my league and would you just help me understand a few things?" approach. With this attitude, the advocate then lulls the expert into a false sense of security; giving the impression that the cross-examination will be easy to withstand. Having created this sense of security the advocate should proceed to make the expert commit himself irreversibly to a position. Once the expert is so firmly committed, he will not be able to extricate himself when the advocate presents him with the impeaching material.

With this technique—as with any other any other—it is important that the advocate ask leading questions and confine the expert to "yes" and "no" answers.

In the following example Lloyd Stryker is cross-examining a specialist in x-rays who has testified on behalf of the plaintiff in a malpractice case. The plaintiff's doctor has testified that the dosage was too great and caused the harm complained of. Stryker's cross does not use the learned treatise *per se* to impeach but rather uses accepted medical practice.

Mr. Lloyd P. Stryker cross-examined Dr. Hood as follows:

Q. *"Doctor, are you admitted to practice in New York State?"*
A. *"Yes, sir."*
Q. *"You believe in X-ray, don't you?"*
A. *"With regard to therapy, you mean?"*
Q. *"You believe in X-ray as a proper therapeutic agency in the practice of medicine?"*
A. *"Yes, I do."*
Q. *"And it is a proper and approved method in assisting the treatment of disease, is it not?"*
A. *"It is."*
Q. *"And there are two types of X-ray therapy, one superficial and the other deep, is that not correct?"*
A. *"That is true."*
Q. *"Did I understand you to say, doctor, on your direct examination that you dealt in superficial X-ray therapy?"*
A. *"While I was connected with the Skin and Cancer Hospital."*
Q. *"So while you were there, you had to do only with the superficial variety of that specialty?"*
A. *"Yes, sir."*
Q. *"What is the difference between superficial and deep therapy?"*
A. *"Superficial therapy is the treatment of lesions on the skin and deep therapy of the deeper structures."*
Q. *"Have you treated the deeper structures as well?"*
A. *"Yes, sir."*

Q. *"You do that now?"*
A. *"I do it now."*
Q. *"Deep therapy is recognized, is it not, as a proper and approved method of treating sarcomatous or malignant conditions?"*
A. *"It is."*
Q. *"In order to reach those conditions and have the X-ray affect them, it is necessary to have the electric X-rays or whatever rays they are, we don't know, do we, what they are—reach into the tissues through the outer skin, the fat and fascia, down to the place where the cancer is?"*
A. *"That is true."*
Q. *"In other words, the X-ray has to find this growth of the cancer in the same way as if it were done by surgery, that a knife would be used to find it? Do I make myself plain?"*
A. *"Yes."*
Q. *"In other words, it has to reach it in order to affect it?"*
A. *"Yes, of course."*
Q. *"How deep the X-rays extend into the body depends upon the particular condition that you are treating, does it not?"*
A. *"The depth of the X-rays depends upon the penetration of them."*
Q. *"The depth of the cancer you are treating or the sarcoma, whatever growth you are treating?"*
A. *"Yes, of course."*
Q. *"So that if you have a deep seated malignant growth, your rays have to go very deep, don't they?"*
A. *"Yes."*
Q. *"You don't criticize sending the rays as deep as the cancer is, do you?"*
A. *"No."*
Q. *"What effect do those X-rays have upon the growths when they reach them?"*
A. *"It causes a death of the new tumor cells."*
Q. *"Sarcoma is a disease of the cells, it is, or of the connecting tissues?"*
A. *"It is of the connective tissue."*
Q. *"And if the connective tissues between the cells are affected, cancerous growths, the X-ray therapist must send his X-ray in as deep as those are, mustn't he?"*
A. *"Yes."*

Q. *"In order to perform X-ray therapy, it is necessary to resort to all the recognized methods of diagnosis available to the medical profession is that correct?"*
A. *"Surely."*
Q. *"And it is proper and approved practice to resort to those methods?"*
A. *"Yes."*
Q. *"Is that not true?"*
A. *"Yes."*
Q. *"And among those methods are the taking of X-ray pictures?"*
A. *"True."*
Q. *"That is correct, isn't it?"*
A. *"Yes, it is."*
Q. *"You don't criticize the doctor here for taking X-ray pictures in connection with his diagnoses, do you?"*
A. *"I do not."*
Q. *"For instance, the deposition which you said you have read of the doctor who has been called as the plaintiff's witness, page 4: 'I made an X-ray examination and I confirmed that diagnosis,' that is proper and approved practice, isn't it?"*
A. *"When these X-rays from this machine reach into the deep tissues, to this cancerous or sarcomatous growth, they destroy the growth? That is the purpose of the rays?"*
A. *"They do, yes."*
Q. *"And sometimes do those rays, when they go very deep, have some effect upon the tissues between the sarcomatous growth and the external part of the body?"*
A. *"Yes."*
Q. *"Sometimes a greater effect than even an ordinary erythema?"*
A. *"On the deeper structures."*
Q. *"Well, on the superficial structures?"*
A. *"I suppose they might have an effect on the skin."*
Q. *"As a matter of fact, they do have, don't they?"*
A. *"Yes, I think I could say yes."*
Q. *"In other words, this heavy voltage of X-ray shot into a depth of the body to attack a cancer will have some effect on that which it goes through, to reach the cancer?"*

A. "Yes."

Q. "In X-ray therapy, deep therapy, where you are after sarcoma, or a cancer, what you are looking for is to get at that cancer, isn't it?"

A. "True."

Q. "In the same way that a surgeon in going after a diseased condition, we will say in the abdomen, will make a slit in the body with his knife to go in for it, isn't that so?"

A. "That is true."

A. "The theory is the same?"

A. "Yes."

Q. "The ultimate object of the doctor is to get at the seat of the disease and attack it and eliminate it? That is the purpose of it all, isn't it?"

A. "Yes, sir."

Q. "The same purpose in X-ray therapy as in surgery, am I right?"

A. "You are right."

Q. "Then, in order to do that, it is proper, isn't it, for the doctor to consider primarily the ultimate enemy that he is attacking, namely, the cancer, that is right, isn't it?"

A. "Yes, sir."

Q. "Sometimes then, in order to make this attack, one of the incidents of the attack is some effect upon the fat and fascia through which you go to get at the cancer, isn't that true?"

A. "That is true."

Q. "Did you assume in this case, that this growth was deep or not deep?"

A. "From my own examination?"

Q. "No, no, not at all, from the facts in this case, the testimony of the doctor who has been called as the plaintiff's witness?"

A. "That it was just below the skin? I understood it to be just below the skin."

Q. "And have you give your whole opinion upon that basis?"

A. "Yes."

Q. "In other words, if this particular mass were not just below the skin, but extended down to the bone, the criticism which you suggested, at least by your testimony, you would naturally take back, wouldn't you?"

A. "Yes, sir."
Q. "I call you attention to the testimony of the doctor in this case, called as the plaintiff's witness: 'A. Did you make a diagnosis independent of Dr. Schwartz? A. I made an X-ray examination and I confirmed that diagnosis. The X-ray examination showed the mass to extend into the soft tissues down to the bone.' Now assuming that to be a fact, you will withdraw your criticism, will you not?"
A. "Yes."

An appeal was taken and thereafter withdrawn.

Principle Six

There Are Few Opinions That Have Not Been Questioned By Another Expert

The advocate's most effective tool in the cross-examination of the expert is provided in the rules of evidence as an exception to the hearsay rule. Rule 803 (18) provides:

To the extent called to the attention of an expert witness upon cross-examination or relied upon by the expert witness in direct examination, statements contained in published treatises, periodicals, or pamphlets on a subject of history, medicine, or other science or art, established as a reliable authority by the testimony or admission of the witness or by other expert testimony or by judicial notice. If admitted, the statements may be read into evidence but may not be received as exhibits.

It is difficult to believe that somewhere in the world another authority that has not written something that is at odds with all or part of the testimony of a particular expert. By quoting these other opinions the advocate will always have at his disposal some means by which to impeach the expert—that is, assuming the advocate has the patience and diligence to find the contrary authority.

To use this rule effectively in cross-examination, the advocate must clearly recognize the difference between the statement of a scientific fact and the statement of an opinion. In the former instance the advocate is wise to leave the matter alone unless he can show the expert wrong. T o use an absurd example, if the medical witness denies the existence of the kidney as part of the anatomy, the advocate clearly should impeach on the subject. But, generally speaking, the scientific fact is not the issue for impeachment. Rather, it is the conclusion drawn from the scientific facts and other material that is the subject of impeachment. The use of learned treatises will always provide the ammunition for impeachment.

Before confronting the expert with the impeaching material it is important to put him in the position of not being able to deny the material's authoritative quality. If confronted too early, the expert may simply say that he does not consider the publication or the author authoritative, thereby denying you the use of the material or requiring you to call witnesses to prove the authoritativeness. The advocate should always force the expert to agree that the organization publishing the material is a recognized organization to which he or other experts of his acquaintance belong. In addition the advocate should get the expert to admit that using a document or book in a teaching situation may speak to its authority. In some cases the advocate may need to ask the expert to admit the authority of other books which in turn cite with approval the book or author the advocate wishes to use. The general guideline is simple: Place the expert in the position of admitting the learned treatise is an authority or appear foolish in the eyes of the jury.

Here is an interesting example of a situation in which an advocate used a treatise to impeach and to conduct one of the experiments contained in the treatise on the witness as part of the cross-examination.

Q. *I suppose, of course, that you are familiar with Professor Munsterberg's recent book,* On the Witness Stand, *which has created comment?*
A. *Yes, indeed.*
Q. *Do you remember the stress he laid on the power of suggestion, and the illusions of memory; and can you recall some of the curious examples he gave of these phenomena?*
A. *Yes; if you will call my attention to them I am sure I will.*
Q. *For instance (reading from the book): "In the midst of a scholarly meeting, the doors open, a clown in a highly colored costume rushes in the excitement, and a Negro with a revolver follows him. They*

both shout wild phrases; then one falls to the ground, the other jumps on him; then a shot, and suddenly both are out of the room. The whole affair, which was prearranged, took not more than twenty seconds. The scholars are then asked immediately to write down a report of what they saw. Out of forty reports there were only six which did not contain positive wrong statements; only four noticed that the Negro had nothing in his hand; the others gave him a derby, or a high hat and so on; different colors and styles of clothing were invented for him; some said he had a coat on, others that he was in his shirt sleeves; and it was determined that a majority of the observers had omitted or falsified about half of the processes which occurred completely in their field of vision." Do you remember that example of the frailty of memory?

A. Yes sir, I remember it well.

Q. Then do you remember this one: "A picture of a room in a farmhouse was shown to a class of picked students; then each was asked questions as to what he had seen. 'Did you see where the stove was located?" Fifty-nine out of one hundred replied and gave the stove a definite place. 'Did you see the farmer's wife winding the clock?' Thirty of the class described the clock, and so on. There was neither stove nor clock shown in the picture." You remember that do you not?

A. Yes, that was one of his examples which quite forcibly impressed me.

Q. I am going to burden you with the relation of one more incident from Munsterberg's book, and then I am going to ask you if you can see the relation of these cases to the one [we are now trying]. Do you remember this further example . . . "A Negro was being tried for murder committed on a highway at night. A disinterested witness, who claimed to have seen the whole occurrence, was asked these suggestive questions on cross-examination;

Q. Did you see by the moonlight, the kind of trousers and coat the prisoner was wearing at the time?

A. Yes, I am sure they were brown or at least dark.'

As a matter of fact there was no moonlight; and all the other witness who had testified earlier said that prisoner's attire consisted of blue trousers, white shirt and no coat." (To witness) Do you remember this example of the remarkable power of suggestion recorded by Professor Munsterberg?

A. Yes, sir, I do.
Q. Do you appreciate, Dr. Allison, that you are yourself easily subject to the power of suggestion?
A. ... Do you mean to imply that I am testifying falsely?
Q. Not intentionally, no; but that you are what is known as a suggestible witness.
A. Prove it!
Q. Very well. Would it surprise you to know that of the three instances I apparently read from Munsterberg's book, all of which you said you remembered perfectly, only the first one was actually in the book, the second was only half true, and the third was an entire fabrication of my own? Here take the book and see for yourself.
A. Mr. Smyth, I am afraid you are making a fool of me.
Q. Not more so than any one of us is liable to be honestly mistaken . . .

Principle Seven

Force The Expert To Commit As Much As Possible Before Impeaching The Opinion

The word *forensic* means pertaining to, connected with, or used in courts of law. When used in conjunction with another word as in "forensic medicine" it means the application of knowledge within a specialty (such as medicine) to questions of law and especially in court proceedings.

This means that the forensic expert is trained not only in the field of expertise but also in the discipline of relating this expertise in a court of law. As such, the expert is a formidable witness and must be treated with special care. He is always on the lookout for opportunities in the cross-examination to elaborate on some point or to clarify seeming contradictions.

When cross-examining this type of witness, the advocate must force the witness to commit as much as possible to a position before impeaching him with other materials. Failing to do so will give the expert the opportunity to explain the contradiction or modify his position to accommodate the impeaching material.

As a general rule the advocate should never launch a frontal assault on the expert witness with the material at hand. The witness must be firmly committed to the opinion the advocate expects to impeach so that when the trap is sprung he will have little chance of using his forensic skills to extricate himself.

Sometimes the lawyer has greater knowledge of the facts than the expert does. In these situations, contrasting the expert's knowledge with that of another witness makes the task even more interesting. In the following example Vincent Hallinan—one of the bar's great champions of justice—shows how he used his own knowledge of medicine to successfully impeach the doctor.

The doctor was asked to draw on the blackboard a picture of the bones as they would appear viewed from the rear. He did so, laughingly disclaiming much skill as an artist.

Q. (By Hallinan) "Now, if we were looking at the back of this child's leg and if all the muscles and other overlying structures were removed, the bones would appear approximately as you have drawn them. Is that correct?"
A. (By the doctor) "Making allowances for my defects as an artist, yes."
Q. "What are the names of those two bones?"
A. "This is the tibia, and this is the fibula."
Q. "This child has a peculiarity of her bone structure, is that correct?"
A. "I don't understand what you mean."
Q. "In most people the fibula is outside the tibia. I notice that you have drawn hers on the inside."
A. "Oh. Oh that is a mistake. I was confused. I thought we were looking at her from in front."
Q. "Let us agree to this, Doctor: that, hereafter, when you answer a question, you will use the correct medical term to describe the part of the body involved. I do not want you to use what you doctors sometimes call 'layman's language,' or what a part 'is sometimes called.' Do you understand?"
Q. "Will you please name the muscles of the leg?"
A. "You mean all of them? There are quite a lot."
Q. "We have time. Go ahead."
A "Well, let me see. There's the sartorius muscle—"
Q. "Pardon me, Doctor, is the sartorius muscle in the leg?"
A. "Why, yes. It is right here" (indicating his thigh.)
Q. "That is not part of the leg. Is it?"

A. "Oh, I see what you mean. Medically, that is the thigh. The leg is the portion below the knee. I was using the ordinary term."
Q. "We agreed not to do that, didn't we?"
A. "Very well, I'll try to avoid that. There's the gastrocnemius." That is the big muscle lying directly under the skin. Under that is the soleus. Then there's the peroneus, and the two muscles which flex the toes and the large toe. They are separate muscles. I forget their Latin names at the moment."
Q. "You mean the flexor hallucis longus and flexor digitorum longus."
A. "Thank you; you have a better memory than I. Then there are the muscles which extend the toes."
Q. "What are they called?"
A. "You just substitute extensor for flexor in the names you just used."
Q. "Are there other muscles in the leg?"
A. "Not at the place where this injury occurred. That is about all."
Q. "The injury was in the upper third of the leg, was it not?"
A. "Yes, that is right."
Q. "Did you ever hear of a muscle in that region called the plantaris?"
A. "Oh yes. I had forgotten that one. However, it is a very small muscle, relatively. It is not a strong muscle. It doesn't have any important function."
Q. "Doctor, I dare say that whatever power designed the human body had a purpose in providing it with a plantaris muscle. At any rate, let's not omit any merely because we are not sure of the function they subserve."
A. "I might say, Counsel, that I did not come here prepared for a memory test in anatomy. I haven't looked into an anatomy book since medical school. If I had known this was to be a quiz, I could easily have brushed up on it last night—just as you have probably done."
Q. "Doctor, you come here, posing as an expert on the particular injury involved in this case. You do not consider it too much that you should be asked to name the very parts concerning which you are testifying as an expert, do you?"
A. "No. Certainly not. Go right ahead. As I say, though, I am somewhat rusty on my anatomy."

- Q. *"Can you tell us the name of the artery which you have described in your direct examination as the main artery, and which you say would be severed by an injury deep enough to expose the bones?"*
- A. *"I believe that it is called the tibial artery."*
- Q. *"That is close enough. It is called the posterior tibial artery. Will you tell us its location in the leg?"*
- A. *"Well, it starts from branches in the foot—down around here—and runs up the leg to the popliteal space—here behind the knee where it joins another artery—I believe, the popliteal."*
- Q. *"Aren't you falling into the same difficulty as you did with the bones? You are not suggesting that there is some anomaly in this child's blood vessels, are you?"*
- A. *"What do you mean?"*
- Q. *"I have never heard of an artery starting in an extremity and flowing toward the heart."*
- A. *"That's being pretty technical. Technically, you are correct. An artery starts at the part nearest the heart, and flows to the extremity. But that's pretty technical."*
- Q. *"What is the correct name of the nerve which you have described in your direct examination as the main nerve, and which you say would be severed by an injury deep enough to expose the bones?"*
- A. *"It is probably called the tibial nerve also. I am not sure."*
- Q. *"The posterior tibial nerve and the posterior tibial artery run side by side throughout the length of the leg. Do they not?"*
- A. *"Yes; I believe they do."*
- Q. *"At the point of this injury, where do they lie with regard to the muscles we have talked about?"*
- A. *"I believe that they are under the gastrocnemius, but I am not sure whether they are above or below the soleus muscle."*
- Q. *"Where are they in regard to the plantaris?"*
- A. *"I am not sure just where that muscle is—as I say, it is a very small muscle. I have forgotten."*
- Q. *"The plantaris lies between the gastrocnemius and soleus muscles."*
- A. *"All right. If you say so, I will accept your statement."*
- Q. *"In brushing up on anatomy last night, as you suggest I have done, Doctor, I learned something which I will ask you now to confirm:*

that in the lower part of the leg this artery and nerve—the posterior tibial—lie between the two big muscles, the gastrocnemius and soleus, but in the lower third of the leg they both bend inward, penetrate through the soleus, and thereafter lie below that muscle also and between the bones of the leg. Will you kindly tell us if that statement is correct?"

A. "I cannot say that that is not so. I had not supposed so, but it may be as you state."

Q. "Who was the author of the anatomy book which you say you looked into in medical school?"

A. "Gray, I believe—or Cummingham."

Q. "Here is a copy of Gray's Anatomy. Please read the passage I am indicating and tell us if it refreshed your recollection that the statement I have just made is correct."

A. (After reading the passage.) "Yes, that is correct."

Q. "So that, at the place where this child's leg was injured, the main nerve and artery lie below the muscles and between the bones of the leg. That is so, is it not?"

A. "Yes, I would say that is so."

Q. "Therefore it is possible that the muscles could have been cut through and the bones exposed, without severing either the main artery or the main nerve. Isn't that so?"

A. "Yes, I would say that is possible."

Q. "You will withdraw your statement that, in this case, the bones of the leg could not have been exposed in the wound without the child either bleeding to death or having her leg permanently shrunken and deformed. Is that right?"

A. "Yes. I will have to amend my opinion. The situation could have been as you say."

Epilogue

When To End May Be The Most Difficult Question Of All

The advocate decides that he must cross-examine the witness and having made that decision will then inevitably have to decide when to end the cross-examination. This is a crucial decision because if it ends to soon it will be of little value and if ends too late is can spell disaster.

While the cross-examination is being conducted the advocate must ask himself:

- Have all the points the advocate can make with this witness been made?
- Are there additional subjects that should be explored?
- Has the jury understood the points that have been made?
- Has the advocate achieved some goal in the cross-examination that he can use later to his benefit?
- Is there a way to end the cross-examination on a high note?
- Is the jury growing impatient or losing interest?

If the advocate has prepared his case properly the answer to these questions will come rather naturally. If the focus of the case has been scattered the answer to these questions will be more difficult.

Before beginning the cross-examination the advocate should have in mind a list of objectives he wishes to accomplish with the witness. He should also have them in a sequence that progresses from least important to most important. When he has achieved these objectives he should end the cross. If issues have been put to the witness in the proper sequence the likelihood is that the cross-examination will end on a high note.

It often happens that the advocate reaches a high note before he has achieved all the objectives in the cross-examination. When this occurs the advocate having finished the cross should take the witness back to the previous subject and recreate the situation to provide the high note upon which to end.

Returning to a previous point in the testimony that was particularly beneficial requires skill to prevent the witness from extricating himself from the trap. To avoid this the advocate should not give the witness an opportunity to answer. The matter should be raised in the form of a summation of the witness's previous testimony and once made the should immediately end the cross-examination.

Any cross-examination involves a balance on the one hand of pursing issues that will help the case, and on the other hand of not being tedious. Exploring every new possibility that presents itself usually leads to being tedious. The advocate must have a keen sense of when some new subject should be explored, and when it should be ignored. This ability is developed with experience and is difficult to define. Nevertheless, the cross-examination that merely throws questions at a witness in the hope that something will come of it will usually fail.

Asking the one question too many has been the downfall of a great many advocates. One test for this is the advocate constantly monitoring his cross-examination using the same criteria he uses to decide whether he should cross-examine at all. It boils down to constantly asking one's self whether the potential for harm in one more question is greater than the potential for benefit. It involves an on the spot determination of whether or not the issue that has been raised buy the answer of the witness can be better exploited in closing argument, or with another witness, than it can by asking the witness additional questions. If the advocate decides he has gotten enough from the witness to maximize his case in closing argument it probably means he should stop.

Often the judge and the jury will give the advocate a good indication of when he should end the cross-examination. If the attention the jury begins to wander, or the judge begins to grow impatient it is a good signal that the advocate should find a good place to stop.

A way to avoid the doubts that plague every advocate in wondering whether he has covered every point of his cross-examination is to develop the skills to hammer in all the nails at the moment the point is being made and have the self confidence that when he leaves a subject it has been fully explored. With this confidence he can safely leave a subject without wondering if he exploited it to its fullest.

Understanding the principles contained in this book and having good working knowledge of them will help any advocate gain the skills to approach each case and each witness with to cross-examine confidently and efficiently.

The cross-examiner, like the writer, must always be left to wonder if he had done all he could do when he ended. Perhaps Herman Melville describes the quandary best in *Moby Dick*.

For small erections may be finished by their first architects; great ones, true ones, ever leave the copestone to posterity. God keep me from ever completing anything. This whole book is but a draught—nay but the draught of a draught. Oh, Time, Strength, Cash, and Patience!

BIBLIOGRAPHY

B.

Bloom, Harold and David Rosenberg, The Book of J, New York, Random House,

Bowen, Catherine Drinker, Miracle at Philadelphia, Boston, Little, Brown and Company, 1966

Bowen, Catherine Drinker, Yankee From Olympus, Boston, Atlantic, Little, Brown and Company, 1944.

Boorstin, Daniel J., The Americans: The Colonial Experience, New York, Random House, 1958.

Boorstin, Daniel J., The Discoverers, Random House, New York, 1983

Bryan, William J., Jr., The Chosen Ones, New York, Vantage Press, 1971.

Busch, Francis X., Prisoners at the Bar, Indianapolis, Bobbs—Merrill, 1952

C.

Cohn, Alfred, and Joe Chisolm, Take the Witness, Garden City NY, Garden City Publishing,1934.

Cooke, Alistair, Generation on Trial, Alfred A. Knopf, New York, 1952

Corbett, Edward P.J., Introduction by, The Rhetoric and the Poetics of Aristotle, New York, Random House, Inc., 1954.

Curiae, Amicus, Edited by, Law In Action, An Anthology of the Law in Literature, New York, Bonanze Books, MCMXLVII.

D.

Darrow, Clarence, Attorney for the Dammed (Arthur Weinberg, editor.) Simon and Schuster, New York, 1957

Diagnostic and Statistical Manual of Mental Disorders, 3rd. Ed. Revised, American Psychiatric Association, Washington, 1987

Dickens, Charles, Pickwick Papers, Oxford, London

Davenport, William H., Edited by, Voices in Court, New York, The MacMillan Company, 1958.

Donovan, James B., Strangers on a Bridge, Atheneum, New York, 1967.

Douglas, William O., An Almanac of Liberty, Garden City, N.Y., Doubleday and Co.

E.

Ehrlich, J. W., The Lost Art of Cross-Examination, New York, G. P. Putnam's Sons, New York, 1970.

Ellman, Richard, Oscar Wilde, Alfred A. Knopf, New York, 1988.

Erskine, Thomas, The Speeches of Lord Erskine, Legal Classics Library, Birmingham, Alabama, 1984.

F.

Fordham, Edward Wilfrid, (Collected and Annotated by), Notable Cross-Examinations, The MacMillan Company, New York; London, Constable & Company, 1951.

Fowler, Gene, The Great Mouthpiece, New York, Blue Ribbon Books, 1931.

G.

Giesler, Jerry, As Told to Pete Martin, The Jerry Giesler Story, Simon and Schuster, New York, 1960.

H.

Hallinan, Vincent, A Lion In Court, New York, G. P. Putnam's Sons, New York, 1963.

Hamlin, Sonya, What Makes Juries Listen, Englewood Cliffs, NJ., Prentice Hall Law and Business, 1985

Heller, Louis B., Do You Solemnly Swear?, Doubleday & Company, Inc., Garden City, New York, 1968.

Herman, Lewis and Mayer Goldberg, You May Cross-Examine!, New York,

The Holy Bible, The Book of Daniel, Chapter 13, Susanna's Virtue, The Catholic Press, Chicago, 1971

Hodge, Harry and James H. Hodge, Editors, Famous Trials, London, Book Club Associates,1984

Hyde, H. Montgomery, Lord Justice, New York, Random House, 1965.

Hyde, H. Montgomery, The Trials of Oscar Wilde, Dover Publications, NY,NY. 1962.

J.

James, Marquis, The Life of Andrew Jackson, New York/Indianapolis, The Bobbs-Merrill Company, 1938.

Jaworski, Leon, The Right and the Power, New York, Reader's Digest Press, New York, 1976.

K.

Kalven, Harry, Jr. and Hans Zeisel,The American Jury, Boston, Little Brown and Co., 1966.

Kunstler, William M., The Minister and the Choir Singer, New York, William Morrow and Company, 1964.

L.

Leibowitz, Robert, The Defender, The Life and Career of Samuel S. Leibowitz 1893-1933, Prentice-Hall, Inc. Englewood Cliffs, Jew Jersey, 1981.

Loftus, Dr. Elizabeth and Katherine Ketcham, Witness for the Defense, St. Martin's Press, New York, 1991

London, Ephraim, Edited by, The World of Law, New York, Simon and Schuster, Inc. 1960.

M.

Marke, Julius J., Vignettes of Legal History, Fred B. Rothman and Co., South Hackensack, NJ., 1965

McDonald, John D., No Deadly Drug, Garden City, NY., Doubleday and Co., 1968.

Munsterberg, Hugo, On the Witness Stand, Clark Boardman Co., New York, 1925.

N.

Nizer, Louis, The Jury Returns, Doubleday & Company, Inc., Garden City, New York, 1966.

Nizer, Louis, My Life In Court, Garden City, New York, Doubleday & Company, Inc., 1961.

P.

Plato, The Days of Socrates, (Translated by Hugh Tredennick), Penguin Books Ltd., Baltimore, 1954.

R.

Reynolds, Quentin, Courtroom, The Story of Samuel S. Leibowitz, Farrar, Straus and Company, New York, 1950

Robbins, Sara (editor), Law, A Treasury of Art and Literature, Hugh Lauter Levin Associates, Inc., New York, 1990.

Rovere, Richard H., Howe and Hummel, New York, Farrar, Straus and Company, 1947

S.

St. Johns, Adela Rogers, Final Verdict, Doubleday & Company, Inc. Garden City, New York. 1962.

Steuer, Aron, Max D. Steuer, New York, Random House, 1950.

Stone, I.F., The Trial of Socrates, Boston, Little Brown and Co.,1988.
Stone, Irving, Clarence Darrow For The Defense, New York, Doubleday and Company, Inc., 1941.
Stryker, Lloyd Paul, The Art of Advocacy, A Plea for the Renaissance of the Trial Lawyer, New York, Cornerstone Library, 1954.
Stryker, Lloyd Paul, For The Defense, Garden City, New York, Doubleday and Company, Inc., 1947.

T.

Train, Arthur, Courts and Criminals, Charles Scribner's Sons, New York, 1923
Tutt, Ephraim, Yankee Lawyer, Autobiography of EphraimTutt, Grosset & Dunlap, New York, 1943.
Tzu, Sun, Translated by Thomas Cleary, The Art of War, Shambhala, Boston & Shaftesbury, 1988.

V.

Vinson, Donald E., Jury Trials, Michie Company, Charlottesville, VA. 1986

W.

Weinstein, Allen, Perjury, The Hiss Chambers Case, Alfred A. Knopf, New York, 1978.
Wellman, Francis L., The Art of Cross-Examination, New York, Macmillan Publishing Company, 1903.
Wellman, Francis L., Day in Court. New York, Macmillan, 1937
Wellman, Francis L., Gentlemen of the Jury, The Macmillan Company, New York, 1936.
Wellman, Francis L., Luck and Opportunity, The MacMillian Company, New York, 1938.
Wild, Roland, and Derek Curtis Bennett, King's Counsel, New York, The Macmillan Co. 1938

Williams, Brad, Due Process, New York, William Morrow and Company, 1960.

Wiliams, Edward Bennett, One Man's Freedom, Atheneum, New York., 1962,

Wouk, Herman, The Caine Mutiny, Doubleday and Company, Inc., Garden City, NY. 1951.

Z.

Zsolt de Haranyi, The Star Gazer, G.P. Putnam's Sons, New York, 1939

Printed in the United States
82801LV00002B/232/A